Bowery to Broadway

Bowery

to

Broadway

*The American Irish in
Classic Hollywood Cinema*

CHRISTOPHER SHANNON

UNIVERSITY OF SCRANTON PRESS

SCRANTON · LONDON

Cover design by Grapevine Design
Typesetting by Bill Powell at Wineskin Media:
wineskinmedia.com

ISBN-13: 978-1-58966-200-1
ISBN-10: 1-58966-200-8

The text of this book was set in Bitstream Charter, using the LaTeX macros and LaTeX
packages, especially *memoir*, with the TeX typesetting engine.

Editing was done with the text editors *Emacs* and *Vim*.

The output PDFs were previewed with the PDF reader *Evince*.

All these programs, as well as the Linux operating system running beneath them,
are professional, open source, and free. These programs are also freely available
for other operating systems, probably including yours.

Library of Congress Cataloging-in-Publication Data

Shannon, Christopher.
    Bowery to Broadway: the American Irish in classic Hollywood cinema / by
Christopher Shannon.
        p. cm.
    Includes bibliographical references.
    ISBN 978-1-58966-200-1 (cloth)
    1. Irish Americans in motion pictures. 2. Motion pictures—United States—
History—20th century. I. Title.

PN1995.9.I67S53 2010
791.43'65299162073–dc21

                                                                    2009045380

Distribution and Order Fulfillment:
Chicago Distribution Center
11030 S. Langley
Chicago, IL 60628
773-702-7000

To the Dewey Ave. Boys

Acknowledgements

THIS BOOK HAS ITS ORIGINS in serendipity. In 1996, I began working in the Motion Picture Department of the George Eastman House in Rochester, New York. In 1997, Kevin Rockett published *The Irish Filmography: Fiction Films 1896–1996*. The Eastman House gave me an opportunity to immerse myself in the legend and lore of American cinema, while Rockett's book gave me an unprecedented guide to the thick Irish underbelly of the golden age of Hollywood. From my time at Eastman House, I would like to thank Paolo Cherchi-Usai, Edward Strattman, Mark Betz, Saundra Peters, Jeffrey Stoiber, Carol Radovitch and all the students who attended the L. Jeffrey Selznick School of Film Preservation in 1997 and 1998. A Rochester native, I grew up a world away from the Eastman House and never made the hike across town to see what was going on. I consider myself fortunate to have discovered, even if late in life, a tremendous cultural treasure right in my own hometown.

I could not have written this book without the use of other archives and the generous assistance of several archivists. I would like to thank Bonnie Coles, Rosemary Hanes, and Josie Walters-Johnston from the Library of Congress; Dorinda Hartmann from the Wisconsin Center for Film and Theater Research; and Sunniva O'Flynn from the Irish Film Institute. In addition, the help I received from the curators of the Film Censorship Records of the New York State Archives was invaluable in providing access to scripts of hard-to-view films.

Funding for research trips came from a Hibernian Research Award from the Cushwa Center for the Study of American Catholi-

cism at the University of Notre Dame, and a Charlotte and Walter
Kohler Fellowship in Family Studies from The Howard Center for
Family, Religion & Society. I owe a very special debt of gratitude
to Allan C. Carlson at the Howard Center. Allan provided essential
funding at a crucial stage in the writing of this book despite the
subject matter being far afield of the policy-oriented work that the
Howard Center usually supports. Allan and I share a common love
for the work of Wendell Berry. I hope he can hear an urban echo of
the great agrarian in this book.

Somewhat of a latecomer to Irish Studies, I have benefited
greatly from the established masters in the field. The work of
William H. A. Williams and Timothy Meagher has been especially influential. James Rogers of *New Hibernian Review* guided me through
the publication of my first article in the field, "Public Enemies, Local
Heroes: The Irish-American Gangster Film in Classic Hollywood
Cinema" *New Hibernia Review* 9.4 (2005): 48–64. Ruth Barton has
worked tirelessly to promote the study of Irish-American film and
was generous enough to include my essay, "The Bowery Cinderella:
Gender, Class and Community in Irish-American Film Narrative" in
her recent collection, *Screening Irish America* (Dublin: Irish Academic Press, 2009). Portions of both of these essays appear in this
book.

On matters Irish-American, I owe my greatest debt to James
T. Fisher. I first encountered Jim while a graduate student in the
American Studies Program at Yale University. He taught American
Catholic history at a time when I was all hot for theory and intellectual history, and he patiently read a dissertation that involved
close readings of the works of very un-Irish figures such as Thorstein
Veblen and John Dewey. After many long conversations at the Fire-
house Tavern, he convinced me that my own background was worth
studying. I hope that some of his spirit has made it into this book.

Beyond the world of Irish Studies, I would like to thank Bill
McClay for his constant intellectual and moral support for my work.
Christopher Blum brought me to Christendom College and has pro-

vided a model of friendship, collegiality, and the Catholic intellectual life. My wife Karen and my daughter Sophronia have put up with long work hours; Karen also has had to endure way too many black-and-white gangster films during those times when I have been able to make it home.

Jeff Gainey of The University of Scranton Press has stuck with me since our days at Notre Dame. He has been a model of patience as I have tried to juggle deadlines with a heavy teaching load. Jeff was also savvy enough to assign me a sympathetic copy editor who had recently survived an Irish-Catholic-movie viewing binge. John Hunckler was an exacting editor who gently reminded me how much I still have to learn about some basic mechanics of the English language. He has made this a much better book than it otherwise would have been.

Most of all, I would like to thank the Dewey Ave. Boys of the 10th Ward in Rochester, New York. Paul Gotham, Len Fetterly, Steve Winter, Greg O'Sullivan, Dan Scheib, Pete Reed, Emmett Connolly, and Joe DiTucci have taught me whatever it is I might know about the city.

Contents

Introduction

The Sidewalks of New York

ON JUNE 28, 1928, AL SMITH became the first Irish-Catholic candidate of a major party to run for the office of President of the United States. Smith's nomination to head the Democratic Party ticket against the Republican candidate, Herbert Hoover, suggested that urban Irish-Catholic America had finally come of age. Such hopes quickly proved illusory. The 1928 contest between Smith and Hoover gave new life to an ethno-religious bigotry the likes of which America had not seen since the heyday of the Know Nothings in the 1850s. Smith went down to defeat in a presidential election that one historian has recently described as "the first truly great hate campaign in modern American history."[1]

Still, for reasons this book wishes to explore, Americans who rejected Irish Catholics in politics embraced them in culture. The twenty years following Smith's electoral defeat saw Irish Americans achieve a privileged place in the most dominant medium of modern American popular culture, Hollywood cinema. In 1945, *Going My Way*, a film about an Irish-Catholic priest's efforts to save a poor urban parish from insolvency, won nearly every major Oscar at that year's Academy Awards ceremony.

How do we account for this seemingly dramatic reversal? Why did Americans who loathed the Irish as politicians love them as gangsters, boxers, working girls, priests, and song-and-dance men?

---

[1] Slayton, *Empire Statesman: The Rise and Redemption of Al Smith*, xiv.

The answer lies less in the personal qualities of these classic urban types than in the stories through which the American movie-going public encountered them. The broad appeal of Irish-American stories in the Hollywood films of the 1930s and 1940s lay primarily in their ability to present the Irish as representative of a broader vision of the city as an urban village—fully ethnic, yet fully American.[2]

This book is an effort to explicate the ethos of Hollywood's image of the Irish-American urban village. It is a study of film narrative, not film production, much less a social history of the Irish through film. Ultimately, it is an exercise in understanding the meaning of the stories on the screen, rather than explaining through concrete extra-textual evidence why Hollywood dedicated so much of its time and talent to telling these stories. Even within these modest parameters, it is very much an introductory study. The Irish are the most represented ethnic group in American film, yet the least represented in film scholarship. The early work in the field focused simply on identifying and cataloging Irish-American performers and directors—along with popular Irish-themed films.[3]

In recent years, scholars have finally started to turn their attention to a close analysis of particular films, yet too often they interpret them through the conventional categories of contemporary cultural studies—categories which, I believe, are very foreign to the spirit of the films themselves.[4] Rather than subject narrative to theory, I will subject theory to narrative. The stories of the Irish-American urban village provide the surest guide to understanding the distinctiveness of the Irish achievement in American popular culture.

---

[2]As a sociological category, the term *urban village* received its classic analysis in Gans, *The Urban Villagers*. I use this term much more loosely and make no claims for sociological rigor in my analysis of Irish-American film narrative.

[3]For a representative survey work, see Curran, *Hibernian Green on the Silver Screen*.

[4]See, for example, Barton, ed., *Screening Irish America*.

Daniel Patrick Moynihan's seminal 1963 essay on the New York Irish contains this suggestive, yet still largely ignored, observation on the cinematic significance of Irish Catholicism:

> For whatever reason, perhaps because of the influence of New York Jews in the film industry, when Hollywood undertook to synthesize the Christian religion, they found it most easy to do in the person of an Irish priest: Pat O'Brien as Father Duffy in the trenches. When it came to portraying the tough American, up from the streets, the image was repeatedly that of an Irishman. James Cagney (a New Yorker) was the quintessential figure: fists cocked, chin out, back straight, bouncing along on his heels. But also doomed: at the end of the movie he was usually dead. The contrast with [Charlie] Chaplin tells worlds.[5]

The failure of film scholars to reflect on this phenomenon also tells worlds.

Moynihan's essay provides a clue to this silence. At once nostalgic and critical, it waxes poetic about the golden age of Irish-American popular culture at the same time that it scolds Irish Americans for their failure to embrace the Irish modernism of Yeats and Joyce, or the homegrown, Irish-American modernism of F. Scott Fitzgerald and Eugene O'Neill. Despite reaching lyrical heights rare for academic prose, Moynihan's essay remains fundamentally a sociological autopsy revealing the inability of Irish-Americans to break out of the repressive cultural restraints of lower-middle-class Catholicism.

Moynihan bemoaned the aesthetic limitations of urban, Irish stereotypes. Film scholars, on the other hand, often prove unwilling or unable to identify certain urban stereotypes as Irish. Peter Quinn has recently identified this blind spot in both popular and scholarly approaches to American urban history.[6] Contemporary viewers of classic Hollywood films are likely to identify certain styles of speech and action as generically urban or working-class rather than distinctly Irish—as if the Irish did not play a central role in creating

---

[5] Glazer and Moynihan, *Beyond the Melting Pot*, 246–47.

[6] Quinn, "Looking for Jimmy," in Quinn, *Looking for Jimmy: A Search for Irish America*, 19–42.

what became a general urban, working-class culture. Too often, the search for Irish ethnic culture becomes a search for immigrant culture, the survival of the old world in the new.

Even worse, the privileged "ethnic" narrative has come to be the story that dramatizes the conflict between the old world and the new. Most scholars in recent film and cultural studies tend to view ethnicity in terms established most clearly in the work of Werner Sollars. For Sollars, the Ur-ethnic scenario consists of an individual caught between two worlds—ethnic and American—struggling to forge some unique identity that could reconcile or transcend the two cultures.[7] Such a tale of ethnicity was in fact present at the creation of the sound era. Alan Crosland's 1927 film, *The Jazz Singer*, tells the story of Jackie Rabinowitz / Jack Robin, the son of a Jewish cantor torn between his duty to follow in his father's footsteps and his desire to pursue his own dreams of success as a popular entertainer.

Scholars looking for an angst-ridden identity crisis of the kind featured in *The Jazz Singer* will be disappointed, and more than a little baffled, by Irish-American films of the 1930s and 1940s. The characters in these films certainly have problems, but identity is not one of them. Irish-American characters may not always know what to do, but they always know who they are. Troubled by conflicting loyalties and obligations within their urban ethnic enclave, they nevertheless understand that they must work out their destiny in terms set by the local community. In these films, ethnicity is not who you are, but where you are.

The Jazz Singer tells a story of ethnicity. The Irish-themed films I will examine tell ethnic stories. Of course, both kinds of stories were available to and experienced by all ethnic groups of the time. Still, the Irish seemed to have a special claim on the ethnic urban village story. The two greatest achievements of Irish-American culture—the Catholic Church (organized by geographic parishes) and the urban wing of the Democratic Party (organized by neighborhood wards)—

---

[7] See Sollars, *Beyond Ethnicity: Consent and Descent in American Culture.*

tie Irish-American identity to place in a way deeper and broader than for any other ethnic group in America. Charles Morris and other scholars have pointed out that even as Irish-American bishops fought against particular ethnic identities in their effort to create a unified "American" Church, they created a whole separate universe of social institutions rooted in local parishes to serve as a firewall against assimilation into mainstream American Protestant culture.[8]

Party and Church linked power and authority to residency in specific local communities; moreover, they sought to link these local communities through an integrated, city-wide organizational structure. This in part explains how the Irish could represent the ethnic city even when they lacked numerical majorities. Every ethnic group could claim one part of the city—a Little Italy, a Chinatown—but only the Irish could consistently claim the whole city for themselves. The classic Irish sections of New York, such as the Bowery and Hell's Kitchen, were much more ethnically diverse than the enclaves of other groups.[9] This mixed settlement pattern gave the Irish a representative status with respect to the city as a whole without diluting the neighborhood loyalties of local attachments.

The authority of place found its way into the stories that shaped American urban popular culture during the period of Irish dominance, from the late-nineteenth through the early-twentieth centuries. The New York plays of Harrigan and Hart and the Chicago journalism of Finley Peter Dunne (under the guise of his Bridgeport South-Side Irish barman, Mr. Dooley) repeatedly satirize efforts at upward mobility that draw people out of their ethnic enclaves.[10] With their light comic touch, these stories avoid both the assimilation anxiety of the early parts of *The Jazz Singer* and the facile synthesis of ethnic and American with which that film concludes.

---

[8]On the separate universe of American Catholicism, see Charles Morris, *American Catholic: The Saints and Sinners Who Built America's Most Powerful Church.*

[9]I would like to thank the author of the anonymous reader's report for reminding me to emphasize this distinctive feature of Irish urban settlement.

[10]See Williams, "Green Again: Irish-American Lace-Curtain Satire."

The happy ending of these Irish-American comic stories comes when failed social climbers realize the error of their ways and return to their relatively unchanged ethnic communities. Some Irish-American performers became very successful by satirizing the American dream of success. By the end of this period, these entertainers seemed comfortable enough with achievement to put success on the stage itself. George M. Cohan, the last dominant Irish-American performer of the New York stage, celebrated the Horatio Alger myth of upward mobility in many of his musicals. Still, for all his national, flag-waving patriotism, Cohan's life and art measured success in terms of a specific—and in retrospect, very local—place: Broadway. Localism of one sort or another continued to place limits on success.

The social and cultural reality of Irish America never fit neatly into the ideals of either Harrigan or Cohan. By the 1930s, the Irish were, as a group, above the tenement squalor of *McNally's Row of Flats*, but they were hardly the plucky Yankee Doodle Dandies of *Little Johnny Jones*. Socially and culturally, the Irish of this time are best understood in terms of the category of lower middle class. The descendents of immigrants who came to America to make a better life for themselves, the Irish understood this betterment less in terms of improvement than security, the achievement of a basic material subsistence denied them in the Old World.

Protestant reformers and other agents of Americanization insisted that immigrants would never rise above poverty if they continued to hold on to Old-World cultural values—most especially Catholicism. The Irish embraced America as a land of economic opportunity and political democracy, yet saw no conflict between patriotism and loyalty to Old-World values—most especially Catholicism. Warts and all, this socio-cultural world found a fairly accurate reflection in the Irish-American city films of the 1930s and 1940s. It was a world still living and vital at the time. Hollywood screenwriters of whatever ethnic background needed no special sociological or anthropological skills to hold up a mirror to this city life.

Indeed, for gritty realism, good humor, triumph, and tragedy, no Hollywood film could ever match the real-life comedy and drama of the man whose political downfall seemed to inaugurate a renaissance in Irish-American popular culture: Al Smith. In nature and nurture, Smith embodied the whole cultural range of the ethnic city. Born of an Irish mother and a father of mixed German and Italian descent, he grew up in the Bowery, a section of New York with a heavily Jewish population. Smith embraced American political democracy and ran for the highest office in the land, but refused to turn his back on his own kind. He campaigned wearing his signature brown derby and chomping on his trademark stogie; most disastrously, he continued to allow himself to be photographed in the company of Catholic priests and bishops. The vote against Smith was as much a vote against his urban world as against any particular policy he advocated.

In a sense, the personal nature of so much of the reaction to Smith was only fitting. From his earliest days in Tammany Hall, the political club that ran the Democratic Party in New York, Smith had come to understand politics in terms of people rather than policies. Tammany held loyalty to friends as the highest political virtue. To outsiders, such loyalty was mere tribalism and a cover for graft and corruption. Smith, for his part, refused to renounce his association with Tammany Hall. Instead, he tried to make the case for loyalty in terms of a deeper ethic of community—an ideal that could appeal to rural WASPs as well as urban ethnics.

Smith made the case for community most eloquently in *Up to Now*, the autobiography occasioned by his presidential run in 1928. Looking back on his childhood, he writes,

> When I was growing up everybody downtown knew his neighbors—not only people who were immediate neighbors but everybody in the neighborhood. Every new arrival in the family was hailed not by the family alone but by the whole neighborhood. Every funeral and every wake was attended by the whole neighborhood. Neighborly feelings extended to the exchange of silverware for events in the family

that required some extraordinary celebration. Today on Manhattan
Island, people live in large apartment houses and do not know the
family living right on the same floor with them.[11]

Here Smith clearly appeals to neighborliness as a kind of common
ground for urban and non-urban Americans. He acknowledges the
growing impersonality of city life, but condemns it and sees it as a
departure from the community ideals that shaped him as a child.

Still, Smith forcefully holds his ground against those reformers
who saw in his childhood world nothing but a bad "environment."
As the historian Oscar Handlin has commented, the very tendency
of reformers to think in abstract, impersonal terms such as "environment" struck Smith as a threat to "family life and religion and all
established social relationships."[12] Against reformers who insisted
that children need official supervision to stay healthy and active,
Smith affirms the free play of the streets: "No gymnasium that was
ever built, no athletic club in the country, could offer to anybody the
opportunities given to the small boy along the water front, using
the bowsprit and the rigging of ships as a gymnasium. When the
ship came to port laden to the water line, trapezes, parallel bars,
everything that would take the place of the modern gymnasium was
available."[13]

Over the course of his career in public life, Smith had actually
proven himself willing and able to work with reformers on a variety
of issues, particularly those relating to the protection of labor. Still,
as an urban ethnic insider, he realized that outsider reformers too
often threw out the baby with the bath water, destroying healthy,
informal community practices in the name of fixing social problems.

Smith defends those community norms most clearly in his account of his family life. By the standards of WASP reformers, Smith
came from a broken home. His father, Alfred E. Smith, Sr., worked
himself into an early grave, dying in 1886 at the age of 46. Al

---

[11] Smith, *Up to Now: An Autobiography*, 25.
[12] Handlin, *Al Smith and His America*, 36.
[13] Smith, *Up to Now*, 17.

was only thirteen years old and had to drop out of school to help support his family through a variety of manual labor jobs. Given his concern to reach out to rural WASP America, Smith could have used his rise from a hardscrabble childhood as an occasion to sing the praises of hard work and self-sufficiency. Instead, reflecting on his life, he gives these individualistic American values their due but subordinates them to the deeper values of community.

Al Sr. had achieved some modest success by the working-class standards of the day (he owned a small trucking company), yet defined his manhood in terms of his personal relations rather than material success. For the elder Smith, a "man who cannot do a favor for a friend is not a man."[14] From his father, Al Jr. learned the joys of Sundays at the beer garden and odd hours at the local volunteer fireman's clubhouse. These and other associations—most especially Smith's childhood parish of St. James—bound the Smith family to their little corner of the Bowery, despite the more unsavory elements that lingered about them on all sides. Raising his family in the shadow of the Brooklyn Bridge, Smith's father refused to succumb to the lure of cheap land in what was then the independent city of Brooklyn.[15] Smith's dwelling on the intense localism of his upbringing bears out Peter Quinn's assessment of his candidacy: "Even when Tammany reached for the White House, its heart was in the neighborhood."[16]

Smith's father may never have wished to venture beyond the Fourth Ward, but Smith himself had to travel far from the neighborhood before he could be in a position to make a claim on Washington. Still, his political journey from Bowery Mick to presidential aspirant took place within the institutional confines of Tammany Hall. Smith's career as a professional politician reflected an ethos of what we could call "mobility within the limits of loyalty"—an ideal

---

[14]Finan, *Alfred E. Smith: The Happy Warrior*, 9.

[15]Smith, *Up to Now*, 5.

[16]Quinn, "Local Politics, Irish-American Style," in Quinn, *Looking for Jimmy*, 104.

central to understanding the Irish-American films of the 1930s and 1940s.

Smith believed in the American dream of working to achieve a better life, but like so many urban Irish Catholics, he understood that dream in communal rather than individualistic terms. Understanding that big-city politics was one of the few areas of life where an Irishman stood a fair chance of rising in the world, Smith placed himself under the mentorship of Henry Campbell, a saloon owner and local Democratic Party operative. He quickly came to the attention of the new Tammany sachem, Charles Murphy, who groomed Smith for service upstate and ran him successfully for a seat on the New York State Assembly.[17] A position in Albany was a death sentence for any true New Yorker. A sleepy town with nothing to do but listen to upstate "hayseeds" and blue-blood reformers drone on about matters of policy, Albany stood in sharp contrast to the rough-and-tumble excitement of New York City ward politics. Still, a solid Tammany man, Smith did his duty.

The qualities that endeared Smith to Tammany threatened to embarrass him in the Assembly. Before leaving for Albany, his mentor Henry Campbell took him to Brooks Brothers to buy new clothes, so that "the old neighborhood would have as well dressed an assemblyman as the uptown folks have."[18] In the eyes of the uptown folks, however, clothes did not make the man. Smith's habit of eating big, messy deli sandwiches at his assembly desk and talking with food in his mouth confirmed the blue bloods' assumptions concerning his city vulgarity. Smith eventually learned to talk without food in his mouth, but never forsook the speaking style that the *New York Times* derisively compared to that of a Coney Island Barker.[19] He was a great joker and storyteller in the city mode; he would often entertain his fellow urban assemblymen with vaudeville routines

---

[17]Handlin, *Al Smith and His America*, 31–32. See also Finan, *The Happy Warrior*, 73ff.

[18]Handlin, *Al Smith and His America*, 47.

[19]Slayton, *Empire Statesman*, 102.

and ethnic imitations. In the end, Smith was happy to have his sartorial transformation remain skin deep.

In one famous incident, some Ivy League assemblymen sought to embarrass Smith by comparing their social and educational pedigrees. Amidst the boasts of Harvard and Yale men, Smith declared himself an FFM man—that is a Fulton Fish Market man, a reference to the dockside market he worked at as a child to help support his family after the death of his father.[20] Proud of his cultural roots, he also fought a political battle for "home rule" for New York City at a time when the state legislature exerted a tremendous degree of power over local city politics. In a famous exchange during the 1915 New York State constitutional convention, Smith responded to the blue-blood reformer Seth Low's claim—that New York City had more self-rule than cities in California—with the defiant boast: "I would sooner be a lamp post on Park Row than the Governor of California."[21] Three years later, Smith would be elected to his first term as governor of New York.

To be sure, Smith could never have won a statewide election on ethnic loyalty alone. During his years in the Assembly, Smith gradually supplemented his local patriotism with a broader reform agenda in tune with the ethos of the Progressive Era—though Smith's brand of Progressivism tended to emphasize protective legislation for workers and the poor rather than the managerial expertise favored by some WASP reformers.

The turning point in Smith's political career came not through any extravagant act of patronage, but through his leadership in the reform response to the catastrophic Triangle Shirtwaist Factory fire of 1913.[22] No turn away from Tammany, Smith's embrace of reform was the brainchild of none other than Charles Murphy himself. "Silent" Charlie was a new breed of Tammany politician, one who

---

[20] Smith, *Up to Now*, 111–12.

[21] Finan, *The Happy Warrior*, 102.

[22] See Slayton, *Empire Statesman*, Chapter 6, "The Triangle Shirtwaist Fire," 89–100.

realized that the organization had to make some kind of peace with the various reform movements afoot. Murphy's strategy was first to minimize the more blatant forms of graft and then to groom certain candidates who would be loyal to Tammany while personally distanced from the other forms of graft that continued to grease the wheels of local New York politics.[23] Murphy had, early on, picked Smith to be one of his "clean" candidates, and the strategy paid off with Smith securing the governor's mansion—without ever having to renounce his loyalty to Tammany Hall.

Still, the synthesis that sustained him at the state level destroyed him at the national level. Smith's refusal to turn his back on his political roots led the mainstream WASP press to brand him a Tammany stooge.[24] The charge was, in the end, cultural as much as political. With the glaring exception of Prohibition, there was very little to distinguish Smith from Hoover on matters of public policy. Both were "Progressives," in favor of some moderate, middle way between the older ideals of the pure free market and newer ideals of state socialism emanating from Europe. Still, with his bowler hat and stogie cigar, Smith would always be, in the words of the influential small-town editor William Allen White, "Al Smith, City Feller."[25] White intended the label as a slur directed at the city as both a cultural and political entity.

For his part, Smith also refused to separate culture and politics. When first nominated for the Democratic presidential ticket in 1920, the convention band starting playing a medley of old Tin Pan Alley, Irish-American popular songs from the turn of the century. Smith adopted one of those songs, "The Sidewalks of New York," as his campaign theme song when he finally won the nomination in 1928.[26] Smith's appeal to city voters lay at least as much in his

---

[23] Slayton, *Empire Statesman*, 84–88.
[24] Ibid., 206.
[25] White, "Al Smith, City Feller," *Colliers* 78 (August 21, 1926): 8–9.
[26] Slayton, *Empire Statesman*, 146.

comfort and familiarity with urban popular culture as with his roots in city politics.

Smith gloried in the amusements of the city and, early on in his life, seriously contemplated pursuing a career in the theater. He grew up idolizing Harrigan and Hart, and got some of his earliest theatrical experience in the church basement at St. James, where he performed in amateur productions of the plays of Dion Boucicault, the Irish nationalist who wrote some of the most popular melodramas produced in the English-speaking world in the late nineteenth century. Smith eventually put aside his theatrical aspirations to pursue the only slightly more stable profession of politics, but he continued to hobnob with New York entertainers. Jimmy Durante used to play piano in the Smith's home; Eddie Cantor stumped for him in 1928 in part to repay Smith's kindness to him as a boy growing up on the Lower East Side.[27]

The affirmation of the popular amusements of the city would be another link between the real-life world of Al Smith and the Hollywood version of the thirties and forties. By 1928, Hollywood was already well on its way to replacing New York as the entertainment capital of America. Despite his reservations about California, Smith extended his love of the stage to the new medium of the screen. The admiration was mutual: Smith had the support of all of the national entertainment celebrities.[28]

As he waited in his governor's mansion in New York to hear the results of the voting at the Democratic national convention in Houston, Smith donned a ten-gallon hat given to him by the Hollywood cowboy star Tom Mix. The gesture was typical of Smith's penchant for humor and love of performance, but it was a gesture with a point. By adopting the costume of a cowboy, Smith offered some symbolic unity to a Democratic Party deeply divided between its Northern/urban/Catholic and Southern/rural/Protestant wings.

---

[27]Ibid., 20, 63.
[28]Ibid., 297.

The particular cowboy hat Smith donned may have only exacerbated some of those fears. It was, after all, the hat of a movie cowboy. As one spokesman for the Ku Klux Klan concluded following Smith's nomination, "He will get the vote of the Jew-Jesuit movie gang who want sex films and Sunday shows to coin millions through the corruption of youth."[29] The Klansman may have been woefully misinformed about Jesuit attitudes toward sex, but his statement reflects an accurate assessment that the modern commercial entertainment industry was largely a creation of Jewish and Catholic immigrants.[30]

Scholars have long acknowledged the role of Jewish Americans in the creation of Hollywood, but the Irish contribution has yet to receive its due. True, all of the major studios were founded by Jewish Americans, but the Hollywood of the first half of the twentieth century starts to look much greener once you look down from the top tier of ownership. The Irish certainly never dominated Hollywood the way that they once ruled the New York stage, but no less a scholar than Kevin Brownlow has argued that the Irish deserve equal credit with the Jews for shaping American cinema, at least through the silent era.[31] Irish-American influence might not have kept numeric pace with the geometric expansion of the film industry during the first decade of the sound era, but even as the percentage of Irish Americans among the ranks of film professionals declined, Irish-American stories achieved a central place in Hollywood film production.

Appreciation for those stories has suffered from a single-minded scholarly obsession with the Irish-Catholic role in film censorship.[32]

---

[29] Ibid., 316.

[30] The Jewish contribution to American popular culture has been extensively documented. On the Jews in Hollywood, see, for example, Gabler, *An Empire of Their Own: How the Jews Invented Hollywood*.

[31] Brownlow, "The Irish in Early Hollywood," delivered at the conference "Screening Irish America," University College at Dublin, April 13, 2007.

[32] For representative works on film censorship, see *Black, Hollywood Censored: Morality Codes, Catholics, and the Movies*; Leff and Simmons, *The Dame in the*

The scholarly consensus that Catholic organizations such as the Legion of Decency used political pressure to impose a Victorian moral code on Hollywood film production has left scholars with little reason to go looking for distinctive Irish cultural traits or stories in the films of the thirties and forties. According to the standard narrative, middle-class Catholics of this period had completely internalized repressive WASP moral standards and used film censorship to impose these old values on an American populace otherwise on a steady march toward modernist liberation. The centralized organizational structures of the Catholic Church enabled Catholic reformers to succeed where earlier, comparatively decentralized Protestant efforts had failed, yet the moral standards Catholics imposed were indistinguishable from those advocated by nineteenth-century Protestant reformers.

That Catholics would emerge in the 1930s as the guardians of American morality so soon after the debacle of 1928 raises questions that cannot be answered by indictments of Irish-Catholic sexual repression. True, on most questions of sexual morality, Catholics held views indistinguishable from those of Middle America. Still,

---

Kimono: Hollywood Censorship and the Production Code from the 1920s to the 1960s; and Walsh, *Sin and Censorship: The Catholic Church and the Motion Picture Industry*. The scholarly bias against censorship reflects the academic professional's class interest in "free" expression; the single-minded focus on censorship reflects interests a bit more sinister. As Al Smith once claimed that assaults on his Tammany connections were really a cover for anti-Catholicism, so I would argue that scholarly attacks on the Production Code Administration, directed by Irish-Catholic layman Joseph Breen, have served as cover for the respectable bigotry of secular anti-Catholic historians. Reading the most respected of these works, one would hardly know that Joe Breen's tenure at the PCA coincided with the golden age of Hollywood, a unique moment that saw both a consistently high quality in artistic and technical standards of production, as well as a never-to-be-repeated harmony between commercial culture and popular moral values. Both aspects were essential to Hollywood's successful claim to represent American culture. The second half of the equation would have been impossible without Joe Breen, the lay Catholic activists of the Legion of Decency, and Fr. Daniel Lord, S.J., the principle author of the censorship code that guided Breen through the early 1950s.

Catholics succeeded where Protestants had failed because of their unique ability to combine concern for moral standards with a genuine openness toward the arts and amusements of modern popular culture.[33] This sensibility enabled Irish Catholics to flourish within the film industry without cutting themselves off from the moral guidance of the Church. Daniel Lord, S.J., may have crafted the censorship code that guided Hollywood through the thirties and forties, but he did so at the request of Martin Quigley, a lay Catholic journalist who ran the influential trade publication *Moving Picture World.*

Quigley solicited Lord's aid for both moral and practical reasons. Personally alarmed by the immoral content of many Hollywood films, he also realized that in the long run, excessive sex and violence would hurt business by undermining Hollywood's appeal to a broader family audience. Earlier efforts at self-censorship had failed, in no small part due to the inept leadership of Hollywood's first morality czar, Will Hays. A former Postmaster General and Republican National Committee chairman, Hays's WASP moral credentials were impeccable. Unfortunately, he had no feel for film as an art or as a business and could not effectively work with the urban ethnics who ran Hollywood. By 1934, Hollywood producers had finally found their man in Joe Breen, the Irish-Catholic layman who directed Hollywood's in-house censorship office—the Production Code Administration—through the golden age of the thirties and forties.[34]

The focus on sexual repression has obscured the persistence of a whole range of issues on which Irish Catholics refused to assimilate to middle-class American norms. Smith biographer Christopher Fi-

---

[33]R. Laurence Moore has made this point in his paper "Tocqueville, American Catholics, and American Democratic Culture," a talk delivered at the Cushwa Center for the Study of American Catholicism, April 12, 2001.

[34]Despite his acceptance of the basic "repression" framework of the existing scholarship, Charles Morris provides a very good short account of this story in Morris, *American Catholic*, 200–209.

nan captures this consensus and conflict when he assesses Smith's response to the dilemma of bachelor boredom during his early years in Albany: "If Smith abjured the brothels, he loved bars."[35] Protestant Americans who might have acknowledged a rough consensus on sexual matters continued to indict Catholics for tolerating and promoting any number of other "immoral" practices, not the least of which was the consumption of alcohol. Smith's opposition to Prohibition was part of his long-standing fight against Protestant moral reformers who sought to impose some kind of prohibition on the whole range of popular amusements so dear to Smith's heart. By the standards of the day, Catholics were a threat to public morality simply because they wished to attend baseball games on Sunday.

It is easy for readers now to dismiss these fears as paranoid or simply silly. For Irish Catholics in the nativist twenties, they were no laughing matter.[36] It was these broader cultural issues, rather than more narrow concerns over sex and violence, which occasioned the first big Irish-Catholic push into film censorship. Organized Irish film activism began in protests surrounding *The Callahans and the Murphys* (George Hill, 1927), a major MGM production that many Irish-American leaders felt perpetuated the negative Irish stereotypes that would only fuel nativist hatred of the Irish and Catholics in general. Not a few of the protesters linked the release of the film to broader efforts to discredit the candidacy of Al Smith, even then the clear favorite for the Democratic nomination in 1928.[37]

Irish fears concerning the political consequences of negative stereotypes proved well-founded. The popular press routinely mocked Smith and his wife Katie as little more than Jiggs and

---

[35] Finan, *The Happy Warrior*, 57.

[36] On nativism, see Higham, *Strangers in the Land: Patterns of American Nativism, 1865–1925*.

[37] See Couvares, "Hollywood, Main Street, and the Church: Trying to Censor the Movies Before the Production Code," in Couvares, ed., *Movie Censorship and American Culture*, 145–52.

Maggie, a reference to the popular comic strip that perpetuated many of the stereotypes on display in *The Callahans and the Murphys*.[38] The comparison points to certain ambiguities in the role of stereotypes in the culture at the time. The comic strip was the creation of George McManus, an Irish-American. Firmly in the satiric tradition of Ned Harrigan and Finley Peter Dunne, most of the strip's stories revolve around the conflict between Maggie's desire for upward mobility and Jiggs's wish to hang out with his buddies in the old neighborhood.

Irish Americans continued to enjoy these stories, even when they perpetuated what most middle-class Irish reformers would deem to be negative stereotypes. Most ordinary Irish Americans recognized the kernel of truth in the stereotype and delighted in the exaggeration. They probably even conceded that the exaggerations themselves often reflected the truth of some Irish Americans. What they could not tolerate was outsiders laughing at them as somehow uniquely foolish—or nativists using the comedy of human weakness as a political tool to deny the Irish status as true Americans.

The Irish succeeded in pressuring MGM to cut the more egregious ethnic stereotyping from *The Callahans and the Murphys* and to remove any disrespectful treatment of Catholicism. Still, much of what remained could hardly be reconciled with the norms of middle-class Protestantism. The Irish who appeared in the final censored version were still very much Paddies and Bridgets—drinking, fighting, and not working too hard. Some thin-skinned Irish continued to take offense and insisted that Irish Catholics were as thrifty, sober, and industrious—that is to say, as American—as any Protestant.[39] Most, however, responded by affirming much of what WASP

---

[38] Slayton, *Empire Statesman*, 314.

[39] Timothy J. Meagher has presented one of the most nuanced accounts of the range of Irish responses to American culture in Meagher, *Inventing Irish America: Generation, Class and Ethnic Identity in a New England City, 1880–1928*. He stresses a tension between an Irish identity rooted in old-world ways and an Irish-American identity profoundly shaped by a stern Victorian moralism, even to the point of

America condemned. Like Smith in his presidential campaign, Irish-Catholic protesters insisted on their proper standing as Americans while refusing to reject their roots.

Of all these roots, Catholicism ran the deepest and inspired the greatest fear and loathing on the part of Protestant America.[40] Smith's nomination seemed to confirm nativist fears of a Catholic takeover of America. Rumors spread that he was secretly digging a tunnel connecting Washington D.C. to the Vatican. Nativists claimed that should Smith win the election, he would then have the pope declare all non-Catholic marriages annulled, thus rendering all Protestant children illegitimate.[41]

And if Catholicism was the single greatest factor in Smith's political defeat, it was also the single greatest factor in the Irish cultural victory in Hollywood film. On the one hand, Catholicism provided a clear firewall against assimilation, one that would most sharply set the Irish apart from WASP America. On the other, Catholicism authoritatively sustained a premodern moral sensibility that tolerated popular amusements within certain limits, sparing the Irish the burden of having to choose between entertainment and faith. In the world of American popular culture, Irish Catholics possessed the unique ability to be at the same time traditional and modern, ethnic and American.

The comparison with the other great ethnic entertainers, American Jews, is instructive. In *The Jazz Singer*, Jackie Rabinowitz has to choose between being a cantor or a jazz singer, while in *Going My Way*, Chuck O'Malley becomes a priest and remains a crooner.

---

advocating temperance. He tends to present the success of the Knights of Columbus at the expense of the Ancient Order of Hibernians as a triumph of middle-class moralism, but again, once one gets past the issue of sex, the drinking and gambling Knights appear quite far from Protestant redemption. On Catholic Americanization programs, see Sterne, *Ballots and Bibles: Ethnic Politics and the Catholic Church in Providence*, especially Chapter 8, "The Force of Compulsion: Americanism and the Wartime State."

[40] Slayton, *Empire Statesman*, 299.

[41] For a good sampling of such scare tactics, see ibid., 305.

That Catholics rather than Jews became the moral guardians of the popular culture of Protestant America reflects less the common ground of Christianity than the uncommon ability of Catholic culture to harmonize the sacred and the profane. Al Smith performed popular melodramas in the basement of St. James Church; under the direction of Fr. Gilbert V. Hartke, the Department of Speech and Drama at the Catholic University of America boasted one of the leading theater programs of any university in the country during the 1930s and 1940s.[42] Secular modernity did much to destroy the festivity that animated premodern European Catholic cultures, but Catholics living in the modern world sustained some of that festivity of old through their participation in the popular arts.

Localism and loyalty, festivity and faith—Al Smith celebrated these ideals in national politics . . . and lost. Hollywood used them to fuel its great American dream machine . . . and won. Why? We might attribute it to higher tolerance or lower expectations in culture as opposed to politics, but we must also acknowledge that in the few short years between Smith's defeat and the first films of James Cagney, American politics itself changed a lot.

The Great Depression called into question some of the most fundamental assumptions of the American dream, most especially the idea that the individual is in control of his own destiny and free to rise in the world as far as his talent and hard work will take him. By the early 1930s, the traditional Irish-Catholic suspicion of individualism and mobility appeared to have found confirmation in the social and economic realities of the day. The times, it would seem, had finally caught up to Irish-American folk wisdom. By linking suspicion of progress to a particular ethnic group, moreover, Hollywood could speak to one undeniable truth of the age without having to challenge the conventional American faith in progress.

To be sure, classic American ideals persisted in film. Scholars have lavished much attention on the links between Hollywood cin-

---

[42]See San Pietro, *Father Hartke: His Life and Legacy to the American Theater.*

ema and the New Deal.[43] Franklin Roosevelt won the hearts and
minds of Americans by appealing to classic, nineteenth-century
American ideals of individual freedom even as he promoted the
construction of a centralized national state that seemed to undermine those old values. Federal agencies such as the Federal Writers'
Project and the Farm Security Administration cultivated the image
of the dust-bowl migrant farmer as a symbol of the resilience of
the human spirit in the face of the economic collapse of urban
industrial civilization—a disjunction ironic at best, deceptive and
manipulative at worst.[44]

On closer examination, this pairing seems quite natural, almost
unavoidable. The extremes of centralized state and isolated individual are the foundational categories of modern liberal political
theory; they have kept a tenacious grip on the American political
and cultural imagination. The rise, during the 1930s, of the idea of
culture as a "whole way of life" marked the most significant effort to
think beyond these traditional liberal categories. Yet, in practice, the
term merely reinforced the conventional liberal alternatives of state
and individual.[45] America has had a much more difficult time with
the middle ground of community. Nostalgia and sentiment abound,
to be sure, but beyond this superficial level, Americans seem inclined
to view community as a threat to individual freedom.[46]

---

[43]For the classic study, see Nick Roddick, *New Deal in Entertainment: Warner
Brothers in the 1930s*. More recent works include Muscio, *Hollywood's New Deal*;
and Giovacchini, *Hollywood Modernism: Film and Politics in the Age of the New
Deal*.

[44]On this issue, the best work remains Stott, *Documentary Expression in Thirties
America*.

[45]Susman, "The Culture of the Thirties," in Susman, *Culture as History: The
Transformation of American Society in the Twentieth Century*, 150–83. Shannon,
*Conspicuous Criticism: Tradition, The Individual, and Culture in Modern American
Social Thought*, Ch. 4, "Patterns of Control."

[46]On this, see Shannon, *Conspicuous Criticism*, Chapter 2, "Middletown as Transition."

The Irish-American films of the thirties and forties stand as one of the few substantial American cultural achievements to elude these liberal cultural antinomies. No minor ethnic genre, the films of the Irish-American urban village created and/or attracted some of the biggest stars and directors of Hollywood's golden age—James Cagney, Spencer Tracy, Bing Crosby, Errol Flynn, Ginger Rogers, Raoul Walsh, and Leo McCarey, to name but a few. These films told the story of Al Smith's ethnic city through a variety of genres covering the whole range of urban life—crime, sports, romance, faith, and entertainment.[47] As an urban village, Smith's city was small-town America with a rougher edge, both tragic and comic—a city where faith and family existed side by side with crime and corruption, where a stiff drink and a night at the fights was a just reward for a hard day's work.

In their only slightly milder forms, the drinking, fighting, laughing, and crying that once marked Irish savagery now stood as a sign of Irish humanity. Redeemed from the slurs of nativists, the Irish nonetheless never became representative Americans. The New Deal, World War II, and Hollywood cinema combined to bring an unprecedented degree of political and cultural unity to American life, but America as a nation is only a minor presence in most of these films. Through it all, the Irish would remain local heroes.

---

[47]The notable exception to this is, of course, politics. Studio heads judged it box-office poison. Preston Sturges had a very difficult time getting any major studio to produce *The Great McGinty*. See Jacobs, *Christmas in July: The Life and Art of Preston Sturges*, 145.

Chapter 1

Hell's Kitchen

THE CULTURAL REHABILITATION OF IRISH AMERICA began in the most unlikely of all genres: the gangster film. For many Americans in 1928, there was little difference between Al Smith and Al Capone. One was an Irish politician, the other an Italian gangster, but as urban, ethnic-Catholic "wets," both appeared equally criminal in their threat to the religious and cultural pre-eminence of rural and small-town Protestant America. Italian Americans won the battle to control the real-life world of gangsters, yet Irish Americans won the battle to represent the big-city gangster in Hollywood film.

From *The Public Enemy* (William Wellman, 1931) through *Angels with Dirty Faces* (Michael Curtiz, 1938), the great Irish-American gangster films render the rich communal ethos of the urban village even as they directly confront the violence so much a part of that world. The characters in these films struggle with, rather than against, violence.[1] Those who triumph do so not by banishing violence from the village, but by transforming it from a force for destruction to a force for redemption. In the best of these films, the Irish-American gangster hero dies a sacrificial death that affirms the primacy of neighborhood ties.

---

[1] For this distinction regarding attitudes toward violence, I am indebted to Alan Erenhalt, *The Lost City: The Forgotten Virtues of Community in America*, especially Chapter 1, "The Limited Life."

For all their sensationalism, gangster films have long invited reflection on some of the most profound themes in Western literature.
Most of the scholarly work on the genre has been little more than a
footnote to Robert Warshow's famous essay, "The Gangster as Tragic
Hero." Warshow established the gangster as a classical American
character: hard-working, self-controlled (in terms of alcohol and
sex, if not violence) and driven to succeed. According to Warshow,
the "gangster's whole life is an effort to assert himself as an individual to draw himself out of the crowd."[2] In his effort to bring the
urban gangster into the great pantheon of American cultural types,
Warshow downplays the ethnic dimension of the gangster stories.
At most, he treats ethnicity as yet another source of alienation.

Some scholars have given greater attention to the ethnic dimensions of the gangster stories, but still follow Warshow in their
concern to locate the gangster either in the tradition of American
individualism or in the new world of corporate capitalism and modern consumerism.[3] To be fair, in two out of the three major works
of the "first wave" of gangster films of the early 1930s—*Little Caesar* (Mervyn LeRoy, 1930), *The Public Enemy* (1931), and *Scarface*
(Howard Hawks, 1932)—ethnicity is little more than local color.
Little Caesar and *Scarface* feature Capone-inspired Italian-American
gangsters who are indeed classic American individualists. Most com-
mentators have followed Warshow in focusing on these films to the
near exclusion of *The Public Enemy* and its distinctly Irish-American

---

[2]Warshow, "The Gangster as Tragic Hero," in Warshow, *The Immediate Experience: Movies, Comics, Theatre, and Other Aspects of Popular Culture*, 133.

[3]See, for example, Munby, *Public Enemies, Public Heroes: Screening the Gangster
from* Little Caesar *to* Touch of Evil. David E. Ruth does identify an ethnic pattern
of sorts, in that Italian gangsters tend to stand for the "modern" ethic of business
organization, while the Irish represent the survival of a "traditional" ethic based
on neighborhood loyalty and friendship. Still, his work, following Warshow, tends
to emphasize the rootless modernity of the gangster film at the expense of the
local. See Ruth, *Inventing the Public Enemy: The Gangster in American Culture,
1918–1934*, 73.

story. This is understandable, since *The Public Enemy* makes very little sense in the terms set by Warshow.

The story of the rise and fall of the Irish-American gangster Tom Powers in *The Public Enemy* could not be any further from the destructive individualism of Italian-American counterparts Rico Bandello (*Little Caesar*) and Tony Camonte (*Scarface*). Despite superficial similarities in style and temperament—such as a desire for fancy clothes and a penchant for impulsive violence—Tom operates according to a social code fundamentally opposed to that of Rico and Tony. If the motto of *Little Caesar* and *Scarface* is "I want to be somebody," then the moral of *The Public Enemy* is "You gotta have friends."

No rootless individual on the make, Tom is a local boy who rises through the ranks of the various neighborhood gangs due as much to loyalties forged in childhood as to the pure "merit," as it were, of his violence. All three characters die at the end of their respective films, but they die for different reasons. Rico and Tony fall at the point when their aggressive individualism finally turns them against their best friend. In contrast, Tom meets his fate when he sacrifices his own life to avenge the murder of his best friend by a rival gang. *The Public Enemy* is less a morality tale on the consequences of blind ambition than a fable of the duties and obligations imposed by membership in a community not of one's own making.

The opening scenes establish the film as a story of a place in time. Following a title card announcing the year 1909, director William Wellman uses stock footage of congested intersections, stockyards, and factories to establish the city itself as the first character in the film. Shifting visual gears from stock to studio, Wellman offers an extended photo essay on a city neighborhood whose whole existence seems to revolve around beer. He presents close-up shots of beer poured into buckets and hauled on trucks in barrels. A tracking shot, spanning several city blocks, reveals one or two saloons on every corner. Men carry buckets of beer on poles through the streets, dodging a Salvation Army marching band singing temperance songs.

The moving camera stops at the "Family Entrance" sign of one bar, as two boys, Tom Powers and Matt Doyle, walk out from the swinging doors with buckets of beer, presumably for their fathers. As they sample the brew in front of the entrance, two neighborhood girls walk past them in a huff, presumably on a similar mission. After the swinging door slams in Matt's face as he tries to sneak a kiss from one of the girls, Tom scolds him for messing with women and reminds him that they have to attend to their "business." The business, of course, is crime.

This opening scene has received much comment from film scholars who wish to read Tom as a sociological or psychological case study. Spanning the interpretive spectrum from prudery to prurience, this scene supposedly reveals Tom as the product of a corrupting social environment or as a sociopath driven to violence by some primal, inexplicable hatred of women. Ultimately, the opening scenes of the film tell us less about individual motivation than cultural milieu. Tom's actions take place in a neighborhood setting that is less a material environment than a web of social relationships to which Tom is (defiantly) accountable. From an early age, crime is social, not individual.

Tom and Matt leave the girls to shoplift at a comparatively upscale department store. What they steal is less important than how they steal it. Their dramatic escape from the floorwalker suggests that the daring camaraderie of crime is at least as attractive as any actual material reward. Back at home, on the wrong side of the tracks, Tom and Matt have their criminal activities exposed by Tom's brother, Mike. Tom's father, a policeman, comes out and, through eye contact alone, orders Tom inside for punishment. Used to the routine, Tom takes his father's razor strap off its hook, hands it to him, and asks defiantly if he wants to whip him with his pants up or down.

The scene plays fairly violently today, but the average movie-goer of the early 1930s would hardly view this sort of corporal punishment as "child abuse" in any clinical sense of that term. The film's treatment of childhood crime and punishment does not explain Tom's rebellious behavior so much as it broadens our awareness of the complex social world in which he lives. It is a world that first and last defies easy sociological analysis.

Tom is poor, but he is from a relatively stable, two-parent home. Despite, or perhaps because of, a strong father figure, he seems to have little respect for authority. Still, his brother Mike, growing up in the same circumstances, seems to have internalized his policeman father's sense of right and wrong. Matt, too, has a good twin of sorts, in the figure of his sister Molly, who returns a gift of roller skates to Tom once she realizes they are stolen. The presence of Mike and Molly, who indeed will become romantically involved as adults, reflects less a WASP moral individualism—the turn to crime is a personal choice in no way determined by social environment—than a social world in which virtue and vice live side by side.

Tom's continued involvement in crime will place him increasingly at odds with Mike, but for much of the film they continue to live in the same house together. Even after Tom makes it big and moves to a fancy apartment, he continues to visit his mother—and continues to argue and fight with Mike. Despite his hostility to authority, Tom needs acceptance by his family and community in order for his success to feel complete.

Indeed, Tom's rise as a criminal appears less an assertion of individuality than a search for legitimate (criminal) authority. We see this search in Tom's relationship with two surrogate criminal fathers, Putty Nose (Murray Kinnell) and Paddy Ryan (Robert Emmett O'Connor). Putty Nose, a Fagin-like character, runs the Red Oaks Club, a local hangout for hoodlum boys. In the scene following Tom's beating by his policeman father, Tom (James Cagney) and Matt (Edward Woods) enter the club with several very expensive stolen watches for Putty Nose to fence. After entertaining the boys with bawdy songs, Putty Nose pays Tom and Matt a mere fifty cents each for the watches and demands most of that back as part of their club dues.

The next scene fast-forwards to 1915, with Putty Nose offering a mature Tom and Matt a shot at their first big job: an armed robbery of a fur warehouse. Excited by the prospect of carrying guns, Tom and Matt accept what they are assured will be an easy job. Breaking into the warehouse at night, Tom mistakes a stuffed bear for a security guard and starts firing his gun wildly. His shots draw the real security guard and, soon, the police. Tom and Matt manage to escape, but find that Putty Nose has skipped town and left them high and dry. Retreating back into the world of petty crime, they vow revenge on Putty Nose for his betrayal.

Putty Nose has his good twin, of sorts, in Paddy Ryan. A gang leader several rungs up the ladder of crime from Putty Nose, Paddy takes a sincerely paternalistic interest in Tom and Matt. Two years after the botched warehouse robbery, Tom and Matt have taken day jobs as truck drivers, but continue to scheme for ways to make a fast buck. Between deliveries, they attempt to interest Paddy Ryan, a local saloon owner, in some "hot" cigars. Paddy declines the offer— "I have my own system, boys. But being a fence isn't part of it"—but gives them the name of an associate who would be interested.

Tom and Matt thank Paddy, who proceeds to give them some friendly criminal advice: "Remember this, boys...you gotta have friends. I've been watchin' you and hearin' about you...and I've been worried. I was worried when you got mixed up with that two-timer Putty Nose. Such guys are dangerous. I'm glad you come to me. So far as Paddy Ryan is concerned, there's only two kinds of people...right and wrong. I think you're right and you'll find that I am...unless you cross me. That's all."

We next see the three together at Paddy's saloon on the eve of Prohibition. True to his earlier promises, Paddy offers to take Tom and Matt under his wing by letting them in on the ground floor of his new criminal enterprise: bootleg alcohol. Paddy offers them a very generous, even, three-way split to steal bonded whiskey out of a government warehouse. The parallels to the Putty Nose fur heist are clear, though under Paddy's guidance, this warehouse robbery is a complete success. On their triumphant return, Paddy, true to his word, splits the money evenly three ways. Tom and Matt are speechless. They have never seen so much money in their lives. Paddy assures them, "You ain't started. I'll make big shots of ya yet." The three then share a toast to their new partnership.

After their false start with Putty Nose, Tom and Matt do indeed seem to be on their way up. Having sealed their partnership with Paddy, they embark on a whirlwind ride through the consumerism that film scholars have seen as central to the appeal of the cinematic gangster. In quick succession, Tom and Matt acquire an expensive wardrobe, a new car, and beautiful women.

Paddy Ryan's alliance with the West-Side gangster, Nails Nathan (Leslie Fenton), brings opportunities for career advancement. Tom and Matt move up from driving liquor trucks to serving as the "trouble squad"—that is, the enforcers—for the expanding distribution network. Tom proves particularly adept at convincing speakeasy owners to buy from him rather than other gangsters. In a scene repeated in countless subsequent films, Tom pulls down the taps from the rival kegs, leaving the beer to flood the bar as he slaps the speakeasy owner into submission.

Tom's rise in the realms of work and leisure bears certain similarities to that of Rico and Tony, but with important differences. Rico's and Tony's advancements always come at the expense of others. In rising to the top, they step over bodies—sometimes living, sometimes dead—within their own organizations. Tom's career path is comparatively modest and bloodless. He gets in on the ground floor and moves up during a period of expansion, rather than within a zero-sum, fixed hierarchy. Most importantly, Tom does not seem to aspire to any more than the fair-dealing Paddy Ryan is willing to give him.

Like a good Irish-American civil servant, Tom seems to prefer security to opportunity. Similarly, in the realm of leisure, Tom enjoys the things that money can buy, but shows none of the obsession with consumer items that we see in *Little Caesar* and *Scarface*. For

Rico and Tony, clothes and cars are part of an effort to fashion a new identity, while for Tom they are simply a display of wealth. Tom knows who he is—no little Caesar, just an ordinary foot soldier.

Accepting a certain sense of limits in his work and leisure, Tom directs much of his social energy toward earning the acceptance of his family and non-criminal childhood friends. Despite exposure to the wider world through his life of crime, the comparatively narrow world of neighborhood remains the basis for his social identity. Tom's character changes little over time, and the basic family conflict remains constant—Tom's criminality versus Mike's virtue. This conflict often turns violent, and Mike (Donald Cook) punctuates several of his lectures with successful knockdown punches.

Mike's physical triumphs over Tom inject a certain manly quality into his nagging moralism, but his character may be the weakest link in the narrative chain of community the film otherwise successfully realizes. Mike is so glum, sober, and self-righteous that it is difficult to accept that he is of the same neighborhood, much less the same family, as Tom. Many working-class Irish Catholics were certainly ready to condemn gangsters, but Mike voices this condemnation in the culturally foreign tones of a WASP moral reformer.

This disconnect is clearest in Mike's outburst at the homecoming party in celebration of his return from service in World War I. As the scene opens, Mike looks on curiously at the elaborate flower arrangements that have been sent to the house in his honor. Some have Irish names like Ryan and Grogan, but one comes from a Samuel Nathan—Paddy Ryan's Jewish partner in crime, Nails Nathan. Mike asks Pat the cop, an old family friend, about the flowers and learns that Tom is one of Paddy Ryan's boys—bootlegging and running around with loose women—all the while telling his mother he is working in politics.

Tom and Matt have, in the meantime, set up a rather large wooden keg of beer in the center of the table. Wellman shoots the dinner scene in such a way as to have the keg completely dominate the frame. Tom and Matt try to maintain a festive air, but Mike broods quietly, staring at the keg with contempt. Tom, somewhat irritated by what he sees as Mike's ingratitude, challenges him to drink. Mike responds, "You murderers! Its not beer in that keg! It's beer and blood! Blood of men!" He then picks up the keg and throws it to the ground.

Though the moral issue is murder rather than alcohol, the keg-smashing scene conjures up the image of a Carrie Nation temperance saloon raid. Mike follows his outburst by collapsing in a daze on a chair. He has been wounded in the war, and we are to understand the collapse as largely the result of his continuing battle fatigue. Taken together, however, the outburst and collapse have the cumulative effect of emasculating Mike.

Still, Tom's victory is not complete. He has power (that is his name, after all), but he needs acceptance. In a later scene, he returns home to give his mother (Beryl Mercer) some money, only to have Mike once again rebuke him. Mike has regained enough self-composure to punch Tom, but the scene ends much like the homecoming. Tom tears up the returned money and throws it back at Mike, sneering, "Money don't mean nothin' to me." It is another stalemate of sorts, with Tom secure in his power yet estranged from his family. Paddy Ryan's gang becomes something of a substitute family for him. Increasingly, crime becomes for Tom less a field for individual advancement and more an opportunity to display the communal virtues—chief among them, loyalty—that Mike and his law-abiding neighbors refuse to acknowledge in him.

The notion of the gang as a substitute family sheds different light on the much debated sexual themes of the film. Middle-class critics and scholars sometimes have trouble imagining a social world in which there are some things more important than sex. The Irish no less than most other urban ethnic groups recognized romantic love as a danger to family and community. The Public Enemy highlights this tension in scenes that show the clear need to subordinate romance—even within legitimate marriage—to broader issues of community order and justice. Matt Doyle has his wedding celebration interrupted when Tom notices Putty Nose sitting at a booth in the nightclub where the reception is being held. As Putty Nose exits the nightclub, Matt leaves his bride to accompany Tom to exact a deadly retribution for the betrayal following the botched warehouse heist.

Tom's own fumbling attempts at romance face a similar challenge from broader communal obligations. As Tom is on the verge of finally breaking down the reserve of Gwen (Jean Harlow), his beautiful, sophisticated, yet sexually uncooperative girlfriend, Matt bursts into the apartment to announce that Nails Nathan has been killed—not by a rival gang, but by being thrown from his horse while riding in Lincoln Park. Once again, duty calls. Tom throws his glass in the fireplace, exits with Matt, leaving Gwen alone. In a scene modeled on a real-life gangster story, Tom and Matt then exact retribution through a gangland-style execution of the homicidal horse.[4]

The death of Nails Nathan sets in motion a series of events that brings about Tom's ultimate downfall. Still, Tom's death appears less as punishment for hubris than as yet another occasion to display the virtue of loyalty. Nails's death creates a power vacuum that a rival gang leader, Schemer Burns, seeks to fill at the expense of Paddy Ryan. Realizing he lacks the manpower to take Burns head-on, Paddy tells his boys to lay low until he can work something out. He fixes them up in a hideout—and confiscates their guns and money to keep them honest. Jane, a middle-aged female friend of Paddy, hosts a night of drinking for Tom, Matt, and some of Paddy's other henchmen.

The next morning, a hung-over Tom discovers that he has spent the night with Jane. Repulsed by the thought of having slept with the older woman, Tom, against Paddy's orders, leaves the apartment.

---

[4]Burns, *The One-Way Ride: The Red Trail of Chicago Gangland from Prohibition to Jake Lingle*, 87.

Matt chases after him to persuade him to return to the safety of the hideout. They talk on the street, unaware that they are being watched by members of the rival gang. From a machine gun nest, set up across the street from the hideout, Burns's men open fire on Tom and Matt, killing Matt. Tom escapes and seeks revenge.

The circumstances driving Tom from the hideout suggest more fodder for a psychosexual analysis of Tom's motivation. A little background on the censorship history of the film suggests a different interpretation. Though the censors allowed the clear suggestion of illicit sex between Tom and Jane, they cut a scene that revealed Jane to be Paddy's mistress.[5] Tom's morning-after disgust is not misogyny, but self-loathing at having betrayed his patron. Given Paddy's role as a surrogate father, Tom's betrayal is tantamount to incest. Tom's reckless response—disobeying Paddy's orders, leaving the hideout—results in a kind of symbolic fratricide, with the death of his surrogate brother, Matt.

Nevertheless, both the incest and the fratricide are unintentional. Jane pursued Tom the whole evening and took advantage of him while he was drunk, and Matt ran after Tom of his own free will. The truly Oedipal dimension of the film lies less in the incest than in the sense of fate surrounding the key events of the story. In *Oedipus*, motivation matters less than action. Oedipus understands that he is no less culpable for not intending to kill his father and sleep with his mother; the appropriate response to the objective situation is not self-justification, but self-mutilation.

Tom Powers responds to Matt Doyle's murder with an act of self-sacrificial revenge that enacts a kind of gangster version of this Oedipal surrender to fate. Tom quickly acquires a small arsenal by robbing a pawnshop. Armed to the hilt, Tom lies in wait in the pouring rain outside of Schemer Burns's headquarters. Burns and some of his men pull up in a car and enter the building. Tom waits until they are all inside, and then follows them in with both guns

---

[5] Cohen, "An Ordinary Thug," in Cohen, *The Public Enemy*, 20.

blazing. We hear shouts and cries amid the gunfire, until Tom finally runs out of the building, only to be shot in the back by one of Burns's men. He stumbles away and falls to his knees by the curb. In a close-up shot, Tom cries out, "I ain't so tough after all," and collapses.

Tom's symbolic death on the street atones for Matt's similar fate, but the story as a whole requires a broader reconciliation. A policeman rescues Tom from certain death at the hands of Burns's men and brings him to the hospital. His mother, Mike and Molly, and Paddy Ryan show their support through regular visits. Tom apologizes to Mike for all he has done wrong and his mother rejoices to see her two sons at peace with each other.

The next scene shows the Powers family at home waiting for Tom's return from the hospital. The doorbell rings and Paddy Ryan arrives to inform Mike that Tom has been kidnapped from the hospital. Mike wants to fight to get him back, but Paddy explains that he has already agreed to pull out of the business and hand over all his territory to Schemer Burns in return for Tom. The phone rings and an anonymous caller tells Mike that Tom is coming home. Ma rejoices and sings a happy Irish song as she prepares his room for his return.

The doorbell rings again. Mike opens the door to find Tom's dead body, wrapped up like a mummy. Standing from being propped up against the door, it teeters back and forth until it falls face first on the floor in a parodic inversion of a resurrection. The physical fall cannot completely negate a certain moral and social redemption. Tom realizes in death what he consistently sought in life: reconciliation with his family. Rico and Tony die alone on the street, rootless wanderers to the very end. Tom dies, or more properly is buried, at home. He never reforms in the conventional sense, yet the state of his mind matters less than the location of his body. Tom has paid for his sins. His fatal homecoming stands as a kind of rough absolution.

If *The Public Enemy* has suffered neglect at the hands of the Warshow tradition, it struck contemporary critics as the most significant of the films comprising the gangster triumvirate of the early 1930s. This preeminence was due less to its distinct story than to the screen presence of the actor who played Tom Powers—James Cagney. In a famous essay for the *Hound & Horn*, Harvard intellectual Lincoln Kirstein singled out Cagney as the model of a new type of popular hero—at once distinctly Irish, yet also representative of a broader urban America.[6]

Edward G. Robinson and Paul Muni, who played the gangster heroes in *Little Caesar* and *Scarface*, easily shed their gangster image for other roles—a testament to limitations of their original performances as much as the range of their acting abilities. Cagney found the gangster image tougher to shake and, often against his desire to expand the range of his acting roles, continued to serve as the gold standard for Hollywood gangsters for the rest of the 1930s. Scholars barely willing to concede Cagney's singular significance as creator of a new urban cinema have yet to acknowledge the distinct nature of the stories that followed Cagney through his Irish gangster roles.[7] The gangster-as-urban-villager story, in which communal obligations trump individual glory, would find its greatest expression in Cagney's 1938 film, *Angels with Dirty Faces*.

Film scholars have tended to situate *Angels with Dirty Faces* in a second cycle of gangster films that began with William Wyler's 1937 film *Dead End*.[8] *Angels* and *Dead End* do indeed share a common basic story—the return of a gangster to his childhood neighborhood— and both feature the irrepressible, scene-stealing Dead End Kids. Still, as with the earlier gangster cycle, there are important distinctions between the films—one Irish, the other non-Irish. *Dead End*

---

[6]Kirstein, "James Cagney and the American Hero."

[7]In *City Boys*, for example, Robert Sklar grants Cagney a certain founding status, but fails to recognize the distinctive Irish narratives that followed Cagney throughout his gangster films. Though Sklar places Cagney in a kind of ecumenical, Catholic-Protestant-Jew grouping that includes Humphrey Bogart and John Garfield, he ultimately follows Warshow in trying to present a generic American type. See Sklar, *City Boys: Cagney, Bogart, Garfield*.

[8]Ibid., 72, 84.

seeks to explain the environmental roots of crime, whereas *Angels with Dirty Faces* dramatizes the genuine social relationships that endure within, and despite, a generally corrosive social environment. The critical reputation of *Angels* has suffered somewhat for its seeming lack of sociological realism. What film scholars have dismissed as intellectual deficiency is perhaps better understood as a consistent Irish cultural difference.

Released within a year of *Dead End*, *Angels with Dirty Faces* is, of course, less a deliberate response to the earlier film than a glorious accident of genre filmmaking. Drawing as freely from *The Public Enemy* as from *Dead End*, *Angels* tells the story of two city boys from childhood to adulthood, as well as the story of one gangster's return to his childhood haunts. Perhaps most significantly, *Angels* introduces a character nowhere to be found in *Dead End* (or *Public Enemy*, for that matter): a Catholic priest.

Pat O'Brien plays Father Jerry Connolly, the priest who serves as a friend and moral guide to Rocky Sullivan, Cagney's newest incarnation of Tom Powers. Hardly a sop to the Catholics who dominated the Production Code Administration, the introduction of a priest into a Cagney gangster film was a move toward a deeper urban realism. The careers of real-life Irish gangsters such as Dean O'Bannion, "the choir boy of Holy Name Cathedral," show how a life of crime did not automatically exclude one from participating in the life of the Church.[9] Earlier films such as W. S. Van Dyke's *Manhattan Melodrama* (1934) and *San Francisco* (1936) had shown that the priest-gangster relationship could be handled in a way acceptable to the censors. The real challenge in making the film came from the ignorance of the non-Catholic writers, producers, and directors trying to represent this Catholic world. Cagney later recalled how

---

[9]For a contemporary account of O'Bannion, see Burns, *The One-Way Ride*, 80. For a comprehensive and illuminating treatment of the history of the Irish-American gangster, see T. J. English, *Paddy Whacked: The Untold Story of the Irish American Gangster*.

he and Pat O'Brien, both cradle Catholics, had to rework much of the script to conform to actual Catholic practice.[10]

Drawing from these various cinematic precedents, *Angels with Dirty Faces* becomes a film all its own, the greatest ethnic gangster story of the 1930s. The film begins with a panning shot of a city street, people walking in every direction, street vendors hawking their wares, and an organ grinder cranking out "The Sidewalks of New York"—a tune celebrating city life, Al Smith's theme song. This is not an environment, but a world of people. Moving up from the streets, panning across a sign for "McConaghy's Groceries" (identifying the neighborhood as Irish), the camera stops on a fire escape occupied by two teenage boys, Rocky Sullivan and Jerry Connolly. Much like Tom Powers and Matt Doyle, Rocky and Jerry are bored and looking for action. Like Tom and Matt, they too have an altercation with some young girls, followed by a crime.

This crime, however, will have vastly greater narrative consequences than Tom and Matt's shoplifting. Rocky convinces Jerry to help him steal some fountain pens from a freight car. Caught in the act, Jerry manages to escape while the police hold Rocky on criminal charges. Later, visiting Rocky at the detention center, Jerry offers to turn himself in, hoping to lighten Rocky's sentence. The two trade boasts of who can sacrifice more for the other. Rocky tells Jerry to "lay low" and not to worry. Jerry's escape is no betrayal, just one of the lucky breaks of life: "Just 'cuz you can run a little faster than me, there's no reason you gotta go around hatin' yourself." Jerry protests, but Rocky insists (clearly disingenuously) that if he were in Jerry's position, he would keep his mouth shut: "Always remember: Don't be a sucker." Rocky finally succeeds in convincing Jerry not to turn himself in. The decision sends them on radically different life paths—Rocky becomes a gangster, Jerry a priest—but the sacrifice cements a bond of personal loyalty that will transcend the moral divide of their adult roles.

---

[10]Cagney, *Cagney by Cagney*, 72.

The film next traces the development of Rocky's criminal career through a briskly paced montage sequence. His meteoric rise turns to a precipitous fall following his conviction for a drive-by car bombing. The sequence ends with an adult Rocky sitting in the visiting room of another detention center meeting with a very different kind of partner in crime, the slick lawyer James Frazier (Humphrey Bogart). Nothing in their conversation indicates common neighborhood ties; they appear to be business partners, pure and simple. Frazier informs Rocky that he will be able to get him off with only a three-year sentence, a good deal given the evidence against him.

In pointed contrast to the childhood scene with Jerry, Rocky at first refuses to take the fall for the both of them. Frazier responds that if the police get him, too, they will both lose everything they have built up. Frazier promises to hold on to Rocky's cut of the job and work to build up their criminal enterprise while Rocky does his time. Rocky grudgingly concedes the logic of the plan, and agrees to take the rap. Still, he warns Frazier, "I know you're a smart lawyer, very smart, but don't get smart with me." As he advised Jerry not to be a sucker, he reminds Frazier that he is nobody's fool. With this scene—the historical section of the film—the very long prologue, if you will, comes to an end.

The present-day action begins with the same visual device that introduced the historical background. The storefronts look pretty much the same, but the organ grinder's "Sidewalks of New York" has given way to swing music. The camera reaches street level to identify the source of the music in a large truck, topped with loudspeakers, winding its way through the crowded streets advertising the new invention of radio. The radio truck drives out of the congested intersection past a building conspicuously absent from the first street scene, a Catholic Church.

This new addition to the film's urban landscape provides the setting for the rekindling of an old friendship in the reunion of Rocky and Jerry. Rocky enters the church to find Jerry, now a priest, leading a group of neighborhood boys in choir practice. He quietly listens from below the choir loft and soaks up the atmosphere of his youth. The choir sings in Latin; an old woman lights a candle at a side altar. As choir practice ends, the urban-Catholic sublime gives way to the urban-Catholic carnivalesque: the boys scramble out of the church, tripping over each other and fighting as they genuflect and dip their hands in the holy-water font. Rocky looks on with amusement, but steps back into the shadows to avoid being seen by Jerry.

Next, we see Jerry alone in the sacristy, putting away some of his priestly vestments. With his back to the door, he hears a knock and invites the unknown visitor into the sacristy.

> *Jerry [with back still turned]:* What's on your mind, son?
>
> *Rocky [walking up behind Jerry]:* Not very much, father. It's just been bothering me for about fifteen years. What'd you do with those fountain pens you stole outta that freight car?
>
> *Jerry:* Rocky! You old . . . *[The two smile and shake hands.]*
>
> *Rocky:* Jerry, I'm glad to see you. Whatta ya hear, whatta ya say?
>
> *Jerry:* Whatta ya hear, whatta ya say? I'm glad to see you.

The non-Catholic screenwriters and director Michael Curtiz initially insisted on staging this scene in a confessional; Cagney and O'Brien realized that such backslapping camaraderie would never occur in such a place. Still, all agreed that the camaraderie itself was true to the relationship established between the characters. The scene clearly subordinates moral judgment to enduring friendship and shared memories. Trying to fathom the time, Jerry muses on not having seen Rocky for fifteen years.

> *Rocky:* I've seen you.
>
> *Jerry:* Yeah, where?
>
> *Rocky:* I was in the stands that day you made that 90-yard run against NYU.
>
> *Jerry:* Why didn't you come back and see me?

> *Rocky:* I couldn't. There were some people waiting for me.
> *[He smiles.]*

The two share a laugh at Rocky's subtle reference to his criminal career and Jerry simply presses Rocky more on why he never stayed in touch. Rocky responds with more delicate references to his life of crime and Jerry acknowledges reading about him in the papers. He then changes the subject to Jerry.

> *Rocky:* Well, you certainly make a good-looking priest.
>
> *Jerry:* Thanks.
>
> *Rocky:* Say, I always knew your mother wanted you to do it, but what finally decided you?
>
> *Jerry:* Well, I was riding along on the top of a bus, looking down, passing the cathedral . . .
>
> *Rocky:* And that gave you the idea, huh? That's funny. I got an idea on the top of a bus one time. It got me six years.

The two share yet another laugh at the reference to Rocky's criminal exploits and Jerry once again passes up what seems to be an occasion to lecture Rocky on the difference between right and wrong. Jerry begins to reminisce about their choir-boy days with old Fr. Boyle. The two soon break into singing "My Merry Oldsmobile," a popular song from their youth that they used to sing when they wanted to disrupt choir practice.

This scene, and Jerry's character in general, mark a sea change in Hollywood's moral evaluation of the gangster. In *The Public Enemy*, Mike Powers is pure Victorian moralism; he seems to inhabit a cultural world completely different from Tom's. In *Angels*, Jerry Connolly serves as the voice of morality, but he speaks the same language as Rocky. Dismissed by Robert Sklar as an effort to evade the socialism of *Dead End*, the introduction of the priest character actually functions to ground the moral battle between good and evil in an indigenous institutional setting—the Church—capable of providing the reformer and gangster with some common ground.[11] Rocky may not be a practicing or even a believing Catholic, but the memories of his Catholic boyhood command some vague, ill-defined institutional loyalty.

Catholicism in *Angels with Dirty Faces* roots the grace of God in the city streets themselves. Jerry knows Rocky's past and has few illusions about his present. Still, at first, he makes no direct plea for Rocky to turn from his life of crime. Rather, as the two walk out of the sacristy, Jerry simply asks Rocky, "Why don't you get a room right here in the parish?" Any possible moral transformation must begin by reestablishing membership in a specific geographic community. Rocky accepts the advice ("There's no place like home"), and Jerry takes him over to Mrs. Maggione's boarding house, right around the corner. As they part, Jerry asks, "See you at Mass on Sunday?" Rocky responds, "Yeah, sure. I'll help take up the collection."

Back in his old neighborhood, Rocky adopts a kind of gangster version of domestic bliss. He strikes up a romantic relationship with Laury Martin (Ann Sheridan), a neighborhood girl he used to tease when he was a boy. He also serves as a kind of father/mentor to a neighborhood street gang, played by the Dead End Kids. Rocky vacillates between educating the boys on the finer points of petty crime—"Never bother anybody in your own neighborhood"—and encouraging them in more wholesome pursuits such as playing basketball at Fr. Jerry's storefront gym.

At the same time, Rocky returns to his "work" and forces his double-crossing lawyer Frazier to stick to their pre-prison business arrangement. Rocky's successful return to crime and increasingly negative influence on the neighborhood boys leads Jerry to initiate a reform movement exposing the collusion between gangsters and local politicians. Rocky continues in crime but refuses to make any direct move against Jerry. When Frazier decides that Jerry must

---

[11] Sklar, *City Boys*, 84.

die, Rocky kills Frazier instead. The gunfire draws the police, who capture Rocky after a daring rooftop chase.

Unlike Tom Powers, Rocky meets his death at the hands of the state, not fellow gangsters. Still, his execution appears ultimately more an occasion for healing broken relationships than affirming abstract principles of justice. The death-row scene opens with a shot of Rocky's pant legs cut open for the electric chair. A prison chaplain enters to inform Rocky that Jerry has received special permission to be with him in his final hour. Rocky welcomes the opportunity to see his friend, but tells the chaplain to tell Jerry, "None of that incense-and-holy-water stuff."

Jerry enters the cell, and Rocky immediately asks how the kids are doing and if they have been following his trial. Jerry assures Rocky that he is still their hero. He tries, unsuccessfully, to hear Rocky's Confession and reconcile him to the Church and to God. Rocky insists he is not afraid: "You have to have a heart to be afraid, and that was cut out of me a long time ago." Then, in perhaps the most ingenious plot twist in all the ethnic gangster films, Jerry asks Rocky to act scared, to pretend to turn "yellow," as he faces the electric chair. He reasons that Rocky's cowardice is the only thing that can break the kids' hero worship and thus the only thing that can prevent them from meeting a similar fate.

At first, Rocky flat-out refuses. "You're asking me to throw away the only thing I've got left." He already did Jerry the favor of naming names in court, but he cannot give up his personal dignity. Jerry presses him, once again asking Rocky to get right with God. Rocky again refuses, but still asks Jerry to accompany him to the electric chair, under one condition: "Promise me you won't let me hear you pray." Jerry agrees.

During their walk, Jerry makes one last plea—"Please, Rocky." Rocky denies him a biblically significant third time—"No!" They shake hands goodbye, and as Rocky walks out of hearing range, Jerry whispers, "May God have mercy." Rocky walks straight into the camera and flashes an ambiguous smile. The execution itself takes place off screen, but we soon hear Rocky begging for mercy and see the shadows of a man being dragged, kicking, into the electric chair. A heavenly light shines on Jerry's face, and a tear wells up in his eye. Rocky has died a coward's death and the boys will never be able to look up to him as a hero.

The film leaves some ambiguity as to the true nature of Rocky's cowardice, but most of the narrative evidence suggests a willful act of deception. Rocky shows no remorse or fear in his final conversation with Jerry. No meek lamb to the slaughter, he punches out a guard who mocks him as he walks to his execution. He is true to himself and at peace with himself. Still, unlike later "existential" death-row stories, personal integrity is not enough in the cultural world of the Irish-Catholic ghetto.[12] For Rocky's death to have meaning, he must be reconciled to his community. In the flash of a smile, Rocky transforms himself from existential hero to something like a Christ figure. His coward's death is both sacrificial and, in a sense, unjust.

As Jesus, the man without sin, dies a criminal's death for the salvation of the world, so Rocky, the man without fear, dies a coward's death to save the Dead End Kids. Rocky, like Jesus, empties himself. The suddenness of his transformation does, in effect, amount to an act of grace, yet anything less than divine intervention would have cheapened Rocky's character. The device of "turning yellow" right before his execution enables Cagney's Irish-Catholic gangster to redeem himself without undergoing the cultural humiliation of a more deliberate, prosaic (one might well say Protestant) conversion experience.

Grace, in the film and to some degree in Catholic theology, functions as a principle of contingency that transcends sociological theories of environmental determinism. In the heat of Jerry's reform campaign, Rocky's girlfriend Laury Martin pleads with Jerry to leave

---

[12]For a sharp point of contrast within the urban crime literature of the period, see the death of Bigger Thomas in Richard Wright, *Native Son*.

him alone. Jerry insists he has no personal grudge against Rocky: "I'm not blaming Rocky for what he is today. But for the grace of God, there walk I." He goes on to explain that he is fighting less to destroy Rocky than to save the hundreds of other kids who grow up in the bad environment of the city streets—though significantly, Jerry conceives of environment in terms of crime and criminals rather than poverty.

Contra Sklar, grace does not render environment irrelevant. It simply provides the language for explaining what environment cannot. Why did Rocky get caught instead of Jerry? How would their lives have been different if Rocky had gotten away? In 1938, Jerry's answers clearly lagged behind the main currents of sociological thinking. His attack on organized crime and political corruption has more the feel of Progressive Era muckraking than New Deal social engineering, and his willingness to slug a pool-hall heckler suggests even older traditions of reform.

Like the real-life Al Smith, the cinematic Fr. Jerry synthesizes an Anglo-American reform tradition with a more indigenous folk theology of urban Irish Catholicism. The ethnic ghettos of the early twentieth century were full of real-life conundrums such as those presented in *Angels with Dirty Faces*. Such paradoxes still confound would-be social engineers.[13]

After the execution, Jerry visits the boys in their basement hide-out. They have just read, in utter disbelief, the newspaper account of Rocky's cowardly death. They ask Jerry if it is true; he says it

---

[13]This problem received its classic formulation in Finley Peter Dunne's famous piece on Petey Scanlan. Scanlan came from a good home. His parents were faithful, practicing Catholics, all of his brothers and sisters turned out well. Still, Petey grew up to be the terror of the neighborhood and a hardened criminal. Dunne has Mr. Dooley pose the question: "Who'll tell what makes one man a thief an' another man a saint? I dinnaw." He never answers the question, but in the folk tradition eloquently poses the problem. Though I know of no paper trail connecting the screen writers of *Angels with Dirty Faces* to Dunne's story, *Angels* certainly belongs in this tradition of folk reflection. See "On Criminals," in Dunne, *Mr. Dooley in Peace and in War*, 74—76.

happened just as the papers reported it. The boys stand shocked in stunned silence, as if Rocky had just been killed again before their eyes.

Jerry then invites the boys to come with him: "All right, fellas. Let's go and say a prayer for a boy who couldn't run as fast as I could." Through prayer, Rocky maintains a presence in the community that transcends death. Jerry leads the boys up the stairs and out to the city streets—out of their basement inferno into the light of, if not paradise, at least purgatory.

Angels with Dirty Faces shows the redemptive possibilities of violence in the Irish urban village. Still, the Irish-American films of this period did not always hold violence to such a high spiritual standard. Sometimes, violence could simply be fun. The enduring image of the "Fighting Irish" reflects a certain Anglo and Anglo-American fear of Irish lawlessness, yet it also reflects a real link between fighting and festivity in Irish culture.[14]

From the emergence of John L. Sullivan in the 1880s to the great Gene Tunney–Jack Dempsey fights of the 1920s, the Irish transformed a negative stereotype into a badge of honor through their dominance of professional boxing. As the Irish lost their grip on the sport in the 1930s, they retained a central place in the stories that continued to surround the sport, most especially in Hollywood boxing films.

---

[14]See the account of the old-world faction fights in Ó Maitiú, *The Humours of Donnybrook: Dublin's Famous Fair and Its Suppression*, 21.

Chapter 2

City for Conquest

AL SMITH USED TO BOAST that the only book he ever read was *The Life and Battles of John L. Sullivan*. Smith's proud association with the first great hero of professional boxing confirmed the prejudices of his WASP detractors even as it endeared him to the urban masses. His boast reflects his deep immersion in turn-of-the-century popular culture even as it reveals the distinctly Irish accent of urban America.[1] Boxing was the first sport to triumph in the new world of commercialized mass leisure. The success, mobility and national celebrity that Irish Americans achieved in the sport were certainly at odds with the urban-village values of localism and loyalty.

Still, in the Hollywood films of the thirties and forties, narrative convention trumped historical reality. Films such as *The Bowery* (Raoul Walsh, 1933), *Irish in Us* (Lloyd Bacon, 1935), and *Gentleman Jim* (Raoul Walsh, 1942) consistently place boxing in the context of a working-class struggle to get ahead and rise to the top. These films translate the general American struggle to a local, Irish one. Ultimately, they judge the success of the boxer by his willingness to subordinate his own desires to those of the community.

The local, communal ambiance of the Irish-American boxing films has deep roots in the history of the sport. Born in Restoration England's revolt against Puritanism, modern boxing drew the opprobrium of a rising middle class that prided itself on its distance

---

[1] Slayton, *Empire Statesman*, 27.

from a whole range of aristocratic blood sports, including cock fighting, bear baiting, and pistol dueling.[2] With respect to those sports, the urban working class of the early nineteenth century retained much of the sensibility of the peasant side of aristocratic society and enthusiastically embraced boxing. In America, the Irish comprised a significant portion of that working class and quickly made the sport their own—at the direct expense of the English. Much "Hibernian crowing" accompanied the rise of "Yankee" Sullivan, who became the first American champion through his victories over Anglo fighters Vincent Hammond (1841) and William Bell (1842).[3]

Sullivan's nickname suggests his desire to use boxing as a way to lay claim to a certain American cultural citizenship, but his supporters were just as likely to emphasize his distinctly Irish identity when faced with the challenge of Anglo-American nativism. Ethnic and local attachments were very much behind the match that put boxing on the national cultural map—the "Great $10,000 Fight" between Sullivan and Tom Hyer.

Up to the 1840s, most boxing matches were little more than slightly regulated street fights, usually pitting the strong men of rival neighborhood gangs against each other. Success in such fights could lead to a career in politics, where both local celebrity and local muscle proved essential to securing votes. Yankee Sullivan parlayed his early fighting success into a successful tavern business, at a time when saloons were becoming a major venue for fights as well as political clubs in their own right.[4]

Sullivan's fight with Hyer in 1849 grew out of a local political battle in New York. Hyer was an Anglo-American butcher, while Sullivan worked for Tammany Hall. He challenged Sullivan in part as a response to Tammany's decision to relax the native monopoly on meat cutting and sell butcher licenses to the Irish.[5] Hyer won

---

[2] Gorn, *The Manly Art: Bare-Knuckled Prize Fighting in America*, 23.
[3] Ibid., 71, 73.
[4] Ibid., 69.
[5] Ibid., 84.

the fight, but there was no turning back the Hibernian tide. The Hyer–Sullivan fight established boxing as the premier spectator sport of the American city, and the future of that city belonged to the Irish. Despite the growing national and professional nature of the sport, the institutional mix of neighborhood, saloon, and political club remained central to boxing well into the period of John L. Sullivan's rise in the 1880s.[6] Though a national hero, Sullivan proudly retained his early nick name, "the Boston Strongboy."

Cultural historians acknowledge the local, community roots of boxing, but generally accept the national trajectory of the sport as natural or inevitable. Today's national sports industry provides the framework for a history of sports understood in terms of an enduring tension between the often conflicting professional ideals of technical proficiency and performance for pay. As much as any contemporary sports talk-show host, historians routinely bemoan the corruption of sport by money.[7]

Carlo Rotella, the most sophisticated cultural historian of boxing, has proved to be an exception through his writing on the sport in the context of the post-industrial city. Still, Rotella sees the local as just that, a context, a setting for the development of the "text" of technical excellence. Rotella's boxers are "good with their hands"; they make their own culture in a social and economic world not of their own making.[8] In boxing, as in so many other areas of culture, production and exchange mark the limits of the American moral imagination.

The Irish-American boxing films of the thirties and forties operate in a very different moral economy. The contrast between the Irish and more generically American stories is clearest in two films

---

[6]Isenberg, *John L. Sullivan and His America*, 89.

[7]See, for example, Pope, ed., *The New American Sport History: Recent Approaches and Perspectives*. Pope begins the volume with a series of essays grouped under the category "National Culture" and ends with one on "Markets and Audiences."

[8]See Rotella, *Good with Their Hands: Boxers, Bluesmen, and Other Characters from the Rustbelt*.

of the early 1930s, *The Champ* (King Vidor, 1931) and its sequel of
sorts, *The Bowery*. Both films feature the adult-child team of Wallace
Beery and Jackie Cooper. Both use the manly world of boxing as a
setting for a father-son solidarity apart from the world of women.
In the first film, however, the boxing backdrop supports the story of
two rootless individuals trying to maintain their connection to each
other; in the second, boxing serves as one means for connecting
people to a place.

The Champ takes place in that most American of settings, the
West. MGM chose Beery, a thuggish-looking actor of Irish descent,
to play the part. Screenwriter Frances Marion gave the character an
Irish last name and made him a drunk. External markers of Irishness
end there.[9] Andy Purcell, "The Champ," is an exile from civilization,
living across the border in Tijuana, Mexico. Once the heavyweight
champion of the world, he lost his title by getting drunk right before
a major fight. His wife ran away and left him with responsibility for
their infant son, Dink. For years, the Champ has tried to support
Dink through boxing.

The film opens with the Champ running on the open road, in
training for a big fight. Despite his hard training, he shows up drunk
at a meeting with the promoters and loses the fight, as he appears
to have done many times before. The Champ is a down-and-out,
rootless man with no ties to any person, place or thing—except his
son, Dink.

Much of the melodrama of the story derives from the Champ's
efforts to hold on to his relationship with Dink after his ex-wife,
Linda (Irene Rich), re-enters their life. The three re-connect through

---

[9]Marion had been the screen writer for *The Callahans and the Murphys*, and
evidence suggests that the controversy over that film may have had a chilling effect
on any plans to develop an ethnic angle in the story. She came up with the story
while traveling in Mexico looking for inspiration for a Western. At one point, she
saw a drunken man staggering out of a bar, propped up by a young boy shouting
"Can't you see the Champ needs some air?" See Beauchamp, *Without Lying Down:
Frances Marion and the Powerful Women of Early Hollywood*, 206, 274.

a chance encounter at a Mexican race track. Linda, now married to a wealthy man of high society, expresses her desire to have custody of Dink. At first, the Champ agrees only to allow a visit—a favor for which Tony (Hale Hamilton), Linda's new husband, pays him generously. This exchange continues for a while, with the Champ drinking and gambling away the money he gets for the visits. Eventually, the Champ loses all he has, including Dink's race horse, Little Champ (a present from the Champ after a successful night of gambling), and ends up in jail after a drunken bar fight. Having hit rock bottom, the Champ finally concedes and surrenders custody of Dink.

The world of Linda and Tony appears sterile and effeminate compared to the hearty masculine camaraderie of the saloon, gym, and racetrack, yet the latter world brings only destruction and death. Dink escapes to be with the Champ, who tries once again to redeem himself through boxing—this time, a high-stakes bout against the heavyweight champion of Mexico. The Champ lands a late-round, knock-out punch to win a dramatic, come-from-behind victory, yet he collapses of a heart attack on the way back to the dressing room. He dies with Dink by his side.

After a long grief scene in which Dink wanders around the dressing room repeatedly crying, "I want the Champ! I want the Champ!" Linda comes in, gives Dink a hug, picks him up and carries him away. The Champ's death is sacrificial, but the sacrifice does not restore social order so much as it brings Dink back from the frontier to civilization. The Champ's death through boxing is much like the cowboy hero's riding off into the sunset: the man of violence enables civilization but cannot fully enter it. Dink experienced the world of violence and intense masculine camaraderie, but must exorcise its spirits—"I want the Champ! I want the Champ!"—and be reborn, civilized, in his mother's arms.

All of this is, of course, classic Hollywood formula storytelling. *The Champ* won Academy Awards for Beery and Marion, and enjoyed a successful career of theatrical re-release through the

1930s.[10] Capitalizing on the success of *The Champ*, producers cast Cooper and Beery together in several films, the best-known being *Treasure Island* (Victor Fleming, 1934). The Robert Louis Stevenson story was a long way from the world of *The Champ*, but Hollywood had already returned to a more proximate boxing milieu by casting the two in Raoul Walsh's *The Bowery*.

With Beery playing saloon keeper and boxing promoter, Chuck Connors, and Cooper his sidekick/adopted son, Swipes McGurk, the stage seems set for another melodramatic tearjerker. Against expectations, the film not only trades melodrama for comedy, but also people for place. Connors and Swipes share some father-son affection, but most of the story focuses on the battle between Connors and his rival Steve Brody (George Raft), two real-life historical characters who spent most of the 1890s vying for the title "King of the Bowery."

The opening scene signals a story rooted in place. As *The Champ* opened on the road, so *The Bowery* opens in a bar, Nigger Joe's, with a singing waiter serenading his clientele with a paean to "The Bowery....The Bowery, they think the things that they used to do...on the Bowery...the Bowery, I'll never go there any more." In contrast to the wide-open spaces of *The Champ*, *The Bowery* presents a world densely packed with people of a wide range of ethnicities. From the bar, the camera takes us to the street, filled with stumbling drunks, prostitutes, and street vendors. Two Jews debate over who is the best tailor in the city, while vendors hawk items such as "solid-gold collar buttons" and "genuine fireproof celluloid" collars. This opening street scene ends with a police raid on "Suicide Hall," some sort of house of ill repute.

Having established the Bowery as a place, the film then shows us the Bowery as a person. As police sirens give way to the background music of "When Irish Eyes are Smiling," the camera stops at the

---

[10]As late as 1939, the story was the subject of a radio play featuring Beery himself once again in the title role.

figure of Chuck Connors, sitting in front of his saloon, getting a shoeshine, and reading a Police Gazette (the leading racy tabloid at the turn of the century) with a picture of John L. Sullivan on the cover.[11] This moment of peaceful urban repose proves short-lived. No sooner does the bootblack finish his work than a Chinaman enters the scene chasing a young boy who has been throwing rocks through the windows of his laundry. The boy, Swipes, turns out to be not just any street urchin, but an orphan "adopted" by Connors.

The first exchange between the two reflects both continuity and change from the earlier relationship between the Champ and Dink. We see a similar gruff affection, but the relationship between Chuck and Swipes carries a new note of conditionality. Chuck took Swipes in off the street as an act of kindness, but the street—or more properly, the Bowery—sets the terms for their relationship:

> *Chuck:* Now listen here, Swipsey. You gotta stop throwing them rocks at those Chinamen's windows or I'm gonna have to throw you out. You can go right back to the gutter where I picked you up at, eatin' out of them garbage cans and sleepin' in the gutters. Hidin' in the cellars from those orphan-asylum coppers.
>
> *Swipes:* But, Chuck, it was only a Chink's winda.
>
> *Chuck:* I know but a winda's a winda. You know when I picked you up you told me you'd be the right kind of a guy wid me. I got a reputation down here. Me friends don't want to see me bein' followed by a litter punk that's always throwin' rocks thru windows [sic]. It ain't refined. Now stop it and be a good boy.

Here Chuck as father instructs Swipes in a moral code rooted in relationships rather than abstract principles. Rock throwing is not wrong in general, it is wrong because it damages Chuck's reputation and because, as Chuck says a bit later, "Them Chinks are my friends." As Chuck sends Swipes home for the night, the boy pleads to be

---

[11]Though written in 1912, "Irish Eyes" would serve as a theme song for many Irish films set in the 1890s.

allowed to "throw just one little rock at the Chink." The indulgent father, Chuck grants him his wish.

The last rock Swipes throws on his way home not only breaks a window, but knocks over a kerosene lantern and starts a fire in the Chinese laundry. Despite Connors's long lecture on rock throwing, Swipes's guilt quickly takes a back seat to the issue of who will put out the fire. Before the establishment of municipal fire departments, volunteer fire companies handled most of the firefighting in American cities. Part sports club, part street gang, these fire brigades provided young city men with the quickest path to local celebrity and often a first step on a career in local politics. The competition among brigades was intense, with buildings often burning down as rival companies fought for the right to put out the fire.

The Bowery recreates just such a classic scene from the folklore of urban America. Connors heads up one brigade and, on the way to the fire, meets his archrival, Steve Brody. The race is on as to whose fire company will arrive at the scene first. Chuck bets Steve, "A hundred dollars I throw the first hose on that fire." Steve's crew arrives first, but Swipes sits on the fire hydrant to hide it and save it for Chuck. When Chuck arrives, Swipes exposes the hydrant. Brody cries foul and a donnybrook ensues.

As the police try to break up the brawl, the camera comically cuts back and forth between the fight for the hydrant and a distraught Chinaman desperately trying to get someone to save his laundry. Chuck wins the fight. As Steve sulks, a friend named Slick introduces him to Googy Cochran, a small-time hustler from Jersey City who, for a fee of five hundred dollars, offers to help Steve get revenge by poisoning Chuck. Steve knocks him out with one punch. Even on the Bowery, there is a code of honor. Hiding a hydrant falls within limits of respectable trickery; poisoning is simply dirty pool.

The next day, Steve quickly sets himself to settling the score through a respectable Bowery challenge. As Chuck sits reading about his firefighting exploits in the paper, Steve approaches him with a boxing proposition. He puts up five hundred dollars that his fighter, the Masked Marvel, "can wipe up the floor" with Chuck's champion, Bloody Butch. The two agree to a Saturday-night match at Chuck's tavern. Honest Mike, the referee who introduces the fight, makes it sound as much like a local battle between Connors and Brody as a boxing match between the two fighters:

> Quiet! Gentlemen in the Fourth Ward and their friends. In this corner, we have the well-known Fourth-Ward boy, Chuck Connors, presenting his undefeated protégé, Bloody Butch. And in this corner, another Fourth-Ward boy, Steve Brody, presenting a man we know nothing about, who looks like a worthy contestant, known as the "Masked Marvel."

This is clearly not a Marquis of Queensbury fight. Honest Mike warns the fighters against the usual offenses of hitting below the belt and kicking, yet adds a special warning to Bloody Butch: "Butch, if you so much as sink a tooth in his ear, I'll lay you out myself." The Masked Marvel makes short work of the local champ, knocking him "out for the night." A stunned Chuck demands to know the identity of the new champ, and Steve takes off the mask to reveal none other than the Boston Strongboy, John L. Sullivan! The event itself has no basis in the real-life rivalry between Connors and Brody, but the poetic license reflects the close ties Sullivan retained to the small-time local world of barroom boxing even into the 1890s. For the purposes of the story, Steve's trick evens the score for Chuck's earlier theft of the fire hydrant. In the ongoing rivalry, however, no victory is final. Chuck lives to fight another day.

Swipes plays no part in the boxing match. Following the fight, a subplot involving a woman reveals just how tenuous the ties that bind Chuck and Swipes are. As in *The Champ*, women represent the forces of civilization that threaten to undermine father-son male solidarity. Still, Chuck neither pursues his love interest nor asserts his parental rights with any particular vigor—both are secondary to his struggle to defeat Steve and regain his Bowery bragging rights.

The woman in question is Lucy Calhoun (Fay Wray), a girl from Albany who has come to New York to pursue a career as a novelist. Naively wandering into Chuck's tavern, Lucy nearly falls prey to the designs of Slick and Googy Cochran, the two lowlifes who offered to poison Chuck for Steve. Now their game is prostitution. Chuck eyes the situation from a distance and assumes the worst of Lucy. Once he realizes her innocence, he rescues her from the seduction. As Lucy leaves the tavern, Chuck restrains Slick and Googy so that she can get away safely. Again, the issue is not defending the abstract ideal of pure womanhood, but simply protecting a business investment, as Chuck explains to Slick and Googy:

> Go on. . . . sit down! Stay where you are. You're going to stay right there until she gets in the clear. It's alright for you to spend your mazuma around here, but don't try to hook no new goils outta dis joint. I know what your traffic is and what you're up to. I don't want to get mixed with the law. See? Drink your slop; it's paid for.

Later, Lucy visits Chuck at his apartment to thank him and ask for help finding a legitimate job. He insists, "I ain't got time for no goils," but he lets her sleep in his spare bedroom.

Swipes returns later that night to find a "strange skoit" in the apartment. He wakes up Chuck and, fearing a threat to their life of bachelor freedom, demands an explanation. Chuck assures Swipes that she is only there for the night: "We'll slip 'er a buck and give 'er the breeze." The next day, he starts to rethink the matter when he sees how Lucy has fixed up the apartment. Impressed by the new look, Chuck offers Lucy a job as his cook and housekeeper; he also gives her Swipes's bedroom.

Swipes resents Lucy's presence and plays tricks to get her to leave. Chuck disciplines Swipes and tries to force him to apologize, but Swipes runs away. Lest it appear Chuck has simply gone soft on a woman, he explains his actions to Lucy in terms of the ethic of local reputation:

> Aw...don't you worry, he and me's had fights before. You
> know I ain't gonna let him get fresh wid no lady like you.
> I gotta make him toe the mark. I want him to grow up to
> be a great guy. I gotta teach him manners or he'll grow up
> to be a bum and people'll say Chuck Connors was no good
> because the kid ain't no gentleman. I've got a reputation to
> think about, and that means a lot down on this Bowery.

Chuck's speech echoes similar sentiments expressed in *The Champ*. Yet, in that earlier film, place—that is, Tijuana—never figures into the moral calculus. The Champ's vulgarity aside, he seems to accept Linda's world as a legitimate standard by which to judge his own. Chuck, in contrast, stays true to local standards of gentility. The distinction between a lady and a tramp is indigenous to the world of the Bowery itself. Chuck knows one when he sees one, and acts accordingly.

Lucy, for her part, must be content with the role of a Bowery lady. Steve learns about Lucy from the runaway Swipes and tries to seduce her as part of his ongoing battle with Chuck. After Lucy proves her virtue, Steve starts to treat her like a lady, and the two quickly fall in love. As the two talk of marriage, Lucy expresses concern over Steve's chosen profession as a gambler. Still, she never tries to uplift Steve to the standards of middle-class respectability. Instead, she suggests that he move up the Bowery hierarchy to an "honest" career in saloon keeping.

Steve agrees, but quickly takes the suggestion as yet another opportunity to continue his battle with Chuck. He resolves not only to get into the saloon business, but to take over Chuck's saloon. Steve will, moreover, win his Bowery prize in Bowery fashion—not through hard work and thrift, but through a publicity stunt. He brags that he will jump off the Brooklyn Bridge, a death-defying feat that Chuck could never top.[12] Knowing such a jump would be suicidal, Chuck thinks it's a hoax and bets his saloon that Steve will

---

[12]This part of the story is based on the supposed jump off the Brooklyn Bridge by the real-life Brody in 1886.

not really jump off the bridge. With Chuck taking the bait, Steve stands poised to win both the saloon and Lucy—if he can survive what everyone assumes will be a fatal jump.

In the nineteenth century, bridge jumping was a fairly common daredevil feat akin to boxing and firefighting. Still, for all the physical skill and courage that Steve's jump would presumably require, *The Bowery* places the social above the technical and individual aspects of the bet. Once again, reputation is everything.

As soon as Chuck and Steve seal the deal, a series of quick shots shows the news spreading across the Bowery. Some say he will do it; some say he will not. Some say he will die; some say he will live. Everybody, however, is talking about it. Hearing the news, Lucy approaches Steve and begs him not to make the jump, but he assures her he will be safe. Later, we learn the reason for his confidence: the jump is a hoax, and Steve has arranged to have a lifelike dummy thrown off the bridge in his place. To add insult to injury, he has as his accomplice in this deception none other than Swipes McGurk, who has been living with Steve since he ran away from Chuck.

Someone gets wind of the hoax and steals the dummy right before the jump. Confusion reigns and the film leaves it an open question whether Steve or another dummy actually makes the jump. Again, reputation matters more than physical prowess. Word spreads that Steve made the jump. And, that evening, no less a figure than John L. Sullivan proclaims Steve "King of the Bowery!"

Steve has Lucy, Swipes, and the saloon. His victory seems complete. Still, the film never develops the romantic/domestic plotline that inspired the bridge bet in the first place. Lucy and Swipes are incidental to the ongoing battle between Chuck and Steve. Following his defeat, Chuck wanders the streets of the Bowery, defeated and alone. Displaced rather than heartbroken, he despairs at the loss of the Bowery. Hearing news of the outbreak of the Spanish-American War, he enlists in the army to get as far away from his troubles as possible.

As the following exchange with the recruiting officer shows, Chuck joins out of desperation, not patriotism:

> *Sergeant:* Sign your name on that line in full!
>
> *Chuck:* Dat's me mark—me name's Chuck Connors— everybody knows me by dat mark.
>
> *Sergeant:* Do you want to go to Cuba?
>
> *Chuck:* Oh, I wanta go anyplace . . . but the Bowery.
>
> *Sergeant:* You're in the army now. Report here tomorrow morning at 10:00 AM for your uniform and equipment.
>
> *Little Fellow: [To Chuck]* Did you enlist?
>
> *Chuck:* Yeah.
>
> *Little Fellow:* So did I! Boy we'll clean 'em up. They can't get away with sinkin' the Maine. We'll teach 'em a lesson they'll never forget—won't we?
>
> *Chuck:* Who is we fightin'?

This brief comic scene shows the clash of two worlds—the national and the local. Chuck approaches the impersonal bureaucracy of the United States Army with his "personal mark." This sort of signature has no meaning outside the Bowery, and Chuck has clearly never bothered to acquire the literacy skills that would enable him to move more freely in the wider world. Though living among avid tabloid readers, he has clearly not heard of the sinking of the Maine. He has followed the fights of John L. Sullivan, but not the war fever stirred up by the yellow journalism of the day. The world beyond the Bowery means social death, and Cuba is just as good or bad as any other place for that.

No sooner does the national give Chuck a way out than the local pulls him back in. Swipes returns to Chuck, explaining, "[I] was never really mad at ya . . . not for keeps anyway. Now that you're sort of down and out an' ain't the big noise anymore, it . . . it didn't seem fair fer me to stay away from ya." The film eschews the sentiment of *The Champ*, but Swipes's return is still enough to inspire Chuck to renew the fight for his honor on the Bowery: "Now that we're back together again, I'm goin' to start climbin' fer de top."

His rash decision to join the army now comes back to haunt him. But looking down at his enlistment papers, he vows to "go back down there an' tell 'em what they can do wit dis t'ing." The local fight thus trumps the national. Chuck is a social climber of sorts, but his goal is "de top" of the Bowery, which remains the limit of his ambition.

Back in the fight, Chuck quickly learns of the trick dummy, confronts Steve with the evidence, and demands the return of his saloon. Steve denies the accusation, but by the Bowery code of honor, the evidence of the dummy casts sufficient doubt for Chuck to demand that they settle the dispute with a fist fight. Given the dubious legality of such an unlicensed fight, the two agree to meet under cover of the night, "at 12:30 on Grogan's barge on de river."

The film creates a sense of the excitement of the fight through quick shots of street buzz and betting, showing the fight to be a battle for reputation rather than a display of athletic prowess. As a barker bills the fight as a battle of brains versus brawn, a friend offers Steve a pair of brass knuckles to even out the brawn department. Steve refuses and thus proves himself a man of honor— but he loses the fight.

Picked up by the police half dead on Grogan's barge, Steve refuses to press charges against Chuck. Chuck gets his saloon back, and appears to be, once again, King of the Bowery. When Steve contests Chuck's victory in the fight, Swipes tries to make peace, telling the two that "the Bowery's big enough for the both of yez."

The peace proves short-lived. Swipes reminds Chuck that he has to report for duty at the armory. Fearing he will lose the Bowery to his archrival, Chuck dares Steve to join the army too. As a point of honor, Steve cannot back down from such a dare, and the two simply export their Bowery rivalry to Cuba.

Steve kisses Lucy goodbye. Chuck gives his blessing, accepting their love as one loss in an ongoing battle bigger than any single victory or defeat. Swipes hides under a blanket as a stowaway on an army wagon, and the film concludes with the three going happily off to war. Whereas *The Champ* ends with Dink's mother carrying him back from the Wild West to the civilized East, *The Bowery* suggests that the world of violent masculine camaraderie is a moveable feast with no end in sight.

Beery spent much of the rest of his career recycling *The Champ*, often through films with explicitly Irish titles such as *O'Shaughnessy's Boy* (Richard Boleslawski, 1935) and *The Mighty McGurk* (John Waters, 1946). As Beery made these father-son boxing films his own, Hollywood looked elsewhere for actors who could better exploit the adult romantic potential of the Irish boxing genre.

Not surprisingly, James Cagney emerged as Hollywood's most popular Irish boxer. Cagney had boxed as a youth and considered pursuing the sport as a profession before settling on acting—he played a boxer in one of his early post-*Public Enemy* films, *Winner Take All* (Roy Del Ruth, 1932).[13] Two later films, *The Irish in Us* and *City for Conquest* (Anatole Litvak, 1941), best develop the distinctly Irish themes of *The Bowery*. Both present boxing as part of a broader struggle for love and glory, yet both affirm the subordination of the individual desire to communal duty.

A contemporary story set in an Irish milieu a few steps above the world of Chuck Connors, *The Irish in Us* nonetheless continues in the light comic vein of *The Bowery*. Judged no more than a "modest, sentimental ethnic comedy" by one leading film historian, the film actually proved more popular at the box office than Cagney's better remembered hit film of earlier in 1935, *G-Men* (William Keighley, 1935).[14] Originally intended to be an Irish family story playing off of Cagney's real-life roots on New York's Lower East Side, *The Irish in Us* quickly developed into a boxing film, but the family story wins

---

[13] On Cagney's early boxing interests, see McCabe, *Cagney*, 24–30.

[14] Sklar, *City Boys*, 48–53

out in the end, with boxing simply a means of overcoming family division.[15]

The O'Hara family contains a fairly broad range of Irish stereotypes, and the clash of these stock characters provides the film with most of its comedy and conflict. Pat (Pat O'Brien) and Mike (Frank McHugh) follow conventional Irish civil-service professions— policeman and fireman, respectively—that offer security but little in the way of money or glamour. Danny (James Cagney) pursues a career as a fight manager in the equally Irish world of boxing, one that offers the prospects of fame and fortune—and absolutely no security.

Much of the family tension focuses on the conflict between Pat and Danny, who represent the two extremes of security and risk in the Irish-American struggle for survival. Ma (Mary Gordon) presides over her boys in accord with all the conventions of a stage-Irish Mother Machree. The absence of a husband (through death, not desertion) lends an additional Irish dimension to the film's family sentiment.

In the opening scene, Ma O'Hara prepares breakfast for her sons. This basic morning ritual reveals the pecking order in the family. Pat, the responsible cop, is the first one up and ready. Mike, having answered a three-alarm fire the night before, has to be dragged out of bed. The struggle to rouse Mike establishes his character as the comic relief and buffer between Pat and Danny. Finally, there is Danny. With the irregular hours that accompany his chosen "career," Ma insists Pat and Mike be quiet so that he can sleep in: "He's a growing boy and he needs his strength."

Pat is clearly fed up with both Ma's indulgence and Danny's chosen career. To his mind, "Danny's no different than the rest of us—except, he won't work." Ma defends Danny by insisting (with

---

[15]McCabe, *Cagney*, 136. Marion R. Casey notes that Warner Brothers marketed the film alternately as either a boxing or an Irish story, depending on the target audience. Casey, "Ireland, New York and the Irish Image in American Popular Culture, 1890–1960," 341.

something less than full conviction), "He ain't gonna give up his career, no matter how long he lays around." The noise from Pat's argument with Ma rouses Danny, and Pat quickly redirects his anger to the cause of it.

As the two brothers argue, Pat reveals the motivation for his attack on Danny: he has found a girl he wishes to marry, so Danny must find a reliable job that can help support the family. Pat tells Danny to take the exam to join the police force; Danny appeals to Ma for relief. She supports his right to choose his own career, but concedes, "Danny, I . . . I was a little hurt when you wouldn't take the Civil Service examination to be a letter carrier."

Despite Pat's self-discipline, he makes his demands on Danny not in terms of the universal moral norm of the work ethic, but in the name of family responsibility. Despite Ma's clear preference for her wild Irish son Danny, she knows that security trumps romanticism. With Danny refusing to seek a steady job, and Ma still offering no stern opposition, Pat storms out the door in anger. Ma calms him down and shows her support for his marriage plans by telling him to invite his girl over for dinner. Pat then leaves for work.

Ma O'Hara is a woman rooted firmly in the world of the fighting Irish. Lucille Jackson, Pat's love interest, is not. The name Jackson is fairly neutral—English-sounding but potentially Irish—and Lucille is the daughter of Pat's superior on the force, Captain Jackson. As played respectively by J. Thomas Farrell and Olivia de Havilland, neither character comes off as particularly Irish. If we give Captain Jackson the benefit of the ethnic doubt and assume him to be Irish, he is a "lace-curtain" Irishman intent on keeping his daughter far away from the shanty-Irish world of the likes of the O'Haras.

Whatever the ethnicity of the Jacksons, Pat's attraction to Lucille introduces a note of class tension into the story. Pat would seem to want to move up in the world as well as out of the house. We first meet Lucille when she stops by her father's office to "wheedle some shopping money out of him." With her father temporarily out of the office, she plays a prank on Pat, issuing an order for him to report

to Captain Jackson's office immediately. Pat thinks he is in trouble
and is pleasantly surprised to find Lucille.

When Captain Jackson arrives, Pat does in fact find himself in
trouble—for his familiarity with Lucille. The father clearly disap-
proves of the two seeing each other and hopes to keep Pat busy
by putting him in charge of the entertainment for the upcoming
annual Police Benefit. Despite the Captain's opposition, Pat later
invites Lucille to his family's apartment for dinner. This sets the
stage for both a comic culture clash and a dramatic love triangle,
as Lucille meets and falls in love with Pat's ne'er-do-well younger
brother, Danny.

Warner Brothers assigned de Havilland the role very early in her
career, before films such as *The Charge of the Light Brigade* and *The
Adventures of Robin Hood*.[16] But in *The Irish in Us*, she already looks
and acts much closer to the world of the English historical dramas
than to the world of the Lower East Side. The class and culture
divide is clear from the first scene with Pat and Lucille together. She
is stylishly dressed and ready to go shopping for more clothes, while
Pat fumbles through their conversation in his working-man's police
uniform. The two make an odd couple, and we soon learn that any
romantic connection between them is mostly in Pat's head.

Lucille is kind and friendly, but nothing in her actions suggests
the closeness Pat assumes by his plans for marriage. Her choice
of the working-class Pat in defiance of her father's wishes invests
the relationship with a quality of youthful rebellion, even a bit of
innocent slumming. Lucille never leads Pat on, but he is within his
rights to feel that her willingness to see him against her father's
wishes suggests something more than casual friendship. Though Pat
misreads Lucille's intentions, he understands the class divide that
separates them. After he invites her to dinner at his home, he asks

---

[16]Both were filmed under the direction of Michael Curtiz—in 1936 and 1938,
respectively.

Ma to have his brothers eat out to spare him the embarrassment of their rough ways.

Ma refuses to send her sons out and assures Pat they will be on their best behavior:

> *Pat:* All right, honey, but for Pete's sake, show Mike the difference between a knife and fork, will you? And for once in his life have him eat those mashed potatoes without a tablespoon!
> *Ma:* I meant to speak to him several times about that, Pat, so you don't need to worry. Tonight I'll absolutely see that he eats them with a teaspoon!

Like Lucy in *The Bowery*, Lucille exists primarily to provide another point of contention/competition between the two male lead characters. Danny at first appears to have no use for women—as evidenced by the scene preceding the family dinner. Out on a training run, Danny lectures his latest protégé, Carbarn Hammerschlog (Alan Jenkins), on the dangers women pose to fighters. The two come across Lucille by the side of the road trying to repair a flat tire on her car. Danny senses Lucille's presence as a threat to Carbarn's training regimen, but gruffly agrees to help fix the car. His fears are confirmed as Carbarn shares cigarettes and lemonade with Lucille and tries to impress her with his physique. Danny yells at Carbarn for breaking training and bids Lucille a very stiff, formal goodbye.

Despite Ma's assurances, Mike's working-class-bachelor table manners are well on display at the dinner. Lucille takes these in stride, with mild amusement. The real threat to Pat's relationship with Lucille comes from another side of working-class life: the danger and excitement of the romantic, roguish Danny.

At dinnertime, Danny arrives home with Carbarn to discover that Lucille is the woman Pat has brought to meet the family. What follows is a pure stage-Irish donnybrook: Pat has to come to dinner in his policeman's uniform because Danny has loaned Pat's blue suit to Carbarn; Ma blurts out Pat's marriage plans to Lucille; Mike embarrasses him by trying to sell Lucille tickets to the Fireman's

Ball; a bell rings, which starts the punch-drunk Carbarn swinging, knocking out Mike and injuring Pat.

Danny agrees to drive Lucille home, and on the way, he learns that she is not in love with Pat. They stop off for a quick dinner. Though less hostile than during their first meeting, Danny is strictly business. He spends most of the meal talking about Carbarn's potential as a fighter and his weakness for wine, women, and song. Talk of festivity leads them to discuss the upcoming Fireman's Ball. Lucille tells Danny that Pat has asked her to go and Danny replies, "I'll probably see you there. Er...I always take Mom, because she...likes the brass buttons and the band and all that, you know." Through the whole conversation, Danny has presented himself as a man with little time for women, but by evening's end, the two clearly share some mutual attraction.

The Danny–Lucille romance will ultimately reveal the strength of the O'Hara family bond rather than the emotional depth of the relationship of the young lovers. At first, of course, the romance threatens to break the family apart. At the Fireman's Ball, Pat arrives with Lucille and Danny fends off a band of female admirers to dance with Ma. Mike, as usual, provides comic relief, this time through his ineptitude on the dance floor.

When Pat takes his turn dancing with Ma, Danny and Lucille end up alone. Danny once again starts to talk boxing, but quickly turns the conversation in a more personal direction. The two go out on the terrace and share a quiet moment alone while the band inside plays "When Irish Eyes Are Smiling." Just as they confess their feelings for each other, Pat discovers them on the terrace. Pat and Danny argue. Lucille tries to intervene, but Pat slugs Danny and walks off in anger.

The next scene shows Pat back at the apartment, packing to leave home, while Ma declares, "All along I knew nothing would break up the family but a thing like this. To think a girl could come between two brothers." Danny comes home, the two argue again and Danny decides that he, not Pat, will move out. Mike arrives home to provide more comic relief, things settle down, and Pat puts Ma to bed to the strains of "Too-Ra-Loo-Ra-Loo-Ra." Danny is gone, however, and Pat expresses no desire for reconciliation.

A woman breaks the brothers apart, but boxing ultimately brings them back together. Captain Jackson has arranged for Joe Delancy, the reigning middleweight champion, to fight an exhibition match for the Police Benefit. Delancy's manager, Doc Mullins, wants an easy opponent. Pat, hoping to get revenge on Danny and gain favor with Captain Jackson, suggests Carbarn Hammerschlog. Pat refuses to speak to Danny, however, so Captain Jackson has to make the arrangements.

On the night of the fight, Carbarn has a toothache. Mike, serving as a second, suggests he apply some gin to the tooth to numb the pain, but Carbarn keeps swallowing the gin until he is drunk. As Delancy waits in the ring, Captain Jackson sends Pat down to see what is holding up the fight. Pat finds Carbarn passed out, argues briefly with Danny over Lucille and challenges him to take Carbarn's place in the ring. Delancy promises to go easy on him to give the crowd a good show, but then he and Mullins decide to end it quick.

With Mike trapped in the crowd, Danny has no second and takes a beating. Mike finally breaks through, but Ma and Lucille convince Pat that Danny needs him. Pat finally accepts defeat in love and rushes down to help. The three brothers reunite and Pat coaches—and taunts—Danny to victory. Ma muscles her way through the crowd to join in the celebration. The reporters ask Danny for a word, to which he responds, "Folks, I want you to meet the champion of the world! My mother!" Lucille finally arrives in the ring as the newest member of the family. She and Danny embrace and the film ends with a shamrock watermark under the closing credits.

Danny's come-from-behind victory might strike the modern viewer as pure Hollywood corn, but in a year that saw James J. Braddock's upset of Max Baer, *The Irish in Us* could strike a viewer in

1935 as a story ripped from the headlines.[17] Issues of realism aside, the significance of Danny's victory lies in the social relations it affirms. In this respect, a comparison with a much later boxing film is instructive.

Sylvester Stallone's Academy Award-winning *Rocky* (John G. Avidsen, 1976) features a similarly improbable matchup between a nobody and a world champion. It also features a similar ending in which personal ties emerge from the swarm of fans who crowd the ring at the end of the fight. The nature of those personal ties marks the gap that separates the ethnic world of the 1930s from that of the 1970s. Rocky's famous cry of "Yo! Adrian!" signals a personal victory amidst professional defeat, but the personal, here, is purely the romantic bond between two individuals. Moreover, these are two individuals who have used the experience of the title fight to break free of the "narrow" confines of the Italian-American world of Philadelphia, a world that considered both of them losers.

In *The Irish in Us*, what happens in the ring is similarly secondary to what happens outside it, but what happens outside is decidedly different. The personal connection that triumphs in the 1930s is a broader family—and, by implication, community—relationship. Yes, Danny kisses Lucille, but only after he has reconciled with Pat and publicly dedicated his victory to his mother. Unlike so many later films, *The Irish in Us* uses boxing as an instrument of community restoration, not a metaphor for personal transformation

Cagney's second major boxing film, *City for Conquest*, continues some of these family themes but more directly addresses the upward-mobility theme (which was, by the end of *The Irish in Us*, somewhat muted). In this later film, Cagney plays a character who combines the virtues of Pat and Danny O'Hara.

Danny Kenny (James Cagney) is a great boxer, but a reluctant one, with no real ambitions beyond keeping his steady job as a

---

[17]On James Braddock, see Schapp, *Cinderella Man: James J. Braddock, Max Baer, and the Greatest Upset in Boxing History*.

truck driver and making enough money to marry his childhood sweetheart, Peggy Nash (Ann Sheridan). Peggy, however, dreams of fame and fortune as a professional dancer, while Danny's brother, Eddie (Arthur Kennedy), struggles to pursue his musical dream of writing a great symphony of the city, a "City for Conquest."

The film is a (not entirely successful) mix of genres and sensibilities: Irish boxing film, women's melodrama, jazz-city symphony, and Popular Front populism.[18] Still, the film finds whatever unity it has in Cagney's performance as Danny Kenny, a boxer whose rise, fall, and redemption stand as a classic urban-Irish cautionary tale of the emptiness found in the quest for fame and fortune.

Following the opening shots of urban-village life, we first see Cagney as Danny working the speed bag at a local gym. His friend, Mutt, played for comic relief once again by the reliable Frank McHugh, stops by to talk. Apparently not for the first time, Mutt encourages Danny to try his hand at professional boxing, but Danny dismisses the notion. The two argue for a bit until Mutt, in frustration, declares, "You could be good, but you don't want to be."

We quickly learn just how good Danny is as an up-and-coming fighter, Kid Callahan, enters the gym and demands that Danny get off the speed bag. Danny says he is almost done and will be off by the time Callahan changes his clothes. When Callahan responds in anger, pushing Mutt down, Danny slugs him, knocking Kid Callahan out. Pinky, a local fight manager, then offers Danny a chance for a professional bout against Callahan. Danny declines, insisting he is just at the gym for some light exercise.

In the next scene, Danny, Mutt, and some friends are hanging out in front of a tailor's shop listening to the Max Baer–Primo Carnera title fight on a radio hooked up to a loudspeaker. Mutt hears the

---

[18] The Gershwin-inspired subplot involving Eddie betrays the pretension of the director Anatole Litvak. The director Elia Kazan, who plays the role of Danny's hoodlum friend Googi, contrasted Litvak's showy, European style with the more straightforward filmmaking of the Irish-American director Raoul Walsh. See McCabe, *Cagney*, 191.

announcer report the prize money the two fighters will split, and once again encourages Danny to try to make it as a boxer. Mutt, of course, wants to serve as Danny's second: "I ain't gonna be a truck driver's assistant all my life. I got ambitions. I want to *be* somebody!" The siren song of Rico Bandello still rings through the city films of the era, but Danny, like other Cagney Irishmen, refuses to answer the call.

Irish women, however, are a different matter. From the musicals of Harrigan and Hart to the comic strips of Jiggs and Maggie, women were the driving force behind social climbing in Irish-American stories. This would often not be the case in the movies, but Danny's love interest, Peggy, performs this conventional Irish female role in *City for Conquest*.

Peggy first appears in the film as she and Danny cross paths on the street. He walks away leisurely from the Baer–Carnera broadcast with Mutt, while Peggy approaches walking briskly, patting her face with a handkerchief, drying the sweat from what we soon learn was a night of vigorous dancing. They are clearly a couple and Danny offers to walk her home. Sitting on the stairway landing outside of her mother's apartment, Danny speaks of their future. He has worked his way up to $27.50 per week as a truck driver, enough for them to start a life together as man and wife.

Before Peggy has a chance to respond, Peggy's mother comes out into the hall and scolds the two, accusing them of being up to no good. Peggy protests that they are sitting on the stairs because there is no decent place for them to sit in her apartment, but the mother replies bitterly that the two are destined for ruin—men promise the world, but marriage only drives women into grueling poverty. Danny says goodnight to Peggy and walks upstairs to his own apartment. The issue of their marriage remains unresolved, but the harsh words of Peggy's mother cast a dark cloud over the future of the couple.

Poverty threatens other dreams as well. Danny enters his own apartment to find his brother Eddie struggling through a piano lesson with a local boy who clearly has no talent for the instrument—and whose mother has little money to pay for the lessons. The scene plays as comedy, and Eddie seems to accept such lessons as part of the dues any young struggling musician must pay. He finds it harder, however, to accept that he will most likely have to give up that life. Due to the hard times of the Depression, his music school has cut his scholarship in half. He needs a hundred and fifty dollars for tuition and sees no other way to get it than by taking a regular working-class job.

Facing his own dashed dreams, Eddie tells Danny of his efforts to write a symphony of the city—of the mad dreams of glory, the Darwinian struggle for existence, and the human wreckage such struggle leaves behind. After he concludes his musical monologue, Danny says, "Hey, Eddie. You have ideas like that, and you're talking about driving a truck?" Danny then asks Eddie to play his favorite part of the composition so far, a very melodramatic passage, full of melancholy minor chording.

As Eddie plays, Mutt bursts into the apartment. Danny shushes him and tells him he will fight Kid Callahan. The reason is clear. He will fight simply to earn enough money to keep Eddie in music school. He is fighting for his brother, not for himself.

Despite the close bonds of brotherhood, Eddie and Danny actually represent two very different visions of the city. For Eddie, it is an arena for glory, a city for conquest. Eddie certainly does not delight in human tragedy for its own sake, but in conventional Romantic/Modernist fashion, he accepts the depths of despair as the necessary counterpart to the heights of glory, which together give depth and dignity to the drama of humanity.

All of this sounds pretty heavy for a working stiff like Danny, for whom the city is a place where a regular guy has a chance to make enough money to get married and support a family. Danny's wishes for himself and Peggy have none of the romantic agony Eddie sees in the city, and Danny's initial rejection of the heroic career of boxing contrasts with Eddie's own pursuit of glory through music. Eddie clearly wants more than the life of a music teacher.

Danny could have counseled Eddie to compose in his spare time, the way he boxes in the gym for exercise. Instead, though he may not want more for himself, Danny seems to want more for Eddie. His brother's ambitions set Danny on a course of action that will lead him to betray his own vision of the world. Ironically, while loyalty to Eddie leads Danny to a fight, his love for Peggy will make him into a fighter.

At first, Danny agrees to the match against Kid Callahan as a one-time deal to earn money for Eddie. He delights in his local-hero status—Callahan is West Side, Danny is East Side—but his stunning victory, by knockout, convinces Scotty McPherson (Donald Crisp), a big-time fight manager, that Danny has the makings of a world champion. Danny declines McPherson's offer to take him under management. He tells McPherson that he has seen too many would-be champions stumbling around gyms punch-drunk the rest of their lives: "A million-to-one odds. I think I'll stick to driving a truck."

After the fight, Danny, Mutt, and Peggy go out to celebrate at the Rose Garden Ballroom. Murray Burns (Anthony Quinn), a local dance champion, asks Peggy to be his partner in a contest. The two win and Murray suggests he and Peggy could be a professional dance team. Murray is arrogant and rude to Danny and makes insulting remarks about his relationship to Peggy. Danny knocks him down with one punch.

Despite Murray's rudeness, Peggy is clearly excited by his offer. After Danny drops Peggy off at her apartment, she sneaks out to call Murray, and she takes him up on his offer to go professional. Peggy soon has no time for Danny, as she spends all her free time competing in dance contests with Murray. Confused and troubled by her distance, Danny seeks solace in Eddie's music. Eddie, for his part, explains that the problem is not Peggy's desire for Murray, but her desire for fame, to see her name in lights.

Armed with this knowledge, Danny tries to lure Peggy away from the bright lights. Just like old times, the two spend a Sunday afternoon at Coney Island. As they return to Manhattan on the ferry at night, they look at the skyline of New York and share their dreams. Peggy says the ferry makes her think of taking an ocean voyage; Danny suggests taking a boat down to Atlantic City for their honeymoon. Peggy explains that she wants to see Europe, South America, the world. The two clearly have different dreams for their future:

> *Peggy:* If I'm successful, I can go anywhere.
> *Danny:* Ah, get off that express and take a local.

When Peggy insists that she wants to be a star, Danny replies, "What do you want that for? We could be happy together without all that noise and fancy stuff." When she tells him she wants to get away from the old neighborhood, he replies that after they marry they could move up to the Bronx. Danny just does not seem to get it, and in exasperation Peggy declares, "You're the only one in this town who doesn't want success!"

Feeling his lack of ambition has lowered his standing in Peggy's eyes, Danny agrees to try to make it as a big-time fighter. She insists that he must do it for himself, not for her. In reply, he asks only that she promise she will always be his girl. He signs with Scotty McPherson. Under the ring name "Young Samson," he quickly rises to the top of the welterweight circuit. Danny's childhood friend, Googi (Elia Kazan), now a big-time gangster, throws him a fancy penthouse party to celebrate. Danny is uncomfortable among the rich and glamorous. Googi offers him caviar, but Danny can only think of the hot dogs and lemonade they used to drink when they were kids.

Danny leaves the party and wanders the streets of Manhattan. His wanderings lead him to Peggy. As he has risen up the ranks of the boxing world, so Peggy has turned pro and steadily worked her way up the vaudeville circuit with Murray. Seeing Peggy's dance act on a theater marquee, Danny visits her in her dressing room. After yet another violent exchange with Murray, Danny takes Peggy back to the old neighborhood, trying one last time to woo her away from the bright lights. They go to a dance at the local Forsythe Street Settlement House, where they both enjoy their status as local heroes. As a bastion of Protestant urban reform, the Settlement House setting seems out of place in an Irish story, but the scene convincingly shows dancing with people in the old neighborhood as more enjoyable than dancing for people on the professional circuit. By the end of the evening, Peggy leads Danny to believe she will give up her career and marry him.

On the verge of domestic bliss, the bright lights once again dash Danny's hopes. Returning to her apartment, Peggy finds Murray and their agent waiting for her with the news that they were finally going to tour at the top tier of the dance circuit. Peggy hates Murray, but she still craves fame, so she signs the contract for the new tour and leaves town without telling Danny of her plans. He thinks she is simply playing out her old contract until he receives a letter telling him of her new tour.

Danny is furious and feels the only way to win her back is by rising to the top of his own field. He demands a match against the reigning champ, Cannonball Wales. Scotty insists Danny still needs another fight before he takes on Wales and warns that Wales is a dirty fighter. Danny ultimately gets his wish, but the fight proves Scotty right.

With Danny getting the best of it through the middle rounds, Wales rubs rosin on his glove thumbs, and then rubs his thumbs into Danny's eyes. Unable to see and unaware of the reason why, Danny fights on. He takes a terrible beating, though, and loses the match— and his sight. Peggy feels it is all her fault and Scotty keeps her from seeing Danny, fearing her presence would only make things worse.

Peggy breaks her partnership with Murray and struggles to find work. Lilly, a friendly chorus girl at a low-level show, takes her in when she has no place to stay. The two read tabloid stories and share girl talk. Lilly laments her lost youth in Jersey City, where she left the chance for marriage and family with a simple mechanic in order to pursue the bright lights of Broadway. Experiencing the shock of recognition, Peggy breaks down crying.

For Danny and Peggy, professional failure sets the stage for social redemption. Still, in the lead-up to their reunion, the film affirms at least one quest for fame and fortune: Eddie's rise through the ranks of the New York music world. Eddie is ambivalent about his success, for he seems to have sold his musical soul by writing commercial swing tunes. Danny, now supported financially by Eddie, encourages him to continue to write his symphony of the city.

By the end of the film, Eddie achieves both commercial and artistic success, debuting his symphony at Carnegie Hall. Danny, fearing his presence would jinx Eddie's big night, listens to the performance on a radio at the newspaper stand where he has been working (despite his continued near-blindness). Peggy attends the performance with her friend Lilly. After the standing ovation following the conclusion of the symphony, Eddie publicly dedicates his performance to Danny. He acknowledges Danny's support for his career, saying, "He made music with his fists so I could make a gentler music."

More importantly, Danny inspired the music itself. An attempt to capture the triumph and tragedy at the heart of New York, the symphony is nothing other than the story of Danny's life. Peggy leaves in tears and goes to Danny at his newsstand. At first, the two talk of Eddie's great success and Danny talks about all their old friends and concludes, "Looks like everyone on Forsythe Street is doin' all right." For Danny, community comes before romance. With both of them reconnected to their neighborhood roots, talk turns to love. The two embrace and Danny assures Peggy, "You'll always be my girl."

The conclusion of *City for Conquest* seems to affirm the best of both worlds, but with a revealing division of labor. The Irish story of Danny and Peggy follows the conventional valuation of the local over the national, stability and security over risk and opportunity. Peggy learns what Danny knew all along: true happiness lies in the simple life of hard work, marriage, and family. The American story of Eddie, however, affirms the legitimacy of striving for success and the real possibility of achieving it.

Eddie never sacrifices personal relationships to win glory, but he does, in a sense, rise to the top on the corpse of his brother. Danny's early sacrifices finance Eddie's education, while his tragic rise and fall in the boxing world provide the inspiration for Eddie's musical masterpiece. Danny represents a certain kind of peasant conservatism in his willingness to settle for the life of a truck driver. As a kind of surrogate father to Eddie, however, he affirms the classic immigrant hope that children will be better off than their parents.

The two brothers represent what in other contexts appears as a generational progress from working class to middle class, from manual to intellectual labor. Danny and Peggy are the humble immigrant parents, and Eddie is the son of immigrants who makes good. Like Jack Robinson/Jackie Rabinowitz at the end of *The Jazz Singer*, Eddie retains an emotional attachment to his childhood roots. But as Jackie's black face marks the distance between a jazz singer and a Jewish cantor, so Eddie's black tie marks the distance between Carnegie Hall and Delancey Street. Though the Irish element injects a strong note of ambivalence into the story, *City for Conquest* seems to affirm the ultimate value of making the move up from—and out of—the urban village.

These narrative tensions would find a much more satisfying resolution in the greatest of all Irish boxing films, Raoul Walsh's *Gentleman Jim* (1942). Like *The Bowery*, *Gentleman Jim* looks back to the golden age of Irish-American popular culture in the 1890s through a fictionalized biography of real-life figures. In this case, however, the subject is not a couple of relatively obscure New York saloon operators, but the great boxing heavyweight champion, James J. Corbett.

Whatever poetic license the film may take with particular details, Corbett's real-life story speaks directly to the conflicts of class and culture at the heart of the Irish-American experience at the turn of the century. Corbett won fame in a sport that in the 1890s was still struggling to overcome its association with the seamier side of urban working-class culture. He earned the nickname "Gentleman Jim" due to his own deeply felt and publicly expressed aspirations to gentility and respectability.

Walsh cast Errol Flynn for the role. Australian by birth and possessing a recognizably Irish last name, Flynn nonetheless rose to fame in Hollywood by playing dashing leading men in English historical dramas such as *The Charge of the Light Brigade* and *The Adventures of Robin Hood*. Flynn brought just the right combination of toughness, humor, and sophistication to the role of Jim Corbett— a role which he later claimed to have been his favorite. He needed all of these qualities to rise to the challenge of the film's desire to celebrate individual advancement and achievement while satirizing the broader class and cultural aspirations that so often drive the pursuit of success.

Brash, conceited, and arrogant, Corbett's saving grace is his loyalty to family and friends. We see this trait evident in the film's opening scene. It is San Francisco in 1887. The city is abuzz with excitement over a secret—because illegal—boxing match between two local sluggers. The fight draws rich and poor—as well as the poor who want to act rich, such as Jim Corbett. He arrives at the fight dapperly dressed, but unable to afford the two-dollar admission. He asks his friend, the far-from-stylish Walter Lowrie (Jack Carson), for a dollar to match his, and pays his way in.

Walter is confused; it appears Jim has left him behind. Jim then approaches the fight organizer, an Irishman by the name of Callahan, and tells him that Walter is an irate patron who has had his pocket picked and plans to call the police. Callahan then goes out and drags Walter into the roped-off area to keep him from blowing the whistle on the fight. As Jim looks on and smiles at the success of his deception, a real pickpocket tries to take his wallet. Without even looking behind him, he slaps the pickpocket's hand away and tells him to get lost.

The scene shows Jim to be both head-smart and street-smart, but above all loyal to friends, even those several levels below him in matters of style and intelligence. One of the great character actors of the golden age of Hollywood, Carson performs the same comic relief role that Frank McHugh did in *The Irish in Us* and *City for Conquest*. The character of Walter Lowrie also provides the occasion for Flynn's Corbett to prove his loyalty to childhood friends despite his desire for upward mobility.

This driving desire is also present in the opening scene. No sooner does Jim get Walter into the fight than he notices the presence of Judge Geary (Wallace Clark), a member of the Board of Directors of the bank where they work as humble tellers. He immediately begins to hobnob with the Judge, despite the reluctance of the tongue-tied Walter. Jim is clearly a man on the make and his social aggressiveness will soon gain him entry into the upper-class world of his dreams.

Police raid the fight and arrest many in the crowd, including Jim, Walter, and Judge Geary. But when brought before a judge for sentencing, Jim gets everyone off the hook with a dramatic speech. The next day, Jim and Walter see Judge Geary enter the office of the bank president. They fear they will lose their jobs for their presence at the fight, but quickly learn that the Judge has paid a visit to commend Jim for getting them all off the hook.

The very next moment, Jim seizes upon another opportunity to ingratiate himself with the elite when a beautiful young socialite, Victoria Ware (Alexis Smith), arrives at the bank to withdraw money for her father who is gambling at the exclusive Olympic Club. She requests the money in silver rather than paper, so Jim offers to help her carry the heavy bag of money—all the way to her father's card table at the club. Abruptly thanked and dismissed by Victoria's father, Jim—dazzled by the elegant interior of the club—tries to prolong his visit by asking Victoria to lunch.

Victoria serves as Jim's romantic sparring partner and social conscience. Walking Jim to the dining area, she tries to shatter his illusions about high society. Jim says he wants it all, she says it does not bring happiness. When he accuses her of taking it all for granted, Victoria reveals the truth behind her own façade of gentility. She grew up in Virginia City and played on a coal slag until she was ten. Her father struck it rich on the Comstock Lode and reinvented himself as a San Francisco gentleman. Driven by his own desire for wealth and success, he has given her everything but love.

Worldly wise rather than bitter, Victoria is unimpressed by Jim's ambition but amused by his naiveté. This early exchange at the Olympic Club sets the dynamic for their relationship through the rest of the film. The harder Jim strives to make it to the top, the more Victoria wants to knock him to the bottom. This conflict will of course inflame their romance, and the battle will not end until both sides win. Round one seems to go to Jim. After their lunch, Jim persuades Victoria to give him a tour of the club. The tour ends at the gymnasium, where Jim comes upon Judge Geary receiving a boxing lesson from the club's new instructor, Harry Watson (Rhys Williams), "the man who taught the Prince of Wales how to box." Jim asks if he can spar with Watson and impresses everyone by landing some solid blows on the boxing master. Earlier in the film, the Judge had given a long speech on the need to get a better class of persons into the fight game. He now sees in the clean-cut Corbett the possibility of realizing his dream of a gentleman boxer. He asks Mr. Ware to sponsor Jim to an "athletic membership" to add prestige to the club. The boxing equivalent of Horatio Alger, Jim has worked his way up in the athletic world of San Francisco through talent, hard work, and clever thinking.

The film quickly deflates the simple sentiments of more conventional American success stories. Whenever Jim takes two steps forward, someone or something—most often, his family—will always take him at least one step back, reminding him of his roots and keeping his head from getting too swelled. After his triumph at the Olympic Club, Jim returns home to share the news with his family. The Corbetts are shanty Irish. They live on the poor south side of San Francisco. The father, Pat Corbett (Alan Hale), is a coachman who runs a livery stable. Jim's brothers are longshoremen. Upon hearing the news of Jim's membership in the elite Olympic Club, Pa Corbett praises Jim for wanting to improve himself; his brothers, George and Pat, mock his pretensions.

As Pa continues his praise, the brothers continue their derision, poking at his high collar and fancy tie. Jim is very sensitive about his clothes, but his brothers keep needling him until he challenges them both to a fight. Everyone gets up from the table and marches off to the barn for the fight. Father Burke (Arthur Shields), the parish priest they have invited for dinner, looks on with excitement. Many neighbors follow them into the barn to see the fight, while one of them announces, "The Corbetts are at it again!" Such donnybrooks will recur throughout the film, constantly drawing Jim back to his roots no matter what success he may achieve.

We never learn who wins the fight, but the outcome is beside the point. Jim may now be able to box with the Nobb Hill crowd at the Olympic Club, but he still has to box with his brothers in the barn. No matter what changes at the level of class, some things will never change at the level of culture.

The Corbett brothers are not the only ones who want to knock Jim down a peg or two. Judge Geary and the leaders of the Olympic Club soon regret their decision to admit Jim to the club. He annoys everybody. He plays tricks on them while they are trying to exercise and constantly has himself paged to appear important. One exasperated member asks, "Do we have to have a boor just to have a boxer?" To put Jim in his place, the Judge and Mr. Ware arrange an exhibition match between Jim and Jack Burke, the former champion of the British Isles and Australia, who is passing through San

Francisco on his way to Chicago to fight Jack Kilrain (one of the great heavyweights of the era).

The night of the fight, we see Jim at home, showing off in his rented top hat and tails. He even manages to impress his usually skeptical brothers. The whole family goes to see the fight. Pa takes bets in the balcony, and Fr. Burke wishes him luck at ringside.

The announcer introduces the fight as an exhibition in the "scientific art of self-defense," the first match in America to be fought under the Marquis of Queensbury rules. Historical accuracy aside, the statement reminds us of Corbett's real-life role in raising the respectability of the sport. To everyone's surprise, Jim not only wins, but knocks out the former champ. Judge Geary changes his tune and beams with pride at the man he now calls his protégé, but others, especially Victoria, fear the victory will only make him even more insufferable.

To get even without directly insulting Jim at his own victory party, disgruntled club members, led by Victoria's male suitor Clinton DeWitt (John Loder), expel Jim's friend, the now drunken Walter Lowrie, for violating the club's dress code. Jim sees the action for what it is, exposes their pettiness, and leaves with Walter.

Between his brothers and the Olympic Club, Jim faces two very different objections to his advancement, and responds accordingly. Jim's boast of earning membership in the Olympic Club falls flat in a family setting where membership is not earned or achieved, but granted by birth. The barn fight serves to remind Jim of this other kind of membership, and he accepts the reminder as legitimate.

The Olympic Club, in contrast, purports to be a meritocracy of sorts. Full of nouveau riche miners with old-money pretensions, the Olympic Club has nonetheless admitted Jim on a special "athletic membership" dependent purely on his merits as a fighter. Through the Burke match, they challenge him on those terms and Jim wins in a fair fight. He celebrates the victory with his usual braggadocio until DeWitt asks Walter to leave.

Previously, Jim had accepted the ill feelings of the club members as the price to pay for trying to break into a new social world. In effect, he was willing to put up with their contempt as he tried to earn their respect. The attack on Walter gives him a new perspective on the club members. They are not simply snobs; they are cowards and unmanly poor sports. Jim walks away from the world of gentlemen in part because it has shown itself to be false, but also because it has tried to separate him from his other world of South Side family and friends. He aspires to upward mobility only to the extent that it does not require him to betray his first loyalties. As Jim makes his public break with the Olympic Club, Victoria looks on, pleasantly surprised that Jim has finally seen through the façade of gentility and chosen the better way.

In the short run, that better way leads only to a big hangover. Jim resolves any remaining doubts about his neighborhood loyalties through a night of good, old-fashioned, working-class barhopping with Walter. In the morning, the two discover they have hopped all the way to a hotel room in Salt Lake City. As they struggle to piece together last night's fun, a stranger named Billy Delaney (William Frawley) bursts into their hotel room and informs Jim that he has finalized arrangements for a boxing match with a local bruiser.

Stunned, with no recollection of having agreed to the fight the night before, Jim nonetheless sees the fight as a way to earn money to return to San Francisco. Tired and hung-over, Jim takes a beating early on in the fight but comes back to win by a knockout. Delaney is impressed and declares, "I ain't seen no one hit like that but John L. Sullivan!" From this point on, the action of the film centers on the buildup to the final showdown between the old and the new, between Sullivan and Corbett.

Ward Bond nearly steals the film from Flynn with his larger than life portrayal of the Great John L. Immediately after Delaney makes his prophetic comparison, the film cuts to a series of scenes that capture the place of Sullivan in the urban sporting culture of the day. Sullivan walks down the street, smiling, trailed by a crowd of young boys thrilled to be so close to their great hero. He then enters a bar and delivers his signature boast: "My name is John L. Sullivan and I can lick any man in the world!" The crowd inside the bar cheers in affirmation. Sullivan shouts that the drinks are on him and proceeds to shake the hand of every man in the bar—including that of Jim's father.

Back in San Francisco, Jim has committed himself to pursuing a career as a professional boxer, but has not yet given up his day job at the bank. At this point, no one, not even his father, would consider him worthy to challenge Sullivan for the title. When Pa Corbett stumbles home after his encounter with Sullivan, we get a sense of the exalted position of Sullivan within the Corbett family. Pa Corbett stares at his right hand and declares, with drunken reverence, "This is the hand that shook the hand of John L. Sullivan!" As he tells his family of his encounter, Jim suggests that someday he might fight the Great John L. himself. Pa Corbett dismisses such talk as fantasy at best, blasphemy at worst.

The rivalry begins to heat up on a more personal level as well. Following a performance in a stage show at a local theater, Sullivan greets his adoring fans on the street—including Miss Victoria Ware. As Jim looks on, Victoria throws herself at Sullivan and asks to feel his bicep. She clearly does this to tease Jim, and their romantic sparring continues to drive Jim on the way to his final showdown with Sullivan. Working his way up the boxing ladder, Jim defeats a local champion, Joe Choynski, in a dramatic (and illegal) barge fight. He becomes a national figure when he defeats the great Jake Kilrain in New Orleans. Sharing his winnings with his family, Jim sets up his brothers and father in the bar business and they open a saloon, which they name "Gentleman Jim's."

Throughout his rise to the top of the boxing world, Jim stays close to both his friends and his enemies from the old days. Though hoping to see him lose, Victoria and the Olympic Club crowd follow Jim's career nearly as intently as does his own family. Jim shows no explicit desire to return to the good graces of his old patrons, but he does use his success in boxing to move his family up to Nob Hill.

On one level, Corbett seems to be following in the footsteps of the nouveau riche miners of the Olympic Club. Yet the film makes clear that the move is only geographic, not cultural. As the Corbetts pack up their worldly belongings on the waterfront, they assure their old neighbors that they will keep in touch. More strikingly, they take their goats with them, tied to the back of their wagons. This slight, comic visual speaks volumes of the cultural continuity that persists in spite of upward economic mobility. The Corbetts will be different from the Olympic Club Irishmen. They will enjoy the things that money can buy, but never try to hide their cultural roots. You can take the family out of the neighborhood, but you cannot take the neighborhood out of the family.

Jim, too, will drag along a billy goat of sorts on his way to the top of the boxing world. A "gentleman" both in his adoption of sophisticated manners and a more disciplined, scientific training regimen, Jim can never quite shake the shanty-Irish influence of his family. On the eve of his great fight with Sullivan, Jim attempts to rest in a hotel room as the streets explode with pre-fight revelry. Delaney congratulates himself on keeping Jim aloof from such distractions, while Jim takes the relative peace and quiet of the hotel room as an opportunity to brush up on his Shakespeare.

Before Jim can complete his first line of poetry, his family bursts into the hotel room and starts an old-fashioned Irish party, complete with traditional dancing to the tune of "Dear Old Donegal." Delaney wants to throw them out, but Jim knows there is no stopping them. Dancing quickly descends into fighting, and someone yells, "The Corbetts are at it again!"

Jim's relationship to Sullivan follows a similar trajectory, though comic regression gives way to a more dramatic reconciliation. At first, Jim shows no respect at all for the Great John L. He taunts Sullivan into agreeing to the match and insults him at every turn.

Prior to the fight, the film makes every effort to emphasize the contrast between the two in both personalities and fighting styles.

The generational divide is perhaps most striking in different attitudes toward alcohol. Jim refuses to drink during training, while Sullivan chugs beers between bouts with the heavy bag as he prepares for the title match. As a final insult to his elder, Corbett even tricks Sullivan into entering the ring first, thus denying him one of the privileges of a champion. The fight sequence gives Corbett's innovative style due attention, and his late-round knockout of Sullivan clearly marks a victory of finesse over brawn.

Still, the film ultimately subordinates the technical to the personal, change to continuity.[19] After the fight, Sullivan, clearly a broken man, shows up at Corbett's victory celebration to concede his defeat in the most personal manner possible. He bestows upon Corbett his own engraved championship belt. The two compliment each other on their boxing prowess: Sullivan says he has never seen a fighter with Corbett's speed, while Jim insists that he could never have beaten Sullivan-in-his-prime. Sullivan then goes on to give his blessing to Jim's "gentleman" persona, conceding that it may be just what the sport needs to lift it to respectability. For all the bad blood between them, the two share common bonds—as fighters and as Irishmen.

Triumphant in his professional life, Jim continues his battle of the heart with Victoria. Once again, progress and improvement give way to cultural roots. At the victory party, Victoria presents Jim with an oversized cowboy hat to accommodate the swelled head

---

[19]In this, *Gentleman Jim* stands in sharp contrast to another film about the "fighting Irish," *Knute Rockne, All American* (Lloyd Bacon, 1940). A biography of the legendary Notre Dame football coach—who, despite his Norwegian ethnicity gets portrayed by Irish-American actor Pat O'Brien—the film very much emphasizes the classic WASP approach to sport as a means of building character and an occasion for technical innovation. This emphasis is faithful to the person of Rockne and the institution of Notre Dame, both of which were far removed from the urban world of boxing and very concerned to promote general American ideals far removed from any taint of ethnic particularity.

he is sure to get from his victory over Sullivan. Still, as Victoria observes Jim's reconciliation with Sullivan, she realizes that she has misjudged him. Jim leaves the party, saddened by seeing Sullivan so humiliated. Victoria follows him out.

After sharing some kind words, the two start their bickering again, trading insults of the shanty-Irish variety. Finally, the two admit their insults are a mask for their love. This love, however, has a particular class and cultural dimension. It does not lift them out of their past, but draws them back into it. Jim finally rejects his middle-class aspirations, asking Victoria, "You didn't really believe all that gentleman stuff, did you?" Victoria smiles and replies, "Well, I'm no lady!" As the two embrace, we hear the hotel party turn into yet another donnybrook, as Walter Lowrie yells, "The Corbetts are at it again!" The moral of the story? You can take the Irish out of the shanty, but you can't take the shanty out of the Irish.

Gentleman Jim presents a resolution to the conflict of class loyalty and upward mobility nothing short of utopian. The relation of this fantasy to reality matters less than the persistence of the fantasy against WASP ideals of upward mobility as a means of cultural assimilation. Still, even as *Gentleman Jim* remains true to older themes of class and cultural loyalty, it revises the conventions of Finley Peter Dunne and Ned Harrigan by making the woman the voice of ethnic conscience. In the films of the 1930s and 1940s, this would prove to be the rule rather than the exception. The first half of the twentieth century would see a flowering of Irish-American women in a genre of their own, one that would hold them up as models of cultural loyalty who consistently reject the glamour of upward mobility in order to stay true to their ethnic roots.

Chapter 3

The Bowery Cinderella

VICTORIA WARE STANDS IN A LONG LINE of Irish-American critics of the civilizing process. As leading rather than supporting characters, Irish-American women dramatized this critique through a genre that offered a distinct twist on the classic rags-to-riches fairy-tale romance of Cinderella, the *Bowery* Cinderella. This urban, Irish-American Cinderella would meet her WASP Prince Charming only to conclude that the romance of high society was a poor substitute for the rich communal life of the ethnic ghetto.[1]

The genre peaked in its popularity with silent-era classics such as *Amarilly of Clothes-Line Alley* (Marshall Neilan, 1918) and *Irene* (Alfred E. Green, 1926). It proved resilient enough to produce one significant echo during the classic sound era, the Academy Award-winning *Kitty Foyle* (Sam Wood, 1940). Drawing on narrative conventions of romantic comedy and women's melodrama, the Bowery Cinderella film nevertheless refuses to champion either romantic love or middle-class domesticity. To be convincingly Irish, a Bowery Cinderella had to be tough, feisty, and, in a certain sense, independent. Still, cinematic Irishness also demanded that women—like men—assert their independence within limits set by the working-class community.

---

[1] I take the name for this genre from one of its less distinguished examples, *A Bowery Cinderella* (Burton King, 1927).

65

In choosing community over independence, the cinematic Bowery Cinderellas proved themselves true to the historical experience
of Irish-American women. Compared to other immigrant groups,
Irish-American women possessed a unique degree of economic
power and independence, yet remained steadfastly Catholic and
refused to embrace feminism. Not surprisingly, feminist scholars
have tended to dismiss Irish-American women as reactionary, or
through tortuous dialectics, to uplift them to contemporary standards of feminist autonomy.[2] The stubborn fact of Irish-American
Catholic conservatism remains and no doubt accounts for the scholarly neglect of Irish-American women in general studies of women
and film.

To be fair, the working-girl films of the thirties and forties tend
to mute themes of ethnicity. In this genre, the Depression broke
down the older Hollywood distinction between middle-class WASP
and working-class ethnic, transforming the working-class woman
into a representative, and thus de-ethnicized, American. Detached
from any ethnic community, the women of these films face a world
in which they define themselves primarily, and often exclusively, in
terms of their relation to men. The screwball comedy may have celebrated "fast-talking dames," independent career women who could
hold their own with any man on the battlefield of love, but the more
pervasive genre of women's melodrama presented a more frighten-

---

[2]On the cultural conservatism of Irish-American women, see Diner, *Erin's
Daughters in America: Irish Immigrant Women in the Nineteenth Century*. For a
representative work reflecting the general marginality of Irish-American women to
mainstream women's history, see Evans, *Born for Liberty*. Evans's work remains the
standard survey history of American women. By its account, Irish women appear
to make positive contributions to American women's history only when they break
out of the confines of their patriarchal ethnic cultures. For examples of efforts to
rehabilitate Irish-American women within the terms set by mainstream scholarship,
see the interesting revision of Irish-American women religious in Fitzgerald, *Habits
of Compassion: Irish Catholic Nuns and the Origins of New York's Welfare System,
1830–1920*.

ing, and in its own way more realistic, view of the vulnerability of women in a world made by men.[3]

As victors or victims, women in these films stand on the other side of a historical divide separating traditional and modern gender relations by their very struggle to achieve fulfillment through work and love. Immigrant groups in America maintained a traditional suspicion of romantic love somewhat longer than mainstream middle-class Anglo-Americans, a suspicion best captured by the Bowery Cinderella film.[4] Here, once again, a distinctly Irish-American story sets itself against mainstream American narrative conventions.

That mainstream story found its classic expression in Israel Zangwill's 1908 play, *The Melting Pot*, in which the triumph of romantic love over ethnic family ties achieves a narrative rapprochement between ethnic and WASP cultures. Zangwill's play tells the story of the inter-ethnic romance between David Quixano, a Russian-Jewish immigrant, and Vera Revendal, a settlement-house worker. Despite opposition from David's family, love eventually conquers all. At the end of the play, David and Vera—Jew and Gentile—embrace and pledge their eternal love to the closing strains of "My Country 'tis of Thee."[5]

The particular ethnicity considered here—Jewish—is significant. From Zangwill to later writers such as Isaac Berkson and Horace Kallen, the mainstream debate over the melting pot has largely been

---

[3]For representative works of feminist scholarship on this period, see Basinger, *A Woman's View: How Hollywood Spoke to Women, 1930–1960*; and Maria Di Battista, *Fast-Talking Dames*.

[4]Even Jane Addams, the most enlightened of the WASP urban reformers, found herself troubled by the degree to which immigrants continued to view marriage and family life primarily in economic terms. Addams rejected the forced-draft assimilation of 100-per-cent Americanism, but still believed that proper adjustment to American society depended on immigrants adopting modern, middle-class ideals of companionate marriage and the child-centered family. See Addams, *Twenty Years at Hull House*, 104.

[5]For a perceptive reading of this play in the larger context of debates over assimilation, see Akam, *Transnational America: Cultural Pluralist Thought in the Twentieth Century*, 49–51.

WASPs versus Jews. The marginality of Irish Catholics to the great WASP-Jewish debate found its symbolic embodiment in Zangwill's character Kathleen O'Reilly, the dim-witted, stage-Irish domestic who works for David's family in *The Melting Pot*.

Jewish writers consistently rejected the simple assimilation of 100-per-cent Americanism. But even at their most pluralistic, they imagined the ethnic and the national in a state of constant dialogue— each changing and transforming the other.[6] Irish-Catholic Americanism, by contrast, imagined the ethnic and the national as parallel worlds, equally good but respectful of boundaries, especially in the area of religion. The distinction between Jewish and Irish-Catholic Americanism is perhaps clearest in their attitudes toward the most significant instrument of Americanization, the public school. For all their suspicions of assimilation, Jews embraced the public school; for all their patriotism, Irish Catholics rejected it in favor of a separate parochial school system.

Two decades after Zangwell's play, the Irish moved from margin to center in a very different kind of melting-pot story, Anne Nichols's *Abie's Irish Rose*. The somewhat improbable story of the marriage of the Jewish Abraham Levy and the Irish Rosemary Murphy was the single most lucrative cultural property in the 1920s—the acerbic critic H. L. Menken named it "America's third-largest industry."[7]

The play opened on May 23, 1922, at New York's Fulton Theatre. Surviving an early round of negative reviews, it played on through 2,327 performances over the next five years (a record it held into the early 1940s). The play's success took Broadway as much by surprise as by storm. Nichols initially found no backers for her play. The Jewish producers who had come to dominate Broadway by the 1920s were offended by the play's use of broad ethnic stereotypes and clearly felt the potential audience would be offended as well.[8]

---

[6]On Kallen, see Akam, *Transnational America*, Chapter 3.

[7]Quoted in Merwin, "The Performance of Jewish Ethnicity in Anne Nichols' *Abie's Irish Rose*," 3.

[8]For the initial Jewish response to the play, see ibid., 14–17.

Scholars look back on the play with similar concerns and have been at something of a loss as to why the story was so popular.

The theme of inter-ethnic harmony carries on the spirit of the earlier, popular *Melting Pot*, yet Abie and Rose appear less as models for a new kind of American than as examples of assimilation to 100-per-cent Anglo-Saxonism. Anxious Anglo-Americans may have taken some comfort in a reassuring fable of assimilation, but the story achieved its greatest success playing to ethnic audiences in New York City. Lest this be interpreted as an embrace of assimilation, we must consider that Abie and Rosie more often than not serve merely as straight men for the broad ethnic humor indulged in by their relatives. On this point, the film history of the story is revealing.

Even before Paramount's highly successful 1929 film adaptation (directed by Victor Fleming), the play inspired a film comedy series, The Cohens and the Kellys, very heavy on slapstick ethnic humor and very light on assimilation ideology. As gangster films would use the moral message that crime does not pay as an excuse for showing how exciting crime can be, so the assimilationist message of *Abie's Irish Rose* served as a license to indulge in the vulgar ethnic humor that continued to prove so entertaining to ethnics themselves.[9]

The Irish story of the Bowery Cinderella offers an alternative to the mainstream options of pluralism and assimilation. The first great Bowery Cinderella film, *Amarilly of Clothes-Line Alley*, incorporates romance into an ethnic cultural ideal somewhere between the peasant Kathleen O'Reilly of *The Melting Pot* and the middle-class, assimilated Rosemary Murphy of *Abie's Irish Rose*.

The character of the Bowery Cinderella could not have asked for a higher profile ambassador than Mary Pickford, who plays the lead role of Amarilly. Pickford was the first true Hollywood star,

---

[9]For a different reading of the film that stresses the Irish as agents of assimilation, see Fiedler, "Fatal Attraction: Irish-Jewish Romance in Early Film and Drama." Diane Negra similarly argues—wrongly—that films of the 1920s present the Irish as an assimilated, model minority. See Negra, *Off-White Hollywood: American Culture and Ethnic Female Stardom*.

the biggest star of the silent era, and quite probably the biggest movie star ever.[10] "America's Sweetheart," Pickford was actually Canadian—born Gladys Louise Smith on April 8, 1892, of Irish descent, in Toronto, Ontario.

Pickford credited the spunk and drive she displayed both on and off the screen to her "fiery ancestors," a line of strong-willed Irish women stretching back to her maternal grandmother, Catherine Faeley.[11] She began her acting career in the heavily Irish world of the Toronto theatre and got her first break in New York performing in *Edmund Burke*, a Chauncey Olcott musical loosely based on the life of the famous eighteenth-century Irish politician.[12] Perhaps best known for her work with the Kentucky-born Anglo-American, D. W. Griffith, Pickford herself repeatedly identified the Irish-American Marshall (Mickey) Neilan as her favorite director. Pickford and Neilan traded good-natured Irish insults—she would call him a bog trotter, he would call her shanty Irish—throughout their collaboration on six major features, all critical and popular successes.[13]

The good fun—and shanty-Irish humor—are on full display in *Amarilly of Clothes-Line Alley*. The film tells the story of Amarilly Jenkins, the daughter of a widowed, working-class Irish washerwoman, who meets her Prince Charming only to reject the life of wealth and ease for the simple, honest pleasures of her Irish ghetto, Clothes-Line Alley. Set in San Francisco, the film opens with a view of the city from the bay, but then quickly moves into a close-up of a building corner with a street sign identifying the area as Clothes-Line Alley. The camera then cuts to a wide shot of the Alley itself, crossed with clotheslines, and bustling with people.

---

[10] For Pickford's standing in film history, see Whitfield, *Pickford: The Woman Who Made Hollywood*.

[11] Ibid., 5.

[12] Ibid., 7–10, 20–21, 23, 49.

[13] Ibid., 166.

Films of the era would generally begin by introducing the performers in poses that best represent their characters; it is not a stretch to say that the opening sequence establishes the alley itself as a leading character. Introductions of the conventional characters follow, with Amarilly cleaning windows, her boyfriend Terry McGowen (William Scott) tending bar, and her mother Mrs. Jenkins (Kate Price)—identified as "maid in Ireland"—doing laundry.

Amarilly's mother receives perhaps the most dramatic introduction. As in his introduction of Clothes-Line Alley, Neilan begins with a close-up of a sign, this time stating, "Honest Wash Done by Mrs. Americus Jenkins." The camera then cuts to a wider shot that establishes the sign as on a door in the hallway of a tenement house. The door opens, a boy runs out. We see other children playing inside the apartment, but at the center of the frame is Mrs. Jenkins, happily tending to a steaming pot of laundry. For Neilan, the shot is clearly iconic, a tribute to the dignity of all Irish washerwomen.

With the main characters introduced, the scene shifts back to the character of place. The intertitle reads, "Sunday . . . soothing syrup to Clothes-Line Alley." Neilan provides a wide shot of the Alley, this time without wash hanging across the street. As befitting the day of rest, adults sit in chairs on the sidewalk while children play in the street. The camera then fades to Amarilly and Terry in church. The view of the pews shows no visible markers of Catholicism, but in the following shot of people leaving the church, we clearly see a priest with a Roman collar. Neilan chooses to shoot the outside of the church at an angle that centers the protruding building corner in the frame, echoing the earlier corner shot of Clothes-Line Alley and establishing the church as located at an intersection or crossroads within the community.

The action abruptly switches to how the other half—the richer half—live. Sunday is apparently a private day for the rich. Mrs. Stuyvesant Phillips (Ida Waterman), a matron of high society, picks up the phone in her luxurious home to check up on her nephew, Gordon Phillips (Norman Kerry), at the elite "Athletic Club." One of the manservants at the club tells Mrs. Phillips that Gordon is in Bible Class (a clear marker of Protestantism as opposed to Catholicism), but we quickly see he is relaxing with a drink and fooling around with his friends.

Religion for the rich is an affair for women, and old women at that; the upper class has not been able to pass its religion on to the next generation. Indulgence in alcohol stands as a rejection of a certain class sense of propriety. For the Irish working class, however, religion is still a communal activity, uniting generations and genders. Alcohol, moreover, is not a sign of decadence. There is no suggestion of hypocrisy in Terry working as a bartender and still going to Mass on Sunday.

True to Catholic understandings of Sabbath observance, a day of rest is a day of play. Following the establishment of Gordon's character as a privileged ne'er-do-well, the action shifts back to Clothes-Line Alley. Having fulfilled their Sunday Mass obligation, Amarilly and Terry meet and agree to go for a Sunday drive. Religious and family leaders of the time often railed against automobiles as providing young couples with a kind of privacy and freedom that would only lead to sin. The following scene with Terry and Amarilly deflects such worries in large part by showing how the very public world of the working class simply does not provide for much in the way of sinful privacy.

With car ownership clearly out of reach for a humble bartender, Terry arrives on a motorcycle. The noise of the engine, suggested in the silent film by an excessive amount of smoke, draws neighbors out into the street. Terry appears proud of his machine, but has trouble starting it up again after Amarilly has hopped aboard. A group of neighborhood girls watching from the street corner laugh at Terry's motorized bluster and suggest that Amarilly's hand muff may actually be the fur of a neighborhood cat that disappeared a few days earlier.

Much has been made of the Irish art of begrudgery, but such ridicule is one time-honored way that traditional cultures enforce community standards. Terry and Amarilly's humble attempt to enjoy their day of rest hardly violates those standards—the scene ends with Ma Jenkins waving goodbye, with approval, from her tenement window as Terry and Amarilly ride off. The comedy deflates the middle-class, romantic ideal of splendid isolation. In the working-class world of Clothes-Line Alley, courtship always takes place under the supervision of the community.

Much of the comedy that follows this scene flows from a more explicit clash of middle-class and working-class cultural values. As Sunday turns into Monday, we see this contrast in different styles of eating. Terry stops by the Jenkins's apartment at dinnertime. He learns that Amarilly has lost her cleaning job and quickly offers her a job selling cigarettes at the Cyclone Cafe, where he tends bar. Far from being insulted by the prospect of her daughter working in a bar, Ma Jenkins responds with joy: "There! Wasn't I after telling ye—the Lord never closes wan door but he opens a window!" She then invites Terry to sit down to eat with them.

Throughout the dinner scene, Neilan once again uses crosscutting to highlight the contrast of class values. After showing Ma and Amarilly preparing dinner, he cuts to Mrs. Phillips inviting Gordon to dinner. He declines, claiming that he has already arranged for Professor Haig, the great prohibitionist, to lecture at his art studio (where he is living in bohemian squalor). This is merely a lie, however, to cover up a night of drinking with another genteel wastrel.

Home life for the upper class is an exclusively feminine domain. In contrast to Gordon, Terry sees no threat to his manhood in sitting down for dinner with Amarilly's mother. The Jenkins family eats with gusto and talks boisterously among themselves, while the Phillipses eat with a reserve best captured by the self-description of the society girl, Colette King (Margaret Landis): "Colette King, a product of social cold storage." The comic contrast leaves no doubt as to the cultural superiority of Clothes-Line Alley.

In the grand tradition of social comedy, worlds that contrast inevitably collide. Slumming one night at the Cyclone Cafe, Gordon meets Amarilly. She rescues him from a bar fight and brings him back to her family's apartment to tend to his wounds—under the watchful eye of Ma Jenkins. When Gordon asks how he can repay their kindness, Ma quickly asks if she can do his laundry—to which Amarilly later complains, "Can't a swell guy come up here without you askin' for his dirty shirts?" In the world of Clothes-Line Alley, love is never very far from laundry and both are in plain view for all to see.

On the street the next day, an obviously proud Ma Jenkins confides to a friend, "Don't breathe it to a soul, Mrs. Finnegan, but Amarilly met a dude last night. She's after his washin'!" The secret quickly spreads throughout the neighborhood, in one scene literally shouted from the rooftops: "Don't breathe it to a soul, but Amarilly's gettin' gay with a dude." The rumor mill transforms laundry into love; word eventually gets to Terry and he breaks up with Amarilly.

With Terry temporarily out of the picture, the story shifts to the budding romance between Amarilly and Gordon. At first, the class divide appears too great for either to consider the possibility of love. Clearly attracted to Gordon on one level, Amarilly brings him his laundry only to drum up more business as his cleaning woman. Gordon, in turn, finds himself attracted to Amarilly, but more as a curiosity than a romantic partner.

For his own amusement, rather than from any concern for her welfare, Gordon suggests that Amarilly move in with his aunt and learn how to be a lady. He explains that his aunt is a leader in "The Society for the Betterment of Humanity" for whom kindness is a sort of business. Gordon calls his aunt, who sees Amarilly as an opportunity to experiment with some of her reform club's theories of social conditioning. She agrees to take in Amarilly, and after some initial resistance, Amarilly accepts the offer.

The culture clash now begins in earnest. Neilan and screenwriter Frances Marion waste no opportunity to skewer the arrogance and pretension of social reformers, whose efforts to "uplift" Amarilly transform the old Pygmalion story into an exercise in social engineering. Of all the immigrant groups, the Irish had a special loathing for reform. On one level, Irish urban political machines were one of the prime targets of the real-life Mrs. Phillipses. At a deeper level, the idea that you can reform human nature simply struck the Irish as against all common sense.

The eminent WASP director D. W. Griffith satirized women reformers in *Intolerance* (1916), but his portrayal suggests, with a tone of high seriousness, that prudery or sexual repression fuel their drive to control people. In *Amarilly*, the folly appears to lie primarily in Mrs. Phillips's "theory that environment makes the woman" and a simple change in environment will bring about a change in personality. Much as with Professor Higgins's efforts to transform another Irish street waif, Eliza Doolittle in George Bernard Shaw's *Pygmalion*, Mrs. Phillips seems more concerned about her own theories than the welfare of the poor.

Amarilly, for her part, wants none of it. She physically resists the army of professional groomers enlisted to give her the appearance of a being a "social equal," declaring, "I don't want to be no lady. I want to go home." In a quieter moment, she sadly confides to the butler, a fellow Irishman and old family friend, "I never knowed what a swell place Clothes-Line Alley was, till they took me away from there. Guess—'cause its home."

Against her intentions, Mrs. Phillips's grand experiment succeeds only in transforming her nephew. After seeing Amarilly's earthy vitality set against the lifeless formality of high society, Gordon falls in love. Mrs. Phillips fears that this budding romance will interfere with her own matchmaking plans. She and Colette King, her desired match for Gordon, decide to invite Amarilly's family to an afternoon tea, confident that the pig-in-the-parlor situation will impress upon Gordon the impassable nature of the social gulf that lies between him and Amarilly.

Through this scheme, Mrs. Phillips wins the cultural battle, but loses the war. Yes, the Jenkinses are loud and friendly beyond all propriety. They dance a jig, blow their noses openly with large, dirty handkerchiefs, and struggle unsuccessfully to converse with the upper-class guests. Even motherhood fails to provide a common bond among the women. One failed exchange between Ma Jenkins and a society woman leaves the audience with the impression that the poor have children, while the rich only have pets.

In the end, the visit clearly affirms the cultural superiority of the working-class Irish. Back in her apartment, Ma jokes with several of her hefty, apron-clad neighbors about her afternoon in high society. She and her sons act out the day's events, mocking the stiff formality of the rich.

Despite the disaster at the tea, Gordon makes one last attempt to win Amarilly's heart. Showing the bourgeois soul that lurks beneath every bohemian façade, Gordon approaches Amarilly in her family's apartment with an offer of uplift indistinguishable in its condescension from his aunt's original experiment in reform: "Give me a chance to educate you—to take you away from...all this." Flattered rather than offended, Amarilly respectfully declines the offer, explaining, "I'm sorry, Mr. Gordon, but I knows now that you can't mix ice cream an'...pickles."

With the moral of the story clear for all to see, Gordon leaves Clothes-Line Alley for good and Amarilly returns to Terry. The film moves on to its inevitable happy ending—with a distinctly Irish twist. After surviving a near fatal shooting accident, Terry lands a job at City Hall—a step up from bartender, perhaps, but certainly no leap into the middle class.

The film ends with another Sunday drive—a few years into their marriage. Aside from having two children and a sidecar, Terry and Amarilly appear to be very much the same people they were at the beginning of the film. After a brief stop on a country road, the happy family drives off, no doubt on their way home to Clothes-Line Alley.

The triumph of social stability over mobility sets *Amarilly of Clothes-Line Alley* apart from other Pickford films that deal with crossing the cultural boundaries of class. Most of these films are straightforward Cinderella stories, such as *Daddy Long Legs* (Marshall Neilan, 1919), in which Mary starts out poor and ends up rich. In some, such as *The Hoodlum* (Sidney Franklin, 1920), Pickford plays a spoiled rich girl who has her pride humbled and personality revitalized through contact with working-class culture.

Pickford played other Irish roles, but did not see herself as an Irish actress and certainly had no desire to limit herself to identifiably Irish stories. The Bowery Cinderella story survived in film apart from the long-term commitment of any one producer, director, or performer.[14] In the 1920s, the story found a worthy heir to *Amarilly* in the 1926 film *Irene*.

Appropriately enough, *Irene* had as its star an Irish-American actress, Colleen Moore, who could rightfully claim to be the heir to Mary Pickford's title of America's sweetheart. At first glance, the two could not be further apart. Their very hair styles spoke of two different cultural eras—Pickford, the girl with the curls, a picture of

---

[14]Though generally associated with high-society melodramas and biblical epics, no less a director than Cecil B. De Mille tried his hand at the genre in his 1922 film, *Saturday Night*. Providing a further twist on the story, *Saturday Night* offers two-way cross-class traffic. Shamrock O'Day (Edith Roberts), the daughter of an Irish washerwoman, falls in love with Richard Wynbrook Prentiss (Conrad Nagel), a wealthy society man. At the same time, Iris Van Suydam (Leatrice Joy), Richard's fiancée, falls in love with her chauffeur, Tom McGuire (Jack Mower), who happens to be Shamrock's neighbor and long-time nemesis. The film announces the dilemma, and its inevitable resolution, early on: "Romance laughs at the heavy Chains of Tradition. But Society metes out swift punishment to those who break the Chains." The comedy and drama that follow flow from the futile efforts of the couples to prove that "oil and water will mix," though by the end of the film, "it's always kind to kind." Like *Amarilly*, the film concludes with an epilogue, seven years later, on a Saturday night: Shamrock, Tom, and their three children frolic at Coney Island, while Iris and Richard, alone in a mansion, finally decide to marry. The picture may give each class its due, but the culture of the fertile poor clearly triumphs over that of the sterile rich.

Victorian feminine purity; Moore, originator of the Dutchboy bob, symbol of the Jazz-Age flapper. Moore's performance in *Flaming Youth* (John Francis Dillon, 1923) did indeed make the term flapper a household word and inspired no less a Jazz-Age luminary than fellow Irish-American F. Scott Fitzgerald to comment, "I was the spark that lit up flaming youth, and Colleen Moore was the torch."[15]

Still, Moore's screen persona—as well as her real-life personality—could not have been further from the brooding, sexual modernism of Fitzgerald's fiction. As portrayed by Moore, the flapper was not a vamp or temptress, but an extension of the rule-breaking tomboy perfected by Pickford. Moore's wholesome, almost sexless, and explicitly Irish appeal carried the day against sexier flappers such as Clara Bow.

Moore was the top box-office draw in 1926, 1927, and 1928 precisely because she proved capable of synthesizing a modern style with Victorian ideals of sexual innocence that maintained their hold on the vast majority of Americans—despite the teleology of "liberation" imposed on the era by film historians.[16] These ideals were neither the creation nor the exclusive property of Irish Americans, but the popular image of the Irish as both modern city-dwellers and devout Catholics placed them in a unique position to perform the task of mediating between the values of the two eras.

Born Kathleen Morrison in Port Huron, Michigan in 1900, Moore grew up in a stable, lower-middle-class household at some remove from the rough-and-tumble world of *Amarilly*. Like Pickford, Moore got her start with D. W. Griffith. Her uncle, Walter Howey, was editor of the *Chicago Examiner* and had used his political connections to help Griffith get his two controversial epics, *Birth of a Nation* (1915) and *Intolerance* (1916), past the local censors. Griffith returned the

---

[15]Basinger, *Silent Stars*, 420.

[16]Diane Negra attacks Moore's screen persona as a retreat from the bold, sexual modernism of the "New Woman." That Moore herself, and most Irish Americans, rejected that type of modernism appears as yet another symptom of Irish-Catholic cultural backwardness. See Negra, *Off-White Hollywood*, 29–30.

favor by giving Howey's niece a contract. Howey suggested she change her professional name to the more Irish-sounding Colleen Moore as a way of attracting attention to herself.[17]

Early in her career, Moore played Amarilly-like roles in films such as *Dinty* (Marshall Neilan, 1920), another Mickey Neilan film of Irish ghetto life in San Francisco. After her breakthrough with *Flaming Youth*, the American press commonly referred to her as the "Irish flapper."[18] Again, in the context of Moore's flapper films, Irishness served primarily as a badge of moral probity. Still, the ethnic coding of her celebrity enabled her to pursue more explicitly Irish stories at no risk to her career.

The most successful of these Irish stories was, no doubt, the Bowery Cinderella tale *Irene*. A classic example of the kind of formula-story recycling that drives popular narrative, the film was based on a popular Broadway musical that was itself a reworking of a much less popular nonmusical comedy, produced by the great Irish-Jewish team of George M. Cohan and Sam Harris.[19] The story shares much with *Amarilly*, though in this case Irene actually does marry her WASP prince. True to the spirit of the genre, however, she does so only after he has conceded the superiority of her Irish ghetto life.

Irene opens much like *Amarilly*, introducing the principle of place even before we meet any characters. More than the earlier film, *Irene* links place to class and comically calls attention to the class divide of its city locale: "The society section of Philadelphia—near City Dump Drive, Boxcar Boulevard, and Vista del Gas House." After some street scenes with children at play, the camera focuses in on yet another earth-mother Irish washerwoman—Irene's mother,

---

[17]Moore tells the story in her memoir: "Over a beer in a friendly neighborhood tavern they [Howey and his friend Teddy Beck, editor of the Chicago Tribune] decided the time had come for introducing an Irish actress to the movies. There was a lot of good publicity in it." Colleen Moore, *Silent Star*, 25.

[18]Basinger, *Silent Stars*, 424.

[19]I take the term formula stories from Cawelti, *Adventure, Mystery, Romance: Formula Stories as Art and Culture*.

Mrs. O'Dare, played by Kate Price in what amounts to a reprise of her role as Mrs. Jenkins in *Amarilly*.

The O'Dares are a somewhat more conventional two-parent household, though the presence of Mr. O'Dare (Charles Murray) hardly introduces any greater stability to this struggling working-class home. He is a classic Irish ne'er-do-well drunk, a stage-Irish Paddy who conforms to all the requirements of the old stereotype short of beating his wife. Still, the film plays this all for light comedy. Irene accepts her family situation as normal and, early on, shows little or no aspiration to any better life, content simply to deliver her mother's laundry.

Irene is more a daydreamer than a dreamer, and her inability to focus on her work causes many mistakes that threaten her mother's reputation in the neighborhood. Her mother finally fires her—and, more significantly, banishes her: "You get a job downtown. Your father'll deliver the wash . . . or I'll give him the finest funeral that ever left the Fourth Ward." Irene has disgraced her mother in her own neighborhood and now she must find work elsewhere. Mrs. O'Dare, in turn, must struggle to regain her local reputation with only a drunken husband to take the place of an absent-minded daughter. Community reputation clearly matters more to Mrs. O'Dare than domestic tranquility, and the home is very clearly an economic institution in which everyone must contribute their fair share in order for the family to survive.

These basic economic concerns start the plot machinations propelling Irene toward her Prince Charming. She gets a job downtown demonstrating mattresses in a department store window, but loses it when she gets distracted by an old friend, Cordelia Smith (Betty Francisco), who stops by for a visit after seeing her in the window. Irene returns home and tells her mother she lost her job. Mrs. O'Dare is furious: "Ye can get out—and don't come back till ye've got a new job."

Irene takes her mother at her word and leaves home. Jobless, with no family to turn to, Irene follows up on an invitation she received from Cordelia earlier in the day. Cordelia has married rich, and, needing a date for a friend of her husband, she lends Irene a fancy dress. Later, the two couples meet at a speakeasy, The Tumble Inn. Irene's date is a visitor from New York, "a Wild Oats boy in a Quaker Oats town." He quickly proves himself a drunken boor.

Irene resists his advances and proves more than capable of handling herself. She runs out on the balcony, climbs down a tree and walks off alone. In the film's first clash of cultures, working-class Irish virtue triumphs over upper-class WASP lechery. Though Irene has retained her purity, she still feels that, without a job, she cannot return home to her parents. Having exhausted her options in Philadelphia, she hitchhikes to New York City—not in search of adventure and greater freedom, but simply to look for a job to help support her family.

In New York, Irene once again finds herself working in a department store, this time making deliveries to high-end customers. As soon as she has a place of her own to live, she writes to her family to come and join her. Lest her mother fear losing her good laundry clientele back in the Fourth Ward, Irene assures her, "People are dirtier [here] than they are in Philadelphia, so business should be good."

On one of her department-store deliveries, Irene becomes involved in a Pygmalion-style scheme that leads her to her WASP Prince Charming, Donald Marshall (Lloyd Hughes). Bob Harrison (Lawrence Wheat), a friend of Marshall and junior partner in a silk firm, convinces him to invest his money in a high-fashion dress designer, Madame Lucy (George K. Arthur). An effeminate man who has inherited his aunt's fashion-design business, Madame Lucy attempts to convince Donald to back him by claiming he can make any woman beautiful.

As Madame Lucy makes his pitch, Irene arrives with a delivery for Donald's mother, Mrs. Warren Marshall (Ida Darling). Waiting for Mrs. Marshall, Irene gets into all sorts of mischief—playing dress-up with drapes and lamp shades, knocking over furniture, etc.

Donald finds himself attracted to her as an earthy, honest alternative to the upper-class trappings that clearly bore him. He decides she would be a perfect test case for Madame Lucy's boast and offers Irene the opportunity.

Irene is skeptical at first. The occupation of fashion model "doesn't sound quite . . . quite . . . er . . . respectable." Irene says she would feel safer if a couple of her female friends could accompany her. Donald agrees, and before Irene leaves, we get some glimpse of why he finds Irene so refreshing. His prospective fiancée, Eleanor Hadley (Eva Novak), is another classic product of upper-class cold storage. Donald shows her no more than the basic courtesy he would show any woman, but Irene clearly feels outclassed.

Irene's experience with Madame Lucy does little to build up her confidence. When he first sees her, he declares, "As I live and hemstitch, she's impossible." Still, Donald holds him to his boast. Madame Lucy's first attempt to transform Irene reveals two of Irene's enduring traits: her modesty and her clumsiness. It also provides reminders of the verbal class divide that separates Irene from the world of fashion.

> *Madame Lucy:* I've seen sausages with more style than you. A little nonchalance . . . diablerie . . . esprit du corps.
>
> *Irene:* I may look like a sausage, but I've never been on a spree in my life—it's my father that does the drinking!

The revolving pedestal on which he dresses her predictably spins out of control, providing more occasions for the kind of physical humor at which Moore excelled. In the end, echoing the ice-cream-and-pickles line from *Amarilly*, Madame Lucy declares, "Even *I* cannot make Peach Melba with Prunes." Still, Donald holds him to his promise.

Irene returns home after a frustrating first day on her new job. Her mother is concerned when she learns of the new modeling position, reminding Irene: "*Remimber Dinty McGinty's daughter?* She wanted to be a *foine* bird—and a *foine bird* she turned out to be!" Irene takes her mother's moral warning seriously, but rather than abandon her modeling job, she recruits her chaperone girlfriends as protection. Significantly, she explains the opportunity to two of her friends in terms of family obligations: "We'll have enough money to give our mothers a real vacation." Despite their family motivations, the three agree to pursue their modeling careers without telling their mothers.

The hatching of the pious plot provides an occasion for one of the most powerful visuals in the film. Irene's girlfriends happen to live in the same building with the O'Dares, and she visits them by climbing up and down a fire escape that becomes something like a character in its own right. The director, Alfred E. Green, provides many side-view shots of the O'Dares' apartment building, with the fire escape connecting the three family apartments—a kind of vertical urban village. The fire escape will be the setting for the romantic climax of the film, and these earlier scenes are important for establishing the communal symbolism. Though the fire escape provides some measure of privacy as the girls plan their strategy for keeping their modeling a secret from their mothers, it also serves to mark the physical boundaries of a moral community presided over by the mothers.

Madame Lucy takes the three women under his wing to prepare them for a major high-society fashion show hosted by Donald's mother. The fashion show serves as the equivalent of the Prince's ball in the original Cinderella story. True to that story, Irene nearly misses the show. Madame Lucy plays the part of the evil stepmother, prohibiting Irene from attending the show in punishment for her accidentally ripping one of his dresses. Donald, in turn, plays the fairy godmother.

Stopping off at the dress shop on his way to the show, Donald finds Irene sitting alone. After she explains what has happened, he tells her she will not only go to the show, but lead it. Irene accepts his support, but fears the romantic motivation behind it. Right before the show begins, she tells him, "We've got to say goodbye...after tonight. I can't lie to Mother any longer. I...I don't belong here." Donald then offers her some jewelry to wear in the show and declares, "You're better than any of them, Irene. Wear these—and later I'll tell you where you belong."

A long fashion-show sequence follows, shot in an early Technicolor process (and looking very much like a silent dry run for the lavish musical productions of the sound era). In the meantime, the mothers discover the true whereabouts of their daughters and storm the mansion to protect their daughters' virtue.

The mothers arrive at the grand finale, the lingerie portion of the show. Just as it appears Irene is going to open her robe, her mother yells from the audience: "Don't ye dare open that coat. Shame on ye—roamin' about half nood!" Irene proves that she was never going to model any of the lingerie, and once again the working-class Irish come across as the guardians of morality.

Mrs. Marshall, on the other hand, approves of risqué lingerie but has no tolerance for working-class rabble. Embarrassed by the disruption, she scolds Donald for lying to her and accuses Irene of "angling for my son." Irene comes to the defense of her mother and herself: "I don't want your son, and you can't insult my mother and me. We're not common, we're just poor—and *that's* no crime." Turning to Donald, she finishes with this: "You made me dream of being a lady, but I'm awake now—and I never want to see you again!"

Unimpressed, Mrs. Marshall tells her butler to escort the "vulgarians" off the premises. Mrs. O'Dare responds, "Bulgarians to you, Mrs. Marshall! I'm Irish, I'll have ye understand!" As her mother defends her ethnic honor, Irene runs off and hails a limousine to take her back to her apartment.

Donald manages to smooth things over with his mother and then escorts Mrs. O'Dare back to her home. As the two step out of the limousine, Ma O'Dare laughs, "Go on with ye. With that gift of blarney, ye'd talk forgiveness out of anyone." Declared honorary Irish by no less an authority than Mrs. O'Dare herself, Donald makes one final effort to win the love of Irene. Donald and Mrs. O'Dare go up to the apartment, where they find Irene crying on the fire escape.

Hearing her mother come in, yet unaware of Donald's presence, Irene stares out at the alley and declares, "Ma, I love Donald Marshall so. Why couldn't he have been just an iceman or a motorcycle cop?" Here, Irene confesses that she loves Donald in spite of, not because of, his high standing in society. Donald finally hears the profession of love he has been waiting for, but their romance is still a family matter. "I heard you, Irene, and you can't take it back now! I've fixed things with Mother, and it's all O.K. with the O'Dares."

The film ends as the two embrace on the fire escape. Their love may conquer the class divide, but only after Irene has proven that she will not turn her back on her class and ethnic heritage in order to rise in the world. Like the Prince Charming of the fairy tale, Donald must seek out his Cinderella. Unlike the fairy tale, the Prince Charming of *Irene* does not whisk her away to a mansion, but rather surrenders and submits to the world of the tenement.

The working-class Irish triumph of the ending appears even clearer when contrasted with *Ella Cinders* (Alfred E. Green, 1926), a non-Irish Cinderella film that Moore made in the same year as *Irene*. Based on a popular comic strip, the film features a modern-day Cinderella who rises from rags to riches by winning a trip to Hollywood. Ella ultimately fails as a movie star, but she is rescued from her life as a charwoman by her small-town, iceman boyfriend, Waite Lifter (Lloyd Hughes). Waite is actually a rich college boy who was slumming as a manual laborer when he met Ella. Revealingly, the film ends with Ella and Waite, elegantly dressed, laughing at their humble beginnings as they watch their young son play at being an iceman.

Like Pickford before her, Moore's non-Irish Cinderella roles tended to favor the happy ending of wealth and success, while her Irish roles tended to favor working-class roots. Hollywood has never tired of rags-to-riches stories, but the sad-rags-to-happy-rags story of *Irene* proved remarkably resilient. Ten years after Moore's hit film, Lux Radio Theatre produced a new version, starring Jeanette MacDonald. In the same year, Warner Brothers recycled the story for their *Colleen*, directed by Alfred E. Green and staring Dick Powell and Ruby Keeler, a remake in everything but name. Finally, in 1940, RKO distributed an explicit remake produced by the small Imperadio Pictures, starring a young Irish actress named Anna Neagle—who (needless to say) did not become the next Colleen Moore.

Despite its enduring appeal, the Bowery Cinderella story had clearly moved from A- to B-picture status by the early 1930s. Aside from narrative exhaustion, the reasons for this decline are not exactly clear. At one level, the era simply did not produce an actress of the stature of Pickford or Moore with a similar personal or artistic attraction to distinctly Irish stories.[20] During the Depression, the flapper gave way to the working girl as Hollywood's representative American woman, yet that very representativeness may have worked against any particular ethnic coding.

The central themes of the working-girl melodrama—a woman's struggle for independence and the ultimate value of romantic love—certainly work against the communal orientation of the Irish women's pictures.[21] Of the classic women's melodramas of the era, only *Mannequin* (Frank Borzage, 1938) comes close to drawing on the narrative conventions of the Bowery Cinderella.

Joan Crawford plays the role of Jessie Cassidy, a slum-dwelling Irish-American factory girl who dreams of a better life beyond the unremitting poverty she has known all her life. No cheerful urban village, Jessie's Hester Street is a textbook case of urban— and especially lazy, drunken, and Irish—pathology. Jessie seeks to escape with a get-rich-quick fight-promoter hustler, but ultimately

---

[20]The three major actresses who could have inherited the role by virtue of their portrayal of working-class women—Bette Davis, Barbara Stanwyck, and Joan Crawford—had little or no ethnic Irish connection. Stanwyck had Scotch-Irish grandparents, and Crawford was raised Catholic, but neither played on these connections in their public personas.

[21]Again, for this genre, see Basinger, *A Woman's View*.

finds redemption through a working-class Prince Charming, John L. Hennessey (Spencer Tracy).

John is a self-made man from Hester Street who parlayed a small tugboat into one of the largest shipping fleets on the docks of New York. Through a variety of melodramatic plot twists—including labor strife and a trip to Ireland—Hennessey loses his fortune but wins Jessie's heart. At the end of the film, the two are back at the bottom, but no longer seek to rise to the top. The accumulation of wealth left Hennessey empty; the desire for romantic escape left Jessie betrayed. Together, they will work to achieve Jessie's dream of "three rooms," the humble security of the lower middle class.

Ultimately, *Mannequin* meets the Bowery Cinderella only half way. It has class, but not community. Jessie and John are two people against the world, with only love to keep them together. The traditional enemy of romantic love, community did not fare well in women's melodrama.

Still, the Bowery Cinderella had a last hurrah of sorts in one of the most highly praised specimens of the genre, *Kitty Foyle*. Nominated for five Academy Awards, including Best Picture, the film tells the story of Kitty Foyle (Ginger Rogers), a shanty-Irish girl from Griscom Street living in a city, Philadelphia, still dominated by the Protestant social elite of the Main Line. The animating drama of the story comes from Kitty's struggle to choose between pursuing an illicit love affair with a wealthy socialite, Wyn Strafford (Dennis Morgan), and settling down to a quiet married life with a humble doctor, Mark Eisen (James Craig), committed to serving the poor.

Kitty Foyle lacks the thickly communal vision of earlier films such as *Amarilly of Clothes-Line Alley* and *Irene*, but offers a powerful echo of that vision through its presentation of the relationship between Kitty and her father, Tom "Pop" Foyle (Ernest Cossart). Much to the dismay of feminist scholars, Kitty forsakes independence for marriage.[22] Still, understood in the context of the Bowery Cinderella genre, her choice affirms the working-class folk wisdom of her father more than any delusions of middle-class domestic bliss.

Genre conventions alone provide the best explanation for a film story that departs so dramatically from its source material and from Hollywood's own marketing efforts. The film is based on a contemporary, bestselling novel of the same title, written by Christopher Morely, a popular novelist of the day. The novel is a sprawling, coming-of-age story in which a young girl's awakening to romance serves as an occasion for commentary on ethnic and racial tensions, regional culture, urban decline, the New Deal, and the emergence of a new sociological type—the White Collar Girl. The novel was very racy for its time. Rogers found the explicit love scenes "quite disturbing," and thought the whole novel "highly suggestive and too lurid," but ultimately accepted the role once she had read Dalton Trumbo's highly bowdlerized script.[23]

In developing her character into an Oscar-winning performance, Rogers focused on Irishness as Kitty's defining characteristic, even to the point of forsaking her Hollywood platinum-blonde hair to look more like a tough Irish girl.[24] Still, the Irish elements of the novel required a bit of editing. The original Kitty was that rarity in American popular culture—an Irish Protestant. The novel makes much of the Catholic–Protestant tensions among the Irish in Philadelphia, but the film ignores these in favor of presenting Kitty and Pop

---

[22] Jeanine Basinger is particularly insistent on this point: "A woman needs to be married, and that is the point of *Kitty Foyle*." See Basinger, *A Woman's View*, 494.

[23] Rogers, *Ginger: My Story*, 220, 221.

[24] Rogers recounts in her autobiography, "By the time we started *Kitty Foyle*, my very dark hair had washed out to a tone I felt would be acceptable. After I had digested the script, I concluded that Kitty couldn't possibly be a blonde. She was the daughter of a proud Irishman, and had to look and act like one. Dark hair, blue eyes, a quick wit, and a stinging tongue . . . that was the way Mr. Foyle saw his offspring. She could take care of herself, 'come hell or high-water.'" Ibid., 225.

as generically Irish.[25] Given Hollywood conventions, this implies Irish-Catholic, but the film never explicitly mentions Catholicism.

Despite retaining the novel's very Irish-sounding title, RKO sought to reach as broad an audience as possible by focusing its marketing efforts on the non-ethnic theme of the White Collar Girl. No less an organ of popular culture than LIFE magazine took it upon itself to instruct the producers on how the film should look. In a March 1940 article on the upcoming film, LIFE declared, "The book is successful not just because the story and the character of Kitty are attractive, but also because it is crammed full of specific details which describe the habits and habitat of an important species of American woman, the White Collar Girl."

With Morely as their guide, LIFE photographers took to the streets of Philadelphia and New York to compile an authentic photographic record of the physical environment of the White Collar Girl. Insisting that Kitty herself dress "neither too grubby nor too glamorous," LIFE employed a Ginger Rogers look-alike to model what it thought would be appropriate clothing for a White Collar Girl on a tight budget. In December, in conjunction with the film's release, LIFE featured Rogers in a cover story that compared the final film version with the "suggestions" offered by the LIFE photo spread in March.[26]

True to RKO's commitment to the White-Collar-Girl hype, the film opens with a narrated dumb show tracing the history of the White Collar Girl from Victorian times to the present. This capsule history satirizes women's advance to equality as a decline from the

---

[25] In the novel, Tom Foyle often gets in humorous fights with the "Papists." Still, he is a cultural Catholic of sorts. He hangs out with members of the Catholic Kelly Street Business Men's Association at Dooner's Hotel, "the only bar in America that didn't have any paintings of women" because "too many priests visit it." Morley, *Kitty Foyle*, 142, 11.

[26] See "White Collar Girl: Research Notes for Ginger Rogers' Film Version of Christopher Morley's Best-Selling Novel, *Kitty Foyle*," LIFE (March 25, 1940): 81–87; and "*Kitty Foyle*: LIFE's Pictures of the U.S. White Collar Girl Reappear in RKO Movie," LIFE (December 9, 1940): 87–90.

bliss of home to the loneliness of work. Kitty works in a variety of white-collar jobs as she struggles to find fulfillment in love, but the White Collar theme falls out pretty quickly, in what can only be seen as a marketing bait and switch.

What the film switches to is both less and more Irish than the novel. Despite its ethnic characters and setting, the novel *Kitty Foyle* is a fairly standard (WASP) coming-of-age story in which the main character encounters a variety of people, places, and experiences—especially romantic love—on the path to forging some sense of an autonomous self in a world not of her own making. Early on, Pop and Griscom Street provide moral and geographic orientation as Kitty navigates her path to maturity. But by the end, they are merely sentimental memories, a childhood ideal of security that she must discard in order to come into full womanhood.

Kitty experiences her first great love with the wealthy socialite, Wyn Strafford, but the class divide and his family obligations prove insurmountable. For the last quarter of the novel, she dallies with the attention of Mark Eisen—a balding, socially clumsy, upwardly mobile Jewish doctor from New York's Morningside Heights—yet seems to prefer a hard-won sense of independence to the love of a man.

The film completely restructures the story, transforming it into yet another variation on the Bowery Cinderella. A less flamboyantly Irish Pop—and through him Griscom Street—provides a clear moral center for the story from start to finish. Pop serves as an enduring guide to Kitty through a kind of coming of age that the film reduces to a choice between two men—Wyn, recast as a Prince Charming, the realization of Kitty's childhood dream to live the life of the Main Line; and Mark, completely de-ethnicized, a symbol of limits, the life of hard work and simple pleasures. Though not from Griscom Street, Mark represents a slightly more polished version of Pop's values. Through a highly controlled use of flashback narrative, the film manages to introduce the moment of decision right at the start of the film, and then keeps the audience guessing for a hundred minutes about which man Kitty will choose.

After the opening sequence on the history of the White Collar Girl, the film shifts to the story of one contemporary embodiment, Kitty Foyle. It is quitting time at the department store, and all of the shop girls complain of "that 5:30 feeling"—loneliness. Two old Irish cleaning ladies look on and laugh as the young women vent their man hunger. Kitty sympathizes with the other women, but is in fact off to meet her man, a young doctor named Mark Eisen.

She waits on the street alone, and Mark shows up in a cab— late, having been held up by an emergency at the hospital. He further postpones their dinner date, asking Kitty to accompany him on a home visit to deliver a baby in a run-down tenement apartment. As she holds the newborn child, Mark asks her to marry him. She accepts, though with little enthusiasm. Mark fears that she still harbors feelings for the great love of her life, Wyn Strafford. Apologizing that he must return to work, Mark tells her that if she truly no longer loves Wyn, she should meet him at the hospital— St. Timothy's Hospital—at midnight and they will find an all-night Justice of the Peace.

Kitty returns home to her apartment only to find Wyn waiting for her with an offer to sail away with him to Argentina where they can finally be free to live their lives in love together. Kitty interprets the invitation as a wedding proposal, only to discover that Wyn has no plans to divorce his society wife; he wishes only to have Kitty live as his mistress.

Overcoming her initial disappointment, Kitty gleefully consents and agrees to meet Wyn on the pier at midnight. As she packs her bags for her new life, she comes across a snow globe of a girl riding on a sled down a snow-covered hill. The toy, later revealed to be a gift from her father, prompts an examination of conscience in which she reviews the course of events that have brought her to this moment of decision.

Kitty's conscience, speaking through her reflection in the mirror, points her back to Griscom Street and Pop. The first actual scene from her childhood, however, places Kitty among the crowd of awestruck onlookers struggling to catch a glimpse of Philadelphia's social elite on the night of the annual Philadelphia Assembly. She returns home to hear her father cursing a broken clock with his trademark expletive, "Judas Priest" (a milder version of the novel's recurring "Jesusgod").

Pop scolds Kitty for gawking at the "Mainline monkeys" and vows to send her to Sunday school so she can get a good Christian upbringing and sense of values. Kitty responds by reciting lines from a romantic poem, Tennyson's "The Lady of Shalott," to which Pop replies, "Judas Priest! If ever a man deserved to be hung, it is the fella that started all that Cinderella stuff." Kitty plays with the snow globe while Pop rants on against fantasy stories that make simple girls "dissatisfied with honest shoemakers and bookkeepers."

He warns Kitty that her obsession with the Main Line is taking her for a ride just as sure as the girl on the sled in the globe. Pop points out that the fairy tales that end "happily ever after" never say what happens after the Prince and Cinderella get married. They would have nothing in common, and Cinderella would soon find herself dying to trade all the strawberries and cream in the world for a decent hamburger with onions.[27] Somewhat dumbstruck by Pop's outburst, Kitty simply replies, "I think you're wrong," and puts down the snow globe in defiance. The film, of course, will prove him right.

This Cinderella frame is almost entirely absent from the novel and clearly reflects the desire of the filmmakers to reduce the novel's pretentious "Natural History of a Woman" into a more manageable popular narrative.[28] In the novel, the romance with the Mainline monkey, Wyn Strafford, is but one of many subplots that weave in

---

[27]This is just what happens in Cecil B. De Mille's Bowery Cinderella film, *Saturday Night*. See note 14.

[28]This phrase serves as the film's subtitle.

and out of Kitty's memory as she recounts her life story. Morley's mildly modernist narrative structure subordinates the story of Kitty's romance with Wyn to the process of her remembrance of things past. Wyn's social standing serves more as an opportunity for Morley (through Kitty) to comment on class differences than as a reflection of any burning aspiration for high society on Kitty's part. Wyn drifts in and out of her life, as do many people, places, and things. The narrative trajectory of the novel points away from people (men in particular) and toward a hard-won, slightly melancholy sense of independence. Kitty associates with Mark largely because she is confident that there will never be anything other than "politeness" between them.

The Bowery Cinderella framework of the film, in contrast, points Kitty away from herself—both forward to a husband and backward to her father. Kitty eventually decides to marry Mark because she realizes he embodies the virtues and values praised by her father. The novel transforms Mark from a pathetic, slightly unsavory, upwardly mobile Jew to a straight-shooting, no-nonsense, downwardly mobile American—in the narrative world of the Bowery Cinderella, an honorary Irishman.

In the novel, Kitty and Mark meet at play, on a cruise to Bermuda—two sad and lonely people in search of distraction from life's disappointments. In the film, they meet at work. Kitty fakes a fainting spell to avoid blame for accidentally setting off the burglar alarm in the department store where she works as a cosmetics salesgirl. Mark, a doctor, arrives to tend to Kitty and blackmails her into a date in exchange for not blowing her cover.

The date consists of a night of playing cards in Kitty's studio apartment as her two roommates, Molly and Pat, hide out in the bathroom. At the end of the evening, Mark announces that the date was in fact a test. Though a doctor, he is not rich, has no use for gold diggers, and needed to see if he could have fun with Kitty without spending any money. She passes his test and he invites her on a date to the movies later in the week.

Wyn and Mark are a variation on the standard bad guy/good guy pairings that run through many of the women's films of the thirties and forties. Conventionally, the bad man offers excitement but heartache, while the good man waits in the wings with the promise of dull security. Through much of the film, Kitty indeed treats Mark as, at best, a consolation prize, but the film presents him as much more.

Conventionally handsome and morally upright, Mark nonetheless has a playful streak often lacking in the straight men of women's melodrama. Riding with Kitty on the subway on their movie date, Mark initiates a game of reading the faces of people, making up stories about their lives. After some funny stories, Mark launches into a critique of the people who look worried about getting ahead. He again tells Kitty that he does not have much money, and adds that he turned down the opportunity for a lucrative practice catering to "Park Avenue neurotics" in order to take a job in a children's clinic. Refreshingly free of self-righteousness, Mark insists he is not an idealist—"they are always patting themselves on the back." Kitty responds that she is an idealist—a declaration that suggests her lingering hopes for fulfillment with Wyn.

The film places Kitty's encounter with Mark right in the middle of her two main episodes with Wyn. Kitty's recollection of her life leaps from the childhood scene with her father on the night of the Assembly to her young womanhood, fresh out of secretary school, still living on Griscom Street. Kitty first encounters Wyn when he pays a visit to her house to interview Pop, the former coach of many of the best cricket players among Philadelphia's social elite, for an article on cricket he is writing for his new magazine, *Philly*. One look at Kitty, and Wyn offers her a secretarial job at the magazine.

The romance blossoms even as the magazine withers, but Wyn does most of his public courting of Kitty in New York, free from the censure of his class peers. Kitty challenges Wyn on his evasive social maneuvers and he promises to take her to the Assembly. Pop observes these developments with concern, and ultimate disapproval.

He lectures Kitty that Wyn is taking her for a ride, just like the little girl in the snow globe. He knows Wyn's kind from his days as a cricket coach—and they never marry outside their class.

Pop tells Kitty that her family and her people are miles above the Main Liners: her grandfather was a real Main Liner, because he helped lay the train tracks that made America great. Kitty remains deaf to this appeal to tradition until Wyn offers to keep her on the payroll after the magazine folds. She then realizes she will never be more than a mistress to Wyn. No sooner does she lose her love than she arrives home to find Pop dead in his chair, whiskey glass in his hand and the snow globe at his feet. Having lost everything, she leaves Philadelphia to start all over again in New York.

Wyn re-enters Kitty's life soon after she meets Mark. The day after the people-reading subway ride, memories of Wyn come rushing back as Kitty, passing a newspaper vendor on her way home from work, spies a headline announcing the annual Philadelphia Assembly. She arrives home to find an apartment full of flowers and an invitation from Wyn to attend their own private Assembly in New York.

They dance until dawn, and Wyn finally asks Kitty to marry him. She refuses, insisting the class and culture divide is too great: "... you're Darby Mill and I'm Griscom Street. We're two addresses, twenty three miles, and five hundred light-years apart." Kitty realizes that while the anonymity of New York has enabled them to transcend these boundaries, they could never bring their private fantasy world back to Philadelphia, where Wyn's family and future waits. Wyn declares they are New Yorkers now and will never live in Philadelphia. He asks the band to play "The Sidewalks of New York," and dubs the tune their theme song. At long last—and unlike in the novel—they marry.

Wyn's courage ultimately reveals itself to be as distressingly place-bound as Kitty feared. Arriving at Darby Mill to meet Wyn's family, Kitty learns that Wyn has failed to be completely honest with either her or his family. Open to accepting the marriage, Wyn's grandmother nonetheless expresses dismay that Wyn has rushed into an elopement against his earlier assurance to them that he would wait a year for Kitty to receive a proper education at a social finishing school.

Shocked and insulted, Kitty tells the family of their plans to live in New York. Wyn's uncle informs her that Wyn's Trust Fund requires him to reside in Darby Mill. Kitty responds with romantic indignation: "You mean all those people who are dead can tell us what to do? You mean that Wyn can't live his own life?" In the face of these family responsibilities, Kitty shouts, "It takes six generations to make people like you and, by Judas Priest, I haven't that much time," and storms out of the room.

Despite Kitty's attack on tradition, a comparison of the novel and film versions of this confrontation show how the Bowery Cinderella story consistently works against romance in favor of family ties. In the novel, the incident plays with more indignation but less drama. Wyn and Kitty are not married. She has made occasional visits to his family and has appeared in public with Wyn at high-society gatherings. Wyn informs Kitty that his uncle has suggested to him that Kitty go to finishing school, to which Kitty replies: "You can tell Uncle Ken he's a white slaver. . . . By God, I'll improve *you* all I want but you can't improve *me*."[29]

Despite the insult, Kitty continues to see Wyn. In the film, however, the finishing-school plan confirms for Kitty the impassability of the cultural divide. Wyn follows Kitty as she storms out of the family parlor and insists that he cannot live without her; he then returns to the parlor to say goodbye to his family. Kitty waits in another room lined with the portraits of all the previous generations of Wyn Straffords, and realizes that she cannot come between Wyn and his family. The Straffords may be snobs, but the traditions of Darby Mill have a certain integrity of their own that must be respected: Wyn

---

[29]Morley, *Kitty Foyle*, 241–42.

belongs in Darby Mill, not with her. Kitty leaves before Wyn can return. The dead can indeed tell the living what to do.

For the rest of the story, the melodrama piles up fast and furious. Kitty obtains a quick divorce and returns to New York. She meets up with Mark again, though she makes clear to him that she does not love him. Wyn calls to meet Kitty just as she discovers she is pregnant. She thinks their stars are realigned until, while waiting for him to arrive at one of their old haunts, she comes across a newspaper announcing Wyn's engagement to a society woman—and leaves without telling Wyn of her condition.

Kitty plans to name the child after her father, but the baby dies in childbirth (in the novel, she has an abortion). Five years later, Kitty is transferred to a department store branch in Philadelphia, where she finds herself waiting on Wyn's wife, who arrives accompanied by their five-year-old son. Overhearing a phone conversation, Kitty learns that Wyn has never taken his wife to an Assembly; looking at his son, she realizes that whatever love he may still have for her cannot take precedence over his—now, even greater—family obligations. Stealing a moment with the newest Wyn Strafford, Kitty gives him a ring Wyn had once given to her and tells him to give it to his father. She then returns to New York, to start all over again, again.

The encounter with Wyn's son brings Kitty out of her flashback and returns the film to the crucial decision. Kitty's efforts at closure have failed. The return of the ring brought Wyn back into her life, though he has misinterpreted the ring as a symbol of Kitty's willingness to be his mistress. Up to this point, Kitty has been willing to interpret such miscommunication as yet another realignment of the stars. At the moment of truth, however, she looks down at the snow globe, packs it away in her suitcase, and walks out the door with an assured, half-smile of determination on her face.

Down on the street, Kitty hails a taxi and tells the doorman to tell Wyn she has left to get married. She then tells the cab driver to take her to St. Timothy's Hospital. Tim the doorman, an Irishman with more than a little facial resemblance to Kitty's father, stands speechless as the cab pulls away. He then utters the last lines of the film: "Well, Judas Priest!"

From the snow globe to the final expletive, the spirit of Tom Foyle guides Kitty's decision to marry Mark, the moral equivalent of those honest shoemakers and bookkeepers recommended to Kitty so long ago by her father. In the best possible way, the dead once again tell the living what to do. You can take the girl out of Griscom Street, but you can't take Griscom Street out of the girl.

In affirming marriage over adultery, *Kitty Foyle* follows the conventions of women's melodrama. By linking Kitty's moral decision to a family tradition rooted in ethnicity and place, it offers a distinctly Irish-American twist on the genre. Scholars who are quick to see in Kitty's decision a submission to patriarchy miss how the relationship between Kitty and Pop works both against popular stereotypes concerning the irresponsibility of Irish-Catholic men and against Protestant conventions concerning the unique moral authority of women.

Nowhere do Irish-Catholic films of the period challenge these conventions more than in the area of religion. Against the feminizing trajectory of so much of American Protestantism, Irish-American Catholicism remained a full-blooded, masculine, fighting faith well into the middle of the twentieth century.[30] In Hollywood films of the period, Irish men would often appear more religious than women.[31]

---

[30] On the feminization of American Protestantism, see Douglas, *The Feminization of American Culture.*

[31] The year of Kitty Foyle saw another Irish-themed film with a strong father-daughter relationship. *Three Cheers for the Irish* (Lloyd Bacon, 1940) stars Thomas Mitchell as Peter Casey, a retired Irish policeman whose daughter Maureen (Priscilla Lane) falls in love with the young Scotsman, Angus Ferguson (Dennis Morgan), who has taken her father's place on the force. A light comedy in the tradition of *Abie's Irish Rose*, the film predictably resolves the inter-ethnic tension through grandchildren. Still, family values alone do not get the final word. After father, daughter, and son-in law reconcile at the hospital following the birth of twins, Peter learns that Maureen and Angus were only married by a justice of the

No minor theme interwoven into otherwise nonreligious plots, Irish male religiosity came into its own through a whole genre of film focusing on the heroism and good humor of Catholic priests.

---

peace. The film ends with Peter running out of the hospital declaring, "I'm going to get Fr. Monahan and make this thing legal."

Chapter 4

The Bells of Saint Mary's

URBAN, ETHNIC, WET, CATHOLIC—Al Smith's cultural sins were legion, but none greater than his religion. Rural and small-town fears of urban corruption found their most powerful galvanizing symbol in the specter of the city as a Catholic domain. Specific moral vices such as drinking and the general perception of cultural backwardness among immigrants had their common root in the overwhelmingly Catholic character of the ethnic city. In the two decades following Smith's defeat, no aspect of urban American Irish life stood in greater need of cultural rehabilitation than Catholicism—and no aspect seemed less amenable to the Hollywood treatment.

Against all odds, the Catholic priest emerged as a major leading character in the Irish-themed films of Hollywood's golden age. Films such as *Boys Town* (Norman Taurog, 1938) and *The Fighting 69th* (William Keighley, 1940) told the stories of real-life Catholic priests who voiced humanitarian and patriotic values that spoke to Americans regardless of religious background. Still, the figure of the Catholic priest found its greatest popularity when presented in a local, thickly Irish-Catholic setting. Generally evasive on matters of theology, Bing Crosby's Father O'Malley films, *Going My Way* (Leo McCarey, 1944) and *The Bells of Saint Mary's* (Leo McCarey, 1945), directly confronted the general American public with the accents, symbols, and landscape of urban Catholic culture. These films expressed general communal values in a way that resonated with Protestant small-town America, but their commitment to a local urban idiom established Irish Catholicism as the dominant religious presence in American popular culture.

Years before the flowering of priest films in the late 1930s, Father Charles Coughlin, the "Radio Priest," proved that Catholic priests could speak to a national audience through the new mass media of American popular culture. Best remembered by secular historians for his anti-Semitic screeds during the late 1930s, Coughlin began the decade as the most popular radio personality in America, perhaps the first true radio celebrity.[1] Coughlin originally took to the airwaves in 1926, delivering a Sunday sermon to defend Catholicism against the attacks of nativists and to help raise funds for his new parish in suburban Detroit. With the onset of the Great Depression, his sermons shifted their focus from the spiritual to the social. Coughlin couched his analysis of the causes and possible cures for the Depression in the explicitly Catholic language of scholastic philosophy and the papal social encyclicals, yet his attack on monopoly power and America's financial elite resonated deeply with a broader American populist tradition rooted in the largely Protestant rural regions of the country.[2]

Coughlin's popularity peaked in the years before and immediately after the election of Franklin Roosevelt. CBS had picked up his local Detroit broadcast in 1930, giving him a national audience of about forty million listeners weekly. One popular story of the time declared that on Sunday afternoons warm enough for radio listeners to have their windows open, one could walk the streets of any American city and never miss a word of Coughlin's sermon. A scant two years after the American electorate resoundingly re-

---

[1] For a good brief account of the career of Coughlin, see Morris, *American Catholic: The Saints and Sinniers Who Built America's Most Powerful Church*, 145–49.

[2] On the link between Coughlin and native Anglo-American populist politics, see Alan Brinkley, *Voices of Protest: Huey Long, Father Coughlin, and the Great Depression*.

jected the prospect of a Catholic president, many Americans looked to a Catholic priest to lead them out of the Great Depression. In 1932, Coughlin took up the cause of Franklin Roosevelt, coining the slogans "Roosevelt or Ruin" and "The New Deal is Christ's Deal."

Before the election, Roosevelt was happy to have the most popular media personality in America on his side; after the election, he quickly distanced himself from the man he feared as a political rival. Like Al Smith, Coughlin soon found himself on the outs with the Roosevelt administration. Like Al Smith, he turned against Roosevelt, an act that signaled his political demise years before he descended into his infamous anti-Semitism. Catholics remained an important part of the New Deal coalition, and Roosevelt appointed several Catholic priests to various New Deal committees, particularly labor boards. Even as Coughlin tried to draw Americans away from FDR, other politically active priests, such as the National Catholic Welfare Conference's John A. Ryan, rushed to his defense. Dubbed derisively by Coughlin the "Right Reverend New Dealer," Ryan became in 1937 the first Catholic priest ever to deliver a benediction at a presidential inauguration.[3]

No New Deal priest ever matched Coughlin in terms of public profile, but just as Coughlin's star was fading, Hollywood began to explore the box-office potential of the Catholic priest. Always ready to exploit a popular trend, Hollywood initially sublimated the timelier political-priest phenomenon within conventional Irish genres and historical pictures that ensured a safe distance from potentially divisive current events. Two MGM gangster films of the mid-1930s, *Manhattan Melodrama* and *San Francisco*, helped to raise the role of the priest to something like a leading-man status. Morally somewhat less complex than the later *Angels with Dirty Faces*, these films established the priest as an urban moral presence who was nonetheless at ease with gangsters and chorus girls. The urban milieu implicitly circumscribed the Catholic priest's moral

---

[3] On Ryan, see Broderick, *Right Reverend New Dealer*, John A. Ryan.

authority within a specific place, and the historical settings lent the films a certain temporal buffer, but the films clearly established the priest as an active, public figure.

In *Manhattan Melodrama*, the priest, Father Joe (Leo Carillo), is Italian and a relatively minor character. The moral battle of the film pits Jim Wade (William Powell), a crusading district attorney, against a childhood friend turned gangster, Blackie Gallagher (Clark Gable). Though a box-office hit in its day, *Manhattan Melodrama* earned its place in film history for being the film that played at the movie theatre when John Dillinger had his fatal run-in with the police. Not so with *San Francisco*, a historical epic that recasts the *Manhattan Melodrama* story in the setting of the great San Francisco earthquake of 1906. Perhaps the first disaster film, *San Francisco* stunned audiences with state-of-the-art special effects that dramatically recreated the earthquake; it also marked the emergence of the Catholic priest in a major, leading role. The film blends the roles of Father Joe and Tim Wade into the figure of Father Tim Mullin (Spencer Tracy), who wages a moral battle against his childhood gangster friend, Blackie Norton (Clark Gable).

The casting of Fr. Tim posed both aesthetic and ethno-cultural challenges. The conventions of the day mandated a pious treatment of clergy of all denominations, but the actor who played Fr. Tim needed to be tough and able to hold his own against a star the stature of Clark Gable. For the director, W. S. Van Dyke, there was no choice but Spencer Tracy.

Hollywood professionals had been in awe of Tracy since his debut in the 1930 prison drama *Up the River*.[4] He impressed both directors and fellow actors with the unprecedented realism of his acting style. Still, by 1936, Tracy had yet to achieve major commercial stardom. Physically, Tracy simply did not look like a Hollywood star. Judging Tracy "a galoot" on their first meeting, Louis B. Mayer

---

[4]Directed by John Ford.

initially refused to consider taking Tracy on at MGM, claiming that "we already have a galoot in the family" (a reference to Wallace Beery).

Eventually, Mayer agreed to sign Tracy after conceding that beyond Gable, MGM was somewhat weak in the he-man department.[5] Tracy distinguished himself from other actors by the emotional depth he brought to conventional tough-guy roles. Van Dyke felt that *San Francisco* needed that depth to set it apart from conventional historical dramas and pleaded with Tracy to accept the role.[6]

Tracy, for his part, was reluctant. Given his already established reputation as a heavy drinker and frequent brawler, he felt there was something a bit sacrilegious in playing a priest. Such sensitivity to matters of religion pointed to another essential quality Tracy brought to the role—his cultural credentials as a cradle Irish Catholic. Louis B. Mayer, no particular friend of Catholicism or Tracy, was especially pleased by Van Dyke's choice, believing that Tracy's ethno-religious background would help to deflect potential Catholic criticism of the film.[7]

After *Manhattan Melodrama* and *San Francisco*, MGM appeared to have been willing to leave the gangster film to Warner Brothers. *San Francisco*, however, suggested the possibility of an entirely new genre: the priest film. Originally brought in as support for the great Gable, Tracy stole the show with his portrayal of Fr. Tim.[8] An actor uniquely resistant to type casting, Tracy scored his next big hit for MGM in *Captains Courageous* (Victor Fleming, 1937), winning an Academy Award for his portrayal of Manuel Fidello, a Portuguese fisherman who helps a young Harvey Cheyne become a man in a

---

[5] Swindell, *Spencer Tracy: A Biography*, 119.

[6] The following quote from Van Dyke gives some sense of the respect with which he viewed Tracy's acting: "There's one important thing [*San Francisco*] has to have . . . and that's humanity. Father Tim has to supply it, and so help me, Spencer, you're the only actor I know who can bring humanity into a part. I don't know where you got it, but you have it." Ibid., 129–30.

[7] Ibid., 130.

[8] Ibid., 133.

Victorian boy's adventure tale based on a Rudyard Kipling novel. By 1938, Mayer had settled on a vehicle that could combine Tracy's ability to portray priests with his proven success at working with children. The film, *Boys Town*, earned Tracy his second consecutive Academy Award for Best Actor.

Boys Town clearly builds somewhat on *San Francisco*, but in terms of the genre of the priest film, it stands as a distinct alternative to the Warner Brothers offering of the same year, *Angels with Dirty Faces*. The film tells the story of a priest, Father Edward Flanagan, who begins his career in the city yet becomes a national hero through humanitarian efforts that seemed to transcend this urban, Irish-Catholic subculture. Tracy's Fr. Flanagan presents an ecumenical image of the Catholic priest as true American, committed to cooperation with non-Catholics in the service of a common public good. In this cinematic ecumenism, Flanagan presents a counterbalance to the more tribal figure of the local priest—in films such as *San Francisco* and *Angels with Dirty Faces*. The distance from the world of gangsters also spared Hollywood writers the moral tight-rope walking needed to present a priest as at once the best friend of criminals yet untainted by crime.

In *Boys Town*, screenwriters had the distinct advantage of being able to do more than rework Hollywood conventions. Screenwriters John Meehan and Dore Schary based their script on the life of a real Irish priest, Father Edward Flanagan, who founded a home for wayward or runaway boys in Omaha, Nebraska, to protect them from the corrupting influences of the city. Much of what may strike a modern viewer as period Hollywood sentimentality—Tracy/Flanagan's repeated insistence that "There is no bad boy"—actually comes from the real-life work and words of Fr. Flanagan himself.

Though the film has outlived the memory of its inspiration, Fr. Flanagan was a highly respected public figure well beyond the confines of the American Catholic subculture. By the late 1920s, America had recognized Fr. Flanagan as a great humanitarian for his work with youth. At Boys Town, he played host to a wide range of celebrities from the world of politics and entertainment, including President Calvin Coolidge, John Philip Sousa, Eamon De Valera, Babe Ruth, and Tom Mix.[9] Flanagan's real-life sanctity only increased Tracy's trepidation at once again playing the part of a priest, but Mayer insisted that Tracy was the only actor technically—and ethnically—capable of pulling it off.[10]

Flanagan's idea of Boys Town resonated deeply with older WASP ideals of social reform even as it drew on indigenous Irish-Catholic traditions. In America, the idea of shipping poor urban youth out to the countryside for moral regeneration has roots in Victorian-era social reform.[11] Flanagan, for his part, saw Boys Town as an opportunity to expose city boys to the benefits of rural living that he experienced growing up in County Roscommon, Ireland.

Born in 1886, Flanagan experienced a very conventional rural Irish childhood at the height of Ireland's Catholic revival. Unlike so many later prominent sons of the Irish countryside, Flanagan remembered his childhood fondly. As he grew, he managed to retain his respect for tradition and authority even as he questioned some of the assumptions of the Victorian Irish education system. Attending school in Sligo, he encountered two problems that he would struggle with for the rest of his life: urban poverty and lock-step institutional discipline. He accepted neither as inevitable. His reading of Dickens profoundly shaped his early thinking on these matters, and his experiences in New York City following his emigration in 1904 would only confirm his initial views.[12]

Secular reformers would forever accuse Flanagan of an overly sentimental, unscientific approach to the problem of youth. For his own part, Flanagan proved more than willing to dialogue with

[9] Ousler and Ousler, *Father Flanagan of Boys Town*, 230.

[10] Swindell, *Spencer Tracy*, 150–51.

[11] For a recent study of this reform movement, see O'Connor, *Orphan Trains: The Story of Charles Loring Brace and the Children He Saved and Failed*.

[12] Ousler and Ousler, *Father Flanagan of Boys Town*, 25, 29, 32, 35, 41, 42.

the cutting edge of scientific reform. He was far more cosmopolitan than the average American-born diocesan priest. His seminary training took him to Mount Saint Mary's in Emmitsburg, Maryland and St. Joseph's at Dunwoodie (in Yonkers, New York), the latter briefly a center of theological Modernism at the turn of the century. He studied for a time in Rome and completed his studies at the Royal and Imperial Leopold Francis University in Innsbruck, Austria. Respiratory problems and family connections landed him in Omaha, Nebraska.

In the American Catholic landscape of the early twentieth century, such an assignment was actually a move into a broader social universe. The minority status of Catholics in the region fostered an ethic of ecumenical cooperation unlike the more closed, tribal world of the east coast. Still, despite his general openness to the non-Catholic world, Flanagan retained a suspicion of academics—in part because they always left out God, and in part because they failed to appreciate the power of Christian love and family life. In response to his academic critics, Flanagan once commented, "Some of the *soi-disant* high-brows tell me I deal in platitudes.... But in reply I quote them another: 'A platitude is an immortal truth become so familiar that we have forgotten its meaning.'" Against the academics, Flanagan insisted that science was not enough. Academics rejected his theories, yet conceded, in bafflement, his success.[13]

Louis B. Mayer certainly did not put his money behind the film to settle any scores on the issue of social engineering. Flanagan's supposed sentimentality simply struck him as a real-life instance of the humanity that the character of Fr. Tim brought to *San Francisco*. Though he would later count it among his favorite pictures, Mayer initially viewed the film as a modest production that would capitalize on Tracy's unique talents while celebrating a much-loved humanitarian.[14]

---

[13] Ibid., 5, 10.
[14] Swindell, *Spencer Tracy*, 151.

Lest the move of a priest from supporting to leading role alienate non-Catholic viewers, the film opens with a declaration that highlights the generically American nature of the story: "This is the story of Father Flanagan and the city for boys that he built in Nebraska.... This picture is dedicated to him and his splendid work for homeless, abandoned boys, regardless of race, creed or color." This opening declaration carefully distances Flanagan from the conventional urban stomping grounds of a Catholic priest and emphasizes his ecumenical outreach beyond the tribal world of city Catholics. The film identifies Flanagan as a great American, only incidentally a Catholic priest.

The American ideal that Fr. Flanagan represents is somewhat at odds with the actual America of 1938. Like so many other Irish-American films of this New-Deal period, *Boys Town* presents an Irishman upholding the ideals of an older, more personal America. In the opening scene, Fr. Flanagan counsels a death-row inmate, Dan Farrow (Leslie Fenton), minutes before his execution. Flanagan has presumably arrived to administer the distinctly Catholic sacrament of last rites. As *Angels with Dirty Faces* deflected attention from theological issues to Rocky's more naturalistic self-sacrifice, so in *Boys Town*, a public execution becomes the inspiration for a more humane vision of social work. In both cases, however, personal ties triumph over the impersonal code of the state.

As Fr. Flanagan enters the holding room, he finds the warden of the prison demanding that Farrow confess his guilt. The warden tries to bribe Farrow with a swig from a hip flask. Flanagan looks at Farrow, shakes his head—no—with a smile; Farrow refuses the drink. With the statement "eternity begins in forty-five minutes," Flanagan begins to counsel Farrow. Gentle and forgiving, Fr. Flanagan nonetheless stresses the need for reconciliation; Farrow, for his part, lacks Rocky's cock-sure defiance.

The warden interrupts the sacramental trajectory of the scene by bringing in reporters and insisting once again that Farrow confess his debt to the state. Respectful to Fr. Flanagan, Farrow nonetheless rages at the warden, "The State! What did it ever do for me?" Farrow then launches into an attack on reform schools and defends himself by insisting, "One friend when I'm twelve years old, and I don't stand here like this." The camera quickly cuts to Fr. Flanagan, whose eyes light up.[15] Farrow eventually settles down and apologizes to Fr. Flanagan—though not to the warden. As a competing authority, Flanagan clearly wins out over the State, but he wins less as a priest than as a friend.

This opening scene places *Boys Town* in dialog with another small but significant film genre of the era: the reform school melodrama. The genre flourished alongside the two waves of gangster films. In the early thirties, there were films such as *Hell's House* (Howard Higgin, 1932), featuring Pat O'Brien, and *Mayor of Hell* (Archie Mayo, 1933), with James Cagney in the title role. The later thirties saw films such as *Crime School* (Lewis Seiler, 1938) and *Reform School* (Leo C. Popkin, 1938). The brief treatment of the reform school in *Angels with Dirty Faces* captures the basic message of the genre—reform schools are crime schools that turn juvenile delinquents into adult criminals.

Most of these films chronicle the deficiencies of existing reform schools only to conclude with an appeal to some sort of kinder, gentler version of the very environmentalist social engineering that produced the reform school in the first place. *Boys Town* differs from

---

[15] Again, as corny as this may play today, such things really happened. Though skeptics might see history retelling a Hollywood story, the journalist Roger L. Treat recounts a very similar story of another tough-guy Irish priest from the 1930s, Bishop Bernard Sheil, the founder of the Catholic Youth Organization (CYO). Treat describes the transforming effect Sheil had on Leo, a death-row inmate: "Within a few moments he had known that this was no sissy priest but a rough-and-tumble scrapper who happened to be fighting with the right gang instead of the wrong gang." Much like Flanagan's mantra, "There are no bad boys," Sheil tells Leo: "There are no problem children, Leo. . . . We are the ones who have failed, Leo." The scene concludes with Leo thanking Sheil: "Thanks, Father. You've been the only person who ever gave a damn about me in all my life." See Treat, *Bishop Sheil and the CYO*, 7–8, 14.

The Sidewalks of New York. Al Smith and family on the steps of 25 Oliver Street. Top row (l to r): Al, Jr., Emily; center: Al, Katie, Catherine; bottom: Walter, Arthur. *Museum of the City of New York*.

Hell's Kitchen. Tom Powers (James Cagney) and Matt Doyle (Edward Woods) shoot it out with the police in *The Public Enemy* (William A. Wellman, 1931). © Warner Bros./Photofest.

City for Conquest. James Corbett (Errol Flynn) strikes a John L. Sullivan pose in *Gentleman Jim* (Raoul Walsh, 1942). © Sunset Boulevard/Sigma/ Corbis.

The Bowery Cinderella. Kitty Foyle (Ginger Rogers) shares her Cinderella dreams with a disbelieving Pops Foyle (Ernest Cossart) in *Kitty Foyle*
(Sam Wood, 1940). © RKO Radio Pictures Inc/Photofest.

The Bells of St. Mary's. Father Chuck O'Malley (Bing Crosby) tries to make peace between Mrs. Quimp (Anita Bolster) and her landlord, Ted Haines, Jr. (James Brown) in *Going My Way* (Leo McCarey, 1944). © Paramount Pictures / Photofest

The Lights of Old Broadway. The Four Cohans—l to r, Josie (Jeanne Cagney), George (James Cagney), Nellie (Rosemary DeCamp), and Jerry (Walter Huston)—dance with style in *Yankee Doodle Dandy* (Michael Curtiz, 1942). © Warner Bros./Photofest.

The Suburbs of America. Jacqueline Kennedy, John F. Kennedy, and
Caroline Kennedy at home in the early 1960s. Photofest.

these films by very quickly moving from problem to solution and focusing most of the drama on the challenge to that solution by one particularly hard case. The eventual vindication of Fr. Flanagan's approach may strike a modern viewer as a sentimental, happy ending, but the achievements of the real-life Boys Town certainly merit the Hollywood treatment they get.

After the dramatic death-row opening, the film picks up with Fr. Flanagan's life as he begins to make the transition from caring for homeless men to sheltering troubled youth. With the words of Dan Farrow ringing in his ears, Flanagan walks the streets and witnesses a violent fight among some street boys. He tries to break it up, only to find himself accosted by a local pawnbroker, Dave Morris (Henry Hull), who blames a broken window at his shop on the troublemaking kids attracted to the neighborhood by Flanagan's homeless shelter, "Flanagan's Refuge."

The next scene shows Flanagan back at the shelter, preaching to cynical or indifferent men. A boy bursts into the shelter pleading with him to help some of his friends whom the police have arrested on charges of stealing and vandalism. Flanagan successfully negotiates with the judge and agrees to take them into his own protective custody. Realizing the boys cannot stay at the adult shelter, he approaches his bishop (Minor Watson) and asks permission to start a boy's home. The bishop at first resists, insisting that he has already decided to assign Flanagan to a parish. Flanagan believes he has a calling to work with young boys because he thinks he has found a way to get through to them. His appeal to the bishop reflects the particular brand of tough love that would animate Boys Town: "I know that a mother can take a whip to the toughest boy in the world and he forgets it because he knows that she loves him."

In a film routinely accused of saccharine sentimentality, this description of love stands out. Fr. Flanagan's love does not preclude violence completely. The real-life Flanagan rejected the martinet discipline favored in the reform schools of his day, but realized

the need for physical toughness in certain situations.[16] This type
of tough love has eluded the moral imagination of progressive
reformers and film historians alike. By the late 1930s, the Catholic
priest seemed to be the most convincing embodiment of this distinct
synthesis of authority and love.[17]

Still, the film presents this synthesis as generically American
rather than distinctly Catholic. Flanagan needs the approval of
his bishop to proceed with his boys' home, but the seed money
comes from non-Catholic sources. Desperate for funds, Flanagan
approaches the most unlikely source—Dave Morris, the pawnbroker
who earlier blamed Flanagan for attracting hoodlum boys to the
neighborhood. In Hollywood films, as in early-twentieth-century
cities, Jews tended to be the ones who operated pawnshops. Flanagan's success in securing a security-free loan from Morris demon-
strates his ecumenical appeal as well as his near miraculous powers
of persuasion. Morris remains a friend and supporter through the
difficult first year.

Flanagan is chronically low on funds and must constantly appeal
to the general public for support. The newspapers report his plight
but do nothing to support his cause. The first Christmas is nearly
a disaster. Fr. Flanagan can afford only cornmeal mush and some
broken toys. The boys sing a listless "Silent Night" and complain
that they would be better off in a reform school or even an abusive
home. Just as Flanagan himself appears to have lost faith in his
project, the pawnbroker Dave Morris arrives with good presents

---

[16]Flanagan's biographers, Fulton and Will Ousler, tell the story of one Boys Town
boy, Stubby—referred to Fr. Flanagan by a hobo the boy had met while traveling
on a freight train. The hobo recommended Boys Town after telling Stubby how
Fr. Flanagan had roughed him up to help him to stop drinking. Ousler and Ousler,
Father Flanagan of Boys Town, 10.

[17]Again, Treat's biography of Sheil is revealing: "How many volumes do you
need to tell of a man who is saying a solemn Mass at a certain moment and two
hours later is prancing around a boxing ring—still in his cassock, with boxing
gloves added, slapping the ears off a fresh young punk who thought he was tough?"
Treat, *Bishop Sheil and the CYO*, vii.

and food to save the day. The singing of the Catholic hymn keeps the scene connected to Flanagan's Catholicism, yet significantly, the true joy comes only when the non-Catholic enables the boys to fulfill the secular rituals of the Christmas season. The real Flanagan never sought to impose Catholicism on any of his boys, but he did insist that each boy attend some religious service in the faith of his birth. The Christmas scene in the film goes beyond Flanagan's religious ecumenism by presenting something like a triumph of a more secular vision of Christmas that Hollywood was just beginning to exploit.

Boys Town survives its first year. Despite his continuing financial struggles, Fr. Flanagan dreams of expanding it both quantitatively and qualitatively. He wants a bigger facility to accommodate more boys, and he wants to establish his new home in the country to shelter boys from the corrupting influence of the city. Flanagan takes his old friend and financial backer, Dave Morris, out for a drive in the country and shows him some farm land he has been looking at. Morris says that this is beyond his means, but suggests that Flanagan approach the local newspaper man, John Hargraves (Jonathon Hale), for support.

The Hargraves character stands in for all of the real-life critics of the real Fr. Flanagan. During the tough first year of Boys Town, his paper seemed more interested in reporting Flanagan's troubles than in using its influence to help him. Hargraves rejects Flanagan's methods and insists his whole approach rests on false foundations; some boys are just savages and must be treated as such. Flanagan responds by citing the example of an eleven-year-old "murderer," a boy who killed his drunken father to prevent him from beating his mother. Flanagan eventually succeeds in drawing support from yet another skeptic, though Hargraves agrees to back Flanagan only to use him as a lesson when the new, expanded Boys Town fails. This gruff editor provides the voice of skepticism.

Next, the film introduces a difficult test case: Whitey Marsh (Mickey Rooney). With the new rural Boys Town up and running, Fr.

Flanagan receives a call from a nearby prison. A convict, Joe Marsh (Edward Norris), has just been sentenced to life in prison and has requested a meeting with Fr. Flanagan. Unlike Dan Farrow at the beginning of the film, Marsh is unrepentant. He wants nothing for himself, but asks Fr. Flanagan to look after his kid brother, Whitey.

Fr. Flanagan then tracks down Whitey, who is living in an apartment above a storefront. He enters the apartment to find the teenage Whitey dressed in grown-up clothes, smoking, and playing cards—an incongruity heightened by the actor Rooney's small size. At first, Flanagan is fairly gentle, but Whitey shows him no respect, sitting with his feet up on the table and talking with a cigarette hanging out of the side of his mouth. Flanagan then knocks his feet off the table and the cigarette out of his mouth. When Whitey gets up and tries to walk away, Fr. Flanagan trips him. Here again, Flanagan's tough love defies the conventional categories of liberal and conservative. Hargraves stands in for the old guard who insist that harsh discipline is the only way to deal with troubled boys. Flanagan preaches love, but understands that force is at times necessary. Whitey will, however, prove to be a hard case.

Whitey's arrival at Boys Town provides the film an opportunity to introduce the viewers to the ethos of the community. Whitey learns that Boys Town functions as a real town, complete with a mayor (elected every six months) and a post office. There are no walls or fences. Boys are expected to follow the rules based on the honor system—with no squealing on rule breakers. Whitey is unimpressed.

No sooner does he receive his introductory tour than he tries to run away—stopped only by an empty stomach and the sound of the lunch bell. Lunch serves as both a base motive and an occasion to reveal yet another defining principle of Boys Town: ecumenism. Fr. Flanagan takes Whitey into the cafeteria and shows him a room full of boys, each praying their own grace before their meal: "Catholic, Protestant, Jew, or nothing, each believes as they wish." True to the real Boys Town, blacks and whites sit together, for Fr. Flanagan refused to segregate African Americans.[18] For all its appeal to the ideals of small-town America, Boys Town and *Boys Town* preach a religious and racial tolerance far ahead of mainstream America.

Finally, Fr. Flanagan takes Whitey to a concert of the Boys Town Choir. As in *Angels with Dirty Faces*, the image of tough street boys singing in a choir strikes the modern viewer as pure Hollywood fantasy, but choir singing was once understood as a normal part of any boy's upbringing. Like so many Catholic priests of his era, Flanagan was perfectly at home in the world of music and entertainment. The real Fr. Flanagan actually formed the Boys Town Choir only after launching a much more lowbrow cultural undertaking: a traveling vaudeville-style review titled "Father Flanagan's Boy's Show—World's Greatest Juvenile Actors." Flanagan organized the show to raise funds to pay for the construction of the main building on his new rural campus. He got the idea for a traveling show after seeing an African-American boy dancing. During a performance of his Boy's Show at a prison, the boys broke into an impromptu chorus of "Ave Maria." The singing so moved the otherwise hardened inmates that Fr. Flanagan decided to form a permanent boys choir.[19]

The cinematic Whitey is at first made of tougher stuff than the real-life prisoners. Unmoved by the choir or by anything else he sees in his first days at Boys Town, Whitey sets himself against the community. Though initially welcoming, the other boys turn against him after he insults a well-liked handicapped boy, Tony Ponessa (Gene Reynolds). Seeing Whitey in need of some ego deflation, the boys begin to subject him to some fairly harmless hazing. At one point, they saw the legs of his cot so it collapses when he goes to sleep on it; later, Mo Kahn (Sidney Miller), the Boys Town barber, gives Whitey a "facial" with black shoe polish. That incident provokes a fight, which in turn provides an occasion for the demonstration of Boys Town justice. Mo and Whitey both appear before a court run

---

[18] Ousler and Ousler, *Father Flanagan of Boys Town*, 4.
[19] Ibid., 206, 209.

entirely by the boys themselves. The boy judge sentences Whitey to a month of cow milking, and both boys receive the most dreaded punishment of all. They must sit with their backs to the screen during movie time![20]

Next, Whitey tries to beat the system from within by running for mayor of Boys Town. The current mayor, Freddie Fuller (Frankie Thomas) runs for re-election on the Conservative ticket. Tony Ponessa, the handicap boy Whitey insulted earlier in the film, runs on the Progressive ticket. Hoping to appeal to the malcontents, Whitey declares himself the candidate of the "Don't-Be-a-Sucker" party. Whitey proves himself a capable candidate, organizing a brass band and all the hoopla associated with an adult mayoral campaign. Fearing Whitey's tactics might carry the day, Freddie and Tony each offer to withdraw from the race to help consolidate the responsible voters into a single bloc.

Freddie succeeds in convincing all his supporters to vote for Tony. When Tony wins the election, Whitey cries foul and tries to start a fist fight with Freddie. Fr. Flanagan intervenes—but only to arrange a boxing match for the two boys to settle their differences in a respectable manner. The boxing match shows the limits of Boys Town's (and *Boys Town*'s) Americanism. Up to the election, Whitey had received an education in the virtues of small-town American governance. The introduction of the boxing match introduces a distinctly urban, Irish element into the moral universe of the small town. The boxing match points to the limits of electoral democracy. Flanagan opposes violent corporal punishment but realizes the limits to rational debate in resolving conflicts. Still, even boxing has its limits. Whitey loses the match and runs away from Boys Town in anger and humiliation.

The next section of the film draws on two themes central to the adult Irish gangster/priest films: the basic humanity of the

---

[20]Though it might appear a plug for movie-going itself, this was in fact the most dreaded punishment administered by the Boys Town court. See Ibid., 249.

criminal and the virtue of loyalty. For all his faults, Whitey has earned the friendship of a small boy, Pee Wee (Bobs Watson). Early on in the film, Pee Wee serves as a kind of comic relief character, always breaking into scenes to ask Fr. Flanagan for candy. He sees something good in Whitey, supporting him in his bid for mayor and even cheering him on in his boxing match against Freddie.

When Whitey runs away after losing the match, Pee Wee chases after him, only to be hit by a car. Despite his sense of guilt, Whitey keeps on running. Wandering through the city streets, Whitey stumbles into a bank robbery in progress—perpetrated by none other than his brother Joe, who has escaped from prison. Whitey gets caught in the crossfire with the security guard. Joe escapes, drops off Whitey at a church and calls Fr. Flanagan to pick him up. As Fr. Flanagan arrives at the church, Whitey lies wounded by a bullet, but deliriously praying for Pee Wee. Fr. Flanagan then brings Whitey back to Boys Town.

Whitey's presence soon threatens the survival of Boys Town itself. The police find his cap at the scene of the crime and want to arrest him for the shooting of the security guard. Once again, the film presents state authorities in a negative light. Fr. Flanagan rejects their demand for extradition, declaring, "I'm the head of a community, with complete autonomy, and a better record than any in the state." He manages to hold off the police temporarily, but quickly presses Whitey to come clean on the shooting.

Flanagan is tough with Whitey, reminding him that his very presence threatens to make Boys Town an accessory to the shooting. He expresses his personal frustration at his inability to get through to Whitey and accuses Whitey of having no heart. He then leaves Whitey alone to make his decision.

Whitey faces a tragic choice between his loyalty to his brother and his loyalty to Boys Town. Hoping to fulfill both obligations, he runs away from Boys Town to warn his brother Joe that he has to name him as the shooter in order to save Boys Town. News of Whitey's escape spreads quickly and the skeptical newspaper editor,

John Hargraves, attempts to exploit the scandal to close down Boys Town.

In the end, the community, not the state, achieves justice and re-stores order. Freddie and Moe have followed Whitey to his brother's hideout and return to Boys Town with the news. Fr. Flanagan leads the boys to the hideout to rescue Whitey and save Boys Town. If not quite vigilantes, Fr. Flanagan and his boys in some sense represent a principle of justice that operates outside of the official institutional channels recognized by the State.

They burst into the hideout. The boys free Whitey as Fr. Flanagan slugs Joe. Physical force, rather than the official rule of law, carries the day. Whitey explains that he did what he did because he could not bring himself to rat on his brother. For this explanation, he receives no correction from Fr. Flanagan on his higher duty to obey the rule of law (no squealing is, after all, a rule of Boys Town). Still, despite this performance of quasi-vigilante—almost tribal—justice, the film concludes with an affirmation of the small-town principles at the heart of Boys Town. Tony Ponessa nominates Whitey as mayor of Boys Town, and Whitey wins the election uncontested. This acceptance by the community finally brings Whitey to tears. Fr. Flanagan looks on and affirms, "There is no bad boy."

As likely to bring sneers today as it brought tears in its own time, the ending of *Boys Town* obscures the fine line between faith and sentiment, hope and optimism. Traditional Catholic teaching concerning human nature insists on both the goodness of creation and the reality of sin. The real Fr. Flanagan's insistence that "There is no bad boy" was an act of faith, not a statement of fact. Clearly there are bad boys in the world. Flanagan simply believed that love and the grace of God could conquer evil.

Boys Town affirms the necessity of a proper environment—thus Fr. Flanagan's pains to construct a model, self-governing village at Boys Town. Still, the film clearly suggests that environment is not enough. Whitey refuses to internalize the rules of Boys Town; the practice of small-town politics has none of the miraculous civilizing powers attributed to it by nineteenth-century reformers. Against the dreams of rational social engineers, the film implies the necessity of violence—and love—in personal transformation.

Whitey never really has a change of heart until his anger leads to Pee Wee's car accident. Pee Wee's sacrifice begins the process of transformation, but sorrow alone will not reconcile Whitey to the community. Whitey must match Pee Wee's sacrifice in physical, bodily terms. Objectively and accidentally, he suffers a bodily wound in the shootout at the bank robbery; subjectively and deliberately, he risks his life by tracking down his brother. *Boys Town* stops short of demanding the ultimate sacrifice presented in a film like *Angels with Dirty Faces*, but the two stories, different in many ways, both refuse to equate redemption with purely rational reform.

The success of *Boys Town* marked a sea change in American attitudes toward Catholic priests. It was one thing to show a priest taming adult Irish gangsters in an urban ghetto; it was something entirely different to trust one with the children of America. The influence of priests over children had been the sharpest point of contention between Catholic and Protestant Americans since the mass immigration of Catholics in the middle of the nineteenth century.

The parochial school system struck most Protestants as at best Popish thought control, at worst, treason. Nuns may have done the teaching in the Catholic schools, but priests supervised the fundraising and the building. Protestants spoke derisively of the parochial school as the most noxious form of "priestcraft" precisely because it targeted the most vulnerable members of society, children. The positive image of priests suggests a rethinking of long-held prejudices at a time when intolerance and prejudice—particularly in the form of anti-Semitism—were sweeping Europe into war.

Historians and film scholars often see the priest films like *Boys Town* as a way of placating the Legion of Decency or a symptom of how assimilated and unthreatening Irish Catholics had become by the late 1930s. They might do better to consider the prominence of Catholic priests as a test case for America's emerging conception of itself as a pluralist democracy.[21] Catholics, not blacks or Jews, were the main targets of the nativist revival of the 1920s. Irish Catholics were the original "other" to Anglo-Protestant society, and America had to come to terms with its oldest prejudice before it could deal with other, seemingly more timely issues.

The international issues of the day did very soon come to shape the emerging image of the priest. *Boys Town* brought the priest out of the ghetto, but it did not quite put him in service to the nation. The film's small-town themes may have helped to bridge the gap between Protestant and Catholic America, but nostalgia for the small town was also one of the cultural forces shaping a growing opposition to the New Deal and to any involvement in the coming European war.

Boys Town moves in two directions. It presents a positive vision of pluralistic America, but roots tolerance in an ideal localism. The cafeteria prayer scene suggests little in the way of unity—the conventional melting-pot pledge of allegiance to the flag, in which political unity trumps religious diversity, is conspicuously absent. The film consistently presents state authorities in a negative light and implies that meaningful change comes only through the close personal relations of a face-to-face community.

Two years after *Boys Town* and *Angels with Dirty Faces*, Pat O'Brien returned to the screen as a very different kind of priest in *The Fighting 69th*. Through O'Brien's portrait of Father Francis Patrick Duffy, chaplain to the "Irish Brigade" during World War I, Hollywood enlisted Catholicism to preach a message of pluralism and tolerance in the context of the nation-state. A film about World War I, *The Fighting 69th* is clearly intended to inspire a willingness to sacrifice in yet another European war, World War II. Still, the

---

[21] On this, see Gleason, *Speaking of Diversity: Language and Ethnicity in Twentieth-Century America*, especially Chapter 6, "Americans All."

film also offers a corrective to simple nation-state nationalism by directing the old Irish themes of loyalty and sacrifice away from the nation-state to the local, ethnic regiment.

Once again, a true story of Irish-American-Catholic history gave Hollywood screenwriters more than enough to work with. The film draws on the real-life exploits of the 69th regiment of the New York National Guard, the so-called "Fighting 69th." Founded during the Civil War, the Fighting 69th earned its nickname for the bravery it displayed during major battles such as Bull Run, Antietam, and Chancellorsville.[22] Song and story sustained its reputation through the late-nineteenth century, until the First World War provided an opportunity for a new generation of Irishmen to live up to the glories of the Irish-American military past.

In both the Civil War and World War I, Irish meant Irish-Catholic. The distinctly Catholic character of the American Irish was even more pronounced in the latter war. The regiment's charismatic leader, Colonel William Joseph "Wild Bill" Donovan, had to share the spotlight with its equally charismatic military chaplain, Father Francis Patrick Duffy.

A Canadian by birth, Duffy emigrated to the United States to study for the priesthood. He received holy orders in 1896 following years of study at St. Joseph Provincial Seminary in Troy, New York. Duffy eventually settled into the life of a New York brick-and-mortar priest, establishing the parish of Our Savior in the Bronx. With entry into World War I imminent, Duffy signed on as chaplain to New York's 69th regiment, (reconstituted under federal authority as the 165th U. S. Infantry Regiment). Though technically a non-combatant (due to his position as chaplain), Duffy could always be found in the thick of battle, ministering to the wounded and dying among the still largely Irish-Catholic regiment.

---

[22]For a general history of the Irish Brigade in the American Civil War, see Jones, *The Irish Brigade.*

Donovan counted his contribution to morale as invaluable; Douglas MacArthur, a Brigadier General during the war, later admitted that Duffy was at one point even considered for the post of regimental commander. The most decorated chaplain in the history of the American military, Duffy earned the Distinguished Service Cross, the Distinguished Service Medal, the Conspicuous Service Cross from New York State, and the Legion d'Honneur and Croix de Guerre from France.[23]

Duffy's military résumé marks him as yet another tough Irish-American priest. Pat O'Brien's portrayal of Duffy in *The Fighting 69th* balances this toughness with sentiment, resulting in a Hollywood priest very much in the mold of *Angels with Dirty Faces* and *Boys Town*. Even more than in the case of Edward Flanagan, screenwriters had to pare away much of the real-life priest in order to arrive at a marketable Hollywood product. Like Flanagan, Duffy was far more educated than the average Irish-American Catholic priest. Before he put in his brick-and-mortar time at Our Savior, he spent several years teaching at St. Joseph's Seminary (Dunwoodie) in Yonkers, New York. At the turn of the century, Dunwoodie was at the center of a fledgling movement to engage recent developments in Christian theology and biblical exegesis that has come to be known as theological Modernism. Duffy served as editor and writer for *The New York Review*, a theological journal that served as a forum for American theologians to explore new currents in theology. Duffy's theological career came to an abrupt end with Pope Pius X's condemnation of Modernism in 1907.[24]

Duffy accepted the theological silencing, but redirected his engagement with the modern world within more practical channels. Like Edward Flanagan, who studied under him at Dunwoodie, Duffy

---

[23]For a recent history of Duffy and the Fighting 69th in World War I, see Harris, *Duffy's War: Fr. Francis Duffy, Wild Bill Donovan, and the Irish Fighting 69th in World War I*.

[24]On Dunwoodie and Modernism, see Appleby, *Church and Age Unite!: The Modernist Impulse in American Catholicism*.

worked to promote a non-theological ecumenism in which Catholics would cooperate with non-Catholics on matters of concern to all Americans regardless of creed. His service in World War I is perhaps the most successful example of this ecumenical Americanism.

Duffy also played a central role in a much more controversial effort at Catholic engagement with America: the presidential candidacy of Al Smith. Before soundly rejecting Smith at the polls, many Protestant Americans questioned whether a Catholic such as Smith had any business even running for the presidency. Smith did his best to ignore the more vulgar attacks on his Americanism, but when Charles Marshall, a retired New York lawyer and prominent Episcopalian laymen, published "An Open Letter to the Honorable Alfred E. Smith" in the prestigious *Atlantic Monthly*, Smith and his advisors knew that he needed to make some formal response.

In questioning Smith's fitness for office, Marshall drew on Catholic social teaching itself, as reflected in the papal encyclicals of the nineteenth and early-twentieth century. As of 1928, the Vatican had yet to express unambiguous support for modern democracy and continued to attack the principle of the separation of Church and State. According to Marshall, the Church's official teaching left Smith with two choices: he could promise to be a good president and a bad Catholic, or a bad president and a good Catholic. Smith's famous, though likely apocryphal, response—"What the hell is an encyclical?"—expressed the frustrations of a practical politician and non-intellectual Catholic who clearly had trouble grasping the nature of Marshall's challenge.

Duffy, a New York priest well versed in the conflict between Catholicism and modernity, intervened to assist Smith in drafting his response. Smith openly admitted his dependence on Duffy, taking the acknowledgment as an opportunity to remind his readers of Duffy's decorated military service in the Great War. Still, Duffy steered Smith clear of abstract theology and kept him to the strengths of his record as a public servant, particularly his three terms as governor of New York State, perhaps the most diverse state in America.

Smith/Duffy concluded their response with a plea for tolerance: "I join with fellow Americans of all creeds in a fervent prayer that never again in this land will any public servant be challenged because of the faith in which he has tried to walk humbly with his God."[25] Duffy and Smith were premature pluralists, and their message fell on deaf ears. Ten years later, Hollywood's version of the Catholic priest would be much more successful at preaching the virtues of tolerance.

The times had changed, but the man and the message stayed the same. Had Duffy lived to see *The Fighting 69th* (he died in 1932), he would have approved of the film's dedication to him as "a beloved Chaplain and a truly great *humanitarian*" (emphasis added). It is an open question as to what he would have made of the story itself.

Reuniting O'Brien and Cagney, the film owes as much to the narrative conventions of their earlier films as it does to the real-life exploits of the Fighting 69th. O'Brien, as Fr. Duffy, once again plays the straight man; Cagney, as Jerry Plunkett, once again plays a wild New York Irishman. Still, the wartime setting of the film serves to invest their battles with broader significance. The opening dedication echoes the patriotic ecumenism of *Boys Town*, but from the very beginning, *The Fighting 69th* is much more self-consciously American and ethnic. Fr. Duffy's efforts to teach Jerry to subordinate his own desires for a higher cause serve as an object lesson to a nation on the brink of yet another European war. In keeping with the localism of Irish-American films, Jerry's commitment to the nation will be mediated through a local community, the Fighting 69th itself.

The film makes clear that the local comes first. The story opens in 1917. The nation is at war and new recruits arrive at Camp

---

[25] Quoted in Morris, *American Catholic*, 160. For a more extensive treatment of this controversy, see Shelley, " 'What the Hell is an Encyclical?': Governor Alfred E. Smith, Charles C. Marshall, Esq., and Father Francis P. Duffy."

Mills, New York, for training. From the very start, Jerry visually establishes himself as a troublemaker with his slow response to the commands of Sergeant "Big Mike" Wynn (Alan Hale). Jerry's misanthropy suggests a disruptive individualism, but another breech of discipline provides an opportunity to celebrate the distinct virtues of the group.

Before Sgt. Wynn finishes dismissing the men, one recruit, with clearly Jewish facial features, steps out of formation. The soldier identifies himself as Mike Murphy (Sammy Cohen). The following exchange ensues.

> *Sgt. Wynn:* Did you say your name was Murphy?
>
> *Murphy:* I did, your worship, saving your presence.
>
> *Sgt. Wynn:* What were you born?
>
> *Murphy:* Sure, I was born a boy.
>
> *Sgt. Wynn:* What name were you born with?
>
> *Murphy:* Mike Moskowitz.
>
> *Sgt. Wynn:* Where'd you get the name Murphy?
>
> *Murphy:* I took it. You see sir, I wanted to go over with the Fighting 69th. Ok? *[smiles sheepishly]*

The Irish-Jewish comedy employed here draws on well-established traditions of stage and screen. The particular situation of a Jew passing for Irish to join the Fighting 69th figured in the plot of a 1926 George Jessel vehicle, *Private Izzy Murphy*.[26] The scene suggests both the continuing appeal of a certain kind of vaudeville ethnic humor and a new role for the Irish as ethnic leaders mediating between the nation-state and the newer ethnic groups. The scene stands out in particular when set against the later tradition of the patrol film, in which the multi-ethnic platoon under the leader-

---

[26]*Private Izzy Murphy* was directed by Lloyd Bacon. Jessel would reprise the role in a sequel, *Sailor Izzy Murphy* (Henry Lehrman, 1927).

ship of a WASP commander serves as microcosm of America as a whole.[27]

The Fighting 69th represents an earlier ideal in which ethnics could still confront America as distinct groups with particular cultural obligations, not as individuals each with an equal opportunity to serve their country alongside individuals from other backgrounds. The Fighting 69th accepts Moskowitz/Murphy on Irish—not Jewish or generically American—terms. He must change his name in order to fit into the group—and he does so gladly.

The film complicates the status of Irishness by presenting a significant dissenting voice, Jerry Plunkett. As Sgt. Wynn exposes Mike's true identity, Jerry delights in Murphy's difference and begins to speak Yiddish with him.[28] Later, Jerry runs into Fr. Duffy. His priestly identity obscured by his uniform, Duffy strikes up a conversation on ethnic identity, not faith. After exchanging names, the two discuss the relative merits of the Irish identity of the unit:

> *Jerry:* Irish, huh? I am too. But I don't work at it. I don't like these flannel-mouthed Micks that go around singing Molly Malone all the time.
>
> *Duffy:* I think maybe you're in the wrong outfit. The regiment has certain traditions.
>
> *Jerry:* Ahh, don't give me that malarkey. We both joined up for the same reason. Come back dripping with medals. Big shots. The world our oyster.

Duffy lets the Irish issue drop and turns to general small talk about New York; they hit it off. As they part company, Jerry even offers Duffy a tip on a horse. Jerry's distance from his Irishness is a symptom of his distance from all group identities and obligations. He clearly states his motives for fighting to be those of individual glory, not loyalty to the Irish military tradition or service to coun-

---

[27] On the patrol film, see Basinger, *The World War II Combat Film: Anatomy of a Genre.*

[28] Cagney knew Yiddish and loved to work it into his films.

try. The moral transformation that drives the plot of the film will require Jerry to make peace with both his particular/ethnic and general/national identities.

Having set up the ethnic dilemma, the film quickly moves to the question of the nation. The Fighting 69th is not the only unit with a proud local tradition. During some downtime, the Irish of the 69th encounter the Southerners of the 4th Alabama National Guard, also stationed at Camp Mills. A fight nearly breaks out after the Alabamans boast of how they whipped the 69th at Marye's Heights in 1862. Fr. Duffy and Col. Donovan intervene to restrain their men.

Donovan then gives a speech calling for both groups to put aside the past and unite as Americans. He begins by giving the Alabamans their due. Donovan concedes that they stopped the 69th at the Battle of Fredericksburg (the Northern name for Marye's Heights)—but adds that the Alabaman soldiers then cheered their heads off because they respected a game enemy. He then reminds both groups that the federal government has reorganized their old local regiments into the United States 165th Infantry of the newly titled "Rainbow Division."

In this rainbow, there is no east or west, or individual state: "Those men are coming here as Americans, to form an organization that represents every part and section of our country, the Rainbow Division. But there is no room in this Rainbow for sectional feuds, because we're all one nation now, one team, an all-American team, pulling together, known as the United States Army." (As a counterbalance to the Irish themes of the film, Donovan renders this "rainbow" fairly monochrome.)

Once in France, Donovan tries to make the Irish brigade fit in by turning to the universal solvent of American culture, work. Plunkett chafes under the discipline, calling the regiment "Wild Bill Donovan's Chain Gang." He is not alone. The other brigades laugh at how hard the 69th has to work. Fr. Duffy himself feels the discipline is excessive and implies that Donovan may be trying too hard to overcome stereotypes concerning Irish laziness. Hoping to return some color to the rainbow, Duffy confronts Donovan:

> *Duffy:* So this is the insignia of the Rainbow Division, huh?
>
> *Donovan:* Every color in the spectrum. What's the matter, don't you like it?
>
> *Duffy:* Indeed I do. I was just thinking the boys in the 69th might like it better if it were a little greener.

Duffy then goes on to ask Donovan to lighten up on the men, linking green/Irish to an appreciation for leisure and good fun. On the eve of moving his men up to the front, Donovan insists that he cannot afford to allow them to let down their guard. Duffy eventually wins the argument for the limitations of the work ethic through an appeal to faith rather than leisure. To be Irish in this world is to be Irish Catholic. The most important thing that the men can do to prepare for battle is go to Confession and attend Mass. The Christmas setting of this part of the film provides an occasion for the particularly dramatic ritual of Midnight Mass.

A deeper shade of green, Duffy's Catholicism nonetheless proves to be the great unifier. It is ecumenical without watering down its distinct traditions. Through Duffy's treatment of the role of faith in the Rainbow Division, he ultimately replaces Donovan's *either/or* with a *both/and*.

As Duffy and Donovan end their discussion of work discipline, Donovan asks for a blessing. At first, Duffy recites a Latin prayer as Donovan kneels. Duffy then turns to the crucifix, kneels, and offers an extemporaneous prayer in English. As the Latin clearly links prayer to Catholicism, so the spontaneous prayer in the vernacular suggests a distinctly Protestant style of prayer.

The theme of Catholic/Protestant coexistence continues later as Duffy meets with the commanding officers while they make final preparations for the move up to the front. One commander asks Duffy if he has made arrangements for Midnight Mass. Duffy says yes, but adds that he has scheduled a Protestant service as well.

Duffy then comments, "You know colonel, if a lot of the people back home knew how well the various faiths get along over here, it would cause a lot of scandal to some pious minds."

Duffy's good-natured barb suggests the universality of the State against the particularity of denominations, but the film stops short of a later civil religion by keeping the religious services separate. The only case of true mixing involves the Jewish Mike Murphy, who asks Fr. Duffy if he can attend Midnight Mass. Duffy welcomes him but makes no adjustments to accommodate his Judaism. Once again, Murphy gains acceptance on Irish-Catholic—not generically American—terms.

The Fighting 69th presents a Catholicism that is both more personal and more political than that in the earlier priest films. The contrast with the film's most direct predecessor, *Angels with Dirty Faces*, is particularly stark. With no common bond of childhood friendship, the relationship between Duffy and Plunkett takes on a much more explicitly theological character than that between Fr. Jerry and Rocky.

Jerry Plunkett scoffs at his cradle Catholicism much as he rejects his Irish identity. After initially hitting it off with Duffy, he feels betrayed when he learns of Duffy's priestly status: "Oh, its Father is it? And who am I? Patty dumb duck, I suppose. Big pal, stringing me along. You can't get away from these *dominus vobiscum* salesmen, even in the army."

Rejected as a friend, Duffy later makes a more explicit effort to save Jerry's soul through the distinctly Catholic means of the sacraments. The night before the men must move up to the front, Duffy invites Jerry to Confession and Mass:

> *Jerry:* I don't go for that Holy-Joe stuff, so there's no use trying to convert me.
>
> *Duffy:* I'm not trying to convert you, son. I'm asking you to come back to your religion and recognize the fact of Almighty God.

At this point, Jerry appears as a more alienated version of Rocky Sullivan; he rejects both faith and friendship. Still, the film clearly identifies Jerry as a cradle Catholic and defuses the specter of Catholic priests using the extreme conditions of war to win converts from other faiths. In one sense, Duffy is, of course, trying to convert Jerry. Catholicism tends to see conversion less as a move from unbelief to belief than as a move from a lax or lapsed faith to a sincere, committed, and active faith. The film does not dwell too deeply on such theological subtleties, but the presence of Catholic screenwriters such as Fred Niblo, Jr. (the nephew of George M. Cohan) on the project undoubtedly reflects the producers' concern to beef up the Catholic content of the story.

This first effort to bring Jerry back to God and man ends with a small victory. Alone, Jerry paces outside the chapel where Fr. Duffy is saying Midnight Mass. As the men sing the Latin hymn "Adeste Fideles," Jerry reluctantly enters the chapel. At the conclusion of the hymn, Duffy, standing at the altar, quotes a bible passage on the return of the lost sheep. Like the earlier scene in which Duffy blesses Donovan, this final, pre-battlefield scene combines elements that connect to both Catholic (Latin) and Protestant (vernacular, biblical) traditions.

Fr. Duffy will eventually lead Jerry back to God, but battle only lengthens the journey. In the great tradition of Christian conversion, Jerry must experience the extremes of alienation before he can achieve reconciliation. In his first night in the trenches, Jerry foolishly fires up a flare so he can get a better view of the enemy. The flare merely reveals the regiment's position, inciting a German bombardment that kills many of his fellow soldiers. Even worse, Jerry proves himself a coward. Nothing in his street-fighting past has prepared him for the horrors of war.

As Fr. Duffy tends to the dying, Jerry tries to run away from the battle—stopped only by a punch from Sgt. Wynn. Though Jerry later admits feelings of remorse in private to Fr. Duffy, he continues to act irresponsibly. On a nighttime reconnaissance mission, Jerry once again turns yellow, with deadly consequences for his companions. Screaming in fear, he reveals the patrol's position. The Germans attack, killing everyone (including Sgt. Wynn's younger brother) except Jerry, who has fled in terror.

This final offense puts Jerry beyond the pale. As the 69th prepares for a major engagement at Argonne, Jerry is court-martialed and sentenced to death. Duffy visits him in his cell and tries to persuade him to make his peace with God. Jerry, still seemingly unrepentant, responds by asking Duffy to help him escape. Duffy refuses and returns to tending the sick and dying. As the battle commences, Germans bomb the town. Duffy returns to Jerry's cell and releases him, challenging him to use his freedom to redeem himself rather than simply run away. Jerry runs away, once again proving Duffy's faith misplaced.

From these depths, Jerry ultimately rises to redemption. With no real safe place to run to, Jerry soon returns to the hospital to find Duffy leading the men in the Our Father. At long last, Jerry finally falls to his knees and begins to pray. The two trade knowing looks, and as Jerry runs off to battle, Duffy recites the bible verse on the lost sheep that he spoke earlier when Jerry snuck into Midnight Mass.

On the front lines, Jerry finally proves himself a hero. With the men of the 69th pinned down by enemy fire, Jerry blasts a hole through the barbed wire with a rocket launcher, enabling the men to advance through the lines and clear out a machine gun nest. As the battle rages, Jerry's rocket position comes under grenade assault from the Germans. When a hand grenade lands in his foxhole, he throws his body on it, saving the life of his old nemesis, Sgt. Wynn.

The Battle of the Argonne would prove to be the final battle of the First World War, but the film ends on a note of personal rather than military victory. Back in the hospital, Jerry apologizes to Sgt. Wynn for causing the death of his brother. He calls for Duffy, states, "I'm ready, Father," and receives final absolution (in Latin). Wild Bill Donovan looks on and says, "I once thought this man a coward."

The film concludes with newsreel footage of soldiers returning home in triumph.

Again, the distinct narrative features of the film appear clearer when set against a non-Irish story covering similar material, *Sergeant York* (Howard Hawks, 1941). Based on the real-life exploits of World War I hero Alvin C. York, the film stands as a Protestant-American counterpart to the Irish-American story of *The Fighting 69th*. York (Gary Cooper) is another reluctant hero, but unlike Jerry Plunkett, his reluctance stems not from pride or fear, but conscience.

Having grown up hunting in the hills of Tennessee, York is an excellent marksman. After a religious conversion experience, however, he is convinced that the Bible prohibits killing and so refuses to participate in the war. The army turns down his request for Conscientious Objector status, and after much individual soul-searching, he agrees to fight because of the justness of the cause, the defense of freedom.

At the Battle of the Argonne, York single-handedly kills twenty Germans and forces another one-hundred and thirty-two to surrender. For his heroism, he receives a French Medal, the Distinguished Service Cross, and the Congressional Medal of Honor. At the end, York returns home to marry his childhood sweetheart and live the simple life of a farmer in rural Tennessee. High ideals, technical expertise, individual achievement, and rural domesticity—*Sergeant York* embodies all the classic Protestant-American values conspicuously absent from *The Fighting 69th*.

Too often dismissed as mere Hollywood sentimentality, the personal, ethnic, and religious themes of *The Fighting 69th* reflect the delicate politics of memory concerning World War I. Americans willing to celebrate the heroism of U.S. soldiers nonetheless remained bitter about the tremendous loss of life that seemed to accomplish little in terms of President Wilson's stated goal of making the world safe for democracy. The "lost generation" of modernist writers such as Ernest Hemmingway could add little to the disillusion found in popular World War I-themed films produced in the late silent era, such as *The Four Horsemen of the Apocalypse* (Rex Ingram, 1921), *The Big Parade* (King Vidor, 1925), and *What Price Glory?* (Raoul Walsh, 1926). The outbreak of yet another major European war some twenty years later only confirmed for many Americans the incurable militarism of old Europe. Isolationist sentiment remained strong up until the attack on Pearl Harbor in 1941. Roosevelt won an unprecedented third term in part by promising to keep America out of the war.

Repulsed by Hitler's anti-Semitic regime, liberals in Hollywood favored intervention but realized that it was a tough sell. *The Fighting 69th* presents the war with no reference to the divisive issues that lingered in the American memory of the First World War. Wilsonian idealism is completely absent. Donovan's theme of national unity falls out of the story once the men arrive in France. Jerry joins the army in hopes of attaining personal glory, but by the film's end, he has learned to surrender his pride to God and subordinate his personal desires to the needs of his regiment—*not* his country.

Nevertheless, the relationship between Jerry and Fr. Duffy serves as an allegory for the struggle between isolationists and internationalists. Jerry embodies two of the great weaknesses of isolationists: excessive (diplomatic) individualism and a failure of nerve.[29] Fr. Duffy, in turn, serves as a crypto-internationalist, investing the war with high moral and spiritual purpose without lapsing into the discredited rhetoric of a Wilsonian moral crusade. He delivers the message of the film with little in the way of Wilson's righteous moral fervor. More importantly, his message of religious/ethnic tolerance could not have been further from Wilson's insistence on "100-per-cent Americanism" as a precondition for democracy.

Warner Brothers considered releasing the film under the title, "Father Duffy of the Fighting 69th," and Duffy really is the lead character. For perhaps the only time in their long partnership, O'Brien

---

[29] For a classic indictment of the failure of liberals to take up the fight against fascism, see Mumford, "The Corruption of Liberalism."

got the better of Cagney, whose Jerry Plunkett pales in comparison to earlier tough guys like Rocky Sullivan. After Jerry dies, the film abruptly cuts to a tribute to the real-life Duffy, with a three-way split screen of O'Brien as Duffy, the statue of Duffy in New York's Duffy's Square (at the north end of Times Square), and marching soldiers.

If World War I made Duffy a national hero, his subsequent career as a parish priest in the Times Square district made him a local one. The transplanted New Yorkers who ran Hollywood shared the loves of their native city. In fact and in fiction, Duffy rooted the universal principles of tolerance in an ethno-religious particularity as no other man of his time could.

The United States entered the Second World War little over a year after the release of *The Fighting 69th*. The attack on Pearl Harbor seemed to erase the disillusionment of World War I and to usher in a moment of national unity never seen before or since. World War II also saw a rather curious triumph for the genre of the priest film.

If *The Fighting 69th* was somewhat ambivalent about the relative value of the national against the local, the two great priest films of the World War II era, *Going My Way* (1944) and *The Bells of St. Mary's* (1945), mark a clear victory for the local. Still, with little or no reference to the world events swirling around them, these light, sentimental comedies seemed to offer a more convincing rationale for "why we fight" than any of the more deliberate propaganda Hollywood produced to support the war effort.

In the figure of Father Chuck O'Malley, the Catholic priest no longer preaches tolerance, he *is* tolerance. Father O'Malley solves every problem that comes his way with gentle persuasion rather than stern discipline. The problems, however, remain local: wayward children, parish politics, paying the mortgage. As a chorus of politicians and intellectuals took up the rhetoric of religious and ethnic tolerance, Father O'Malley seemed to argue that tolerance begins at home—not with how we treat strangers, but how we treat our friends and (sometimes, not-so-friendly) neighbors. At the end of an era of unprecedented nationalization through the New Deal and mobilization for World War II, the character of an Irish-Catholic priest carried the torch for localism in American popular culture.

Director Leo McCarey's vision of a Catholic priest—Fr. Chuck O'Malley—required a different kind of Hollywood actor. True, Mc-Carey first envisioned Spencer Tracy in the role, but MGM refused to allow him the part for fear that it would lead to his being typecast as a priest.[30] After a brief consideration of James Cagney, McCarey decided on Bing Crosby.

In one sense, bringing Crosby on board was quite a coup. In the early 1940s, Crosby was the most popular entertainer in America. He topped the music charts as a singer and reigned as the box-office champion at Paramount Studios. Still, he never quite shook his early nickname, "the Crooner," which he earned for his central role in developing the new, more personal style of singing made possible by advancements in microphone and recording technology. The new style of romantic singing had received harsh condemnation from some prominent Roman Catholic Church leaders, most notoriously Boston's Cardinal William O'Connell.[31]

By the early forties, Crosby had sufficiently distanced himself from the more negative connotations of his nickname, but most executives at Paramount seriously doubted whether he could bring the requisite dignity to the role of a Catholic priest.[32] McCarey remained committed to Crosby and proved the studio executives wrong.

In retrospect, Crosby appears as nothing less than the perfect choice to seal the cultural triumph of Irish Catholicism in American popular culture. He was, by birth and culture, a man of two worlds— Irish-Catholic and American—who felt no need to choose between

---

[30]Gehring, *Leo McCarey: From Marx to McCarthy*, 181.

[31]Giddins, *Bing Crosby, A Pocket Full of Dreams: The Early Years, 1903–1940*, 202.

[32]Gehring, *Leo McCarey*, 181.

them. A believing—if not always devout—Catholic, Crosby was also, in the words of the Jewish-American big-band leader Artie Shaw, "the first hip white person born in the United States."[33] His Anglo-Protestant father, Harry Lowe Crosby, appears to have been the model for the popular persona he developed as a screen star for Paramount during the 1930s—a happy-go-lucky Everyman, a slightly roguish, Tom Sawyer-like trickster who always preferred to get other people to work for him rather than to do the work himself.

This was, of course, a persona that required a lot of hard work to develop and refine. In something of a cultural role reversal, Crosby's Irish-Catholic mother, Catherine Helen Harrigan, instilled in him a strong work ethic so noticeably lacking in his father. His mother embodied all the harsh traits of a Victorian Irish Catholicism whose emphasis on moral self-control more than matched the rigor of its Protestant detractors. Throughout his childhood in Spokane, Washington, Crosby was constantly on the go, working a staggering range of odd jobs, including newspaper boy, grocery-truck driver, and lifeguard. For a time, he even worked as an early morning janitor at a notorious flophouse on Spokane's skid row.

Catherine encouraged this culturally Protestant work ethic only to the extent that it did not interfere with her son's practice of the true faith. Crosby made sure to finish his flophouse duties in time to serve the 6:30 Mass at St. Aloysius Parish, located near the Jesuit college of Gonzaga. The combined influence of his mother and the Jesuits more than compensated for the deficiencies of Spokane's Catholic culture in comparison with that of the great cities of the east coast and Midwest. Attending Gonzaga through his high school and college years (though he never completed his undergraduate degree), Crosby received a classical education in Latin, along with training in elocution, public speaking, debate, and drama. Gary Giddins, Crosby's biographer, has stressed that Crosby's Jesuit train-ing in speech and dramatics contributed greatly to his success in

---

[33] Quoted on the back dust jacket of Giddins, *Bing Crosby, A Pocket Full of Dreams*.

developing the new spoken style of singing with which he would forever be associated: the croon.[34]

Of course, Crosby never publicly acknowledged his debt to the Jesuits during his rise to the top of the entertainment world in the 1930s. In public, Crosby was a swing-era version of the All-American man-child: full of mischief, sexual and otherwise, but not the slightest hint of ethno-religious particularity. Even as Hollywood turned progressively greener through the decade, jazz and swing music continued their steady march away from the Irish-American traditions that had dominated American popular music during the late-nineteenth and early-twentieth centuries.[35] In this musical climate, Crosby would have had nothing to gain and everything to lose by identifying himself with Irish Catholicism.

Crosby's public embrace of this aspect of his heritage began several years before he received the invitation from McCarey to play Father O'Malley. By the late 1930s, Father Charles Coughlin's increasingly hysterical attacks on Franklin Roosevelt and his public descent into anti-Semitism had destroyed his own radio career and ushered in a mini-revival of the kind of public anti-Irish-Catholic bigotry aimed at Al Smith in 1928. Crosby decided to take a public stand in defense of his people in the best way he knew how— through song. Against the advice of all the executives at Decca Records, he dipped back into the treasure chest of Tin-Pan-Alley Irish Americana and recorded his first two Irish-American hits: "Did Your Mother Come from Ireland?" and "Where the River Shannon Flows." By the time McCarey was casting for the film that would become *Going My Way*, these songs, along with along with recordings of Catholic Christmas hymns "*Adeste Fidelis*" and "Silent Night," had

---

[34]For this general overview of Crosby's life, I draw on Giddins, *Bing Crosby, A Pocket Full of Dreams,* and a talk, "Bing Crosby's Identities," that Giddins delivered at the University of Notre Dame on October 12, 2001. For a report on that talk, see my account, "Hibernian Lecture," *American Catholic Studies Newsletter* 29, no. 1 (Spring 2002): 4–5.

[35]On these traditions, see Chapter 5.

gone a long way toward narrowing the gap between "the crooner" and the priest.[36]

In Crosby's portrayal of Father O'Malley, the crooner and the priest meet somewhere in the middle. Since the 1960s, where one stands on Crosby's O'Malley has become a fairly accurate indicator of how one views mid-century American Catholicism in general. For critics, *Going My Way* represents all the worst in this cultural moment: it is both sentimental and authoritarian.[37] For partisans, it represents the best in this moment: sentimental and authoritarian.

Both sides are at least half right. The film is undeniably, and intentionally, sentimental. Still, the image of the film as reflecting a culture secure in bedrock moral and spiritual certainties speaks more to the fears and hopes of a later generation than to the text of the film itself. Produced at a time when the cultural cohesion of American Catholicism could be taken for granted, the film has no axe to grind that would serve the contemporary agenda of Catholic liberals or conservatives. Still, if the film leans in any direction, it is much more toward the liberal side of the spectrum. Just as Bing was the first hip white man in America, he was also, as Anthony B. Smith has recently observed, the first hip priest.[38] But O'Malley's hipness had nothing to do with theological innovation per se. Much to the dismay of contemporary liberals, the film leaves every article of orthodoxy intact by refusing to even consider if any point of faith could be in question. Still, a contemporary conservative might be dismayed at the film's suggestion that baseball games and pop songs

---

[36]On Crosby's early ventures into Irish and Catholic music, see Giddins, *Bing Crosby*, 378–79, 555–58.

[37]For a representative attack on the film from a post-1960s liberal perspective, see Mary Gordon, "Father Chuck: A Reading of *Going My Way* and *The Bells of St. Mary's*, or Why Priests Made Us Crazy."

[38]Smith, "Entertaining Catholics: Bing Crosby, Religion and Cultural Pluralism in 1940s America."

provide all the discipline necessary to remain faithful to the wisdom of the ages.[39]

The political and theological debates of a later period do little to help us understand the appeal of the film at the time. Unabashedly sentimental, the film directs its sentiments not toward metaphysical certainties but toward the whole way of life of the urban Irish-Catholic ghetto. If it is a life that achieves a happy ending, it nonetheless faces struggles along the way. The film begins with a problem, a very practical, material problem of a sort that most urban Catholics struggled with in the war years. After an opening shot that introduces the Church of Saint Dominic in the visual context of a bustling urban environment, the film shifts to the office of the pastor, Fr. Fitzgibbon (Barry Fitzgerald), who is discussing finances with a local banker.

The church needs a new furnace, but it is already five payments behind on its mortgage with the (very Protestant-sounding) Knickerbocker Savings and Loan. The banker, Ted Haines, Sr. (Gene Lockhart), accompanied by his son, Ted Haines, Jr. (James Brown), not only refuses further credit, but demands past payment: "We've made a bad loan and we want our money back!" Fr. Fitzgibbon makes vague assurances of future payment and Haines warns him that this is his last chance. Outside, Ted Jr. reminds his father, "There's never been a Catholic Church foreclosure in the history of New York." Ted Sr. suggests there is a first time for everything.

To the rescue, cowboy-style, comes Father Charles Francis Patrick "Chuck" O'Malley. With a white boater standing in for a white cowboy hat, Fr. Chuck arrives on the scene as an outsider of sorts. The film gives few details on his background, but soon after his arrival at St. Dominic's we learn that he attended East St. Louis High School with a fellow New York priest, Father Timothy O'Dowd (Frank McHugh), and that earlier in his priestly career he used to

---

[39]Wes Gehring notes that McCarey envisioned his Fr. O'Malley as a "gently disrespectful" priest. See Gehring, *Leo McCarey*, 183.

work out with the St. Louis Browns baseball team. Still, it is very clear and very significant that he has no childhood ties to Fr. Fitzgibbon or to St. Dominic's. Though he develops a deep affection for the parish and its pastor, Fr. Chuck is free from any association with the kind of tribal loyalties that defined earlier city priests. Sociologically, he is a cinematic hybrid: a Fr. Flanagan in the milieu of a Fr. Jerry.

Introducing a new kind of priest, *Going My Way* also introduces a new kind of struggle. The old conflict between good and evil represented by the priest/gangster pairing gives way to a generational conflict between old and new, represented by the two priests, Fr. O'Malley and Fr. Fitzgibbon. St. Dominic's financial woes are the result of the failing capabilities of Fr. Fitzgibbon. The bishop has sent Fr. Chuck in to take over the parish and put its finances in order, though Fr. Chuck tries to keep this a secret out of respect for his elder. Fr. Chuck, moreover, is not simply a younger, more capable version of Fr. Fitzgibbon. Even as their initially adversarial relationship develops into a true friendship, the two represent stark opposites in terms of their priestly style. The warmth of the friendship obscures the film's gently presented harsh judgment that in the end, Fr. Fitzgibbon's idea of the priesthood is obsolete.

What endures, however, is the life of the parish itself, lived out on the streets for all to see. The first scene with Fr. Chuck finds him somewhat lost on the streets of his new parish, looking for the church. This confusion reinforces his standing as an outsider but provides the occasion to show Fr. Chuck as a man at ease with strangers. Passing two women sitting out on windowsills cleaning windows, Fr. Chuck introduces himself and asks for directions. One woman, Mrs. Quimp (Anita Bolster), snaps at him with a heavy Irish accent: "The new assistant, eh? And you can't even find the church." The other woman comes to Fr. Chuck's defense by giving him the lowdown on Mrs. Quimp: "You'll see a lot of her, you will, at St. Dominic's. She's a regular two-a-dayer. Very religious. Burns candles." Mrs. Quimp expresses yet more righteous indignation and bangs her head while leaving the windowsill. The other woman laughs and gives Fr. Chuck directions to St. Anthony's.

This exchange with the window ladies reflects the tone of gentle disrespect that McCarey strove to bring to the film. The city Catholic parish life of *Going My Way* is a world that respects piety and devotion but understands the fine line between righteousness and self-righteousness. That Mrs. Quimp gets her comeuppance from a fellow laywoman rather than a cleric suggests the ability of parishioners to keep each other in check. All this reflects the reality of parish life at the time. Fr. Chuck's befuddlement, however, deviates from this reality as well as from Hollywood's earlier treatment of priestly authority. If audiences could laugh *with* Fr. Jerry and Fr. Flanagan, Crosby gives them many occasions to laugh *at* Fr. Chuck.

Before the viewer has time to ponder Fr. Chuck's priestly style, the film throws him into another classic scenario of city life: the stickball game. As he wanders toward St. Anthony's, a little boy asks him to cover right "field" while he goes inside for a minute. The batter hits the ball over Fr. Chuck's head. It breaks a window and the children scatter. Fr. Chuck finds himself confronting yet another cranky denizen of the parish boundaries. In response to his second scolding of the day, Fr. Chuck simply insists that he is sorry and assures the man he will pay him for his window.

Just as Fr. Chuck's standing as a priest and a man seems at its lowest, McCarey pulls out the heavy artillery. As security for the window, Fr. Chuck offers the man his rosary—the prayer beads for the popular devotion to the Virgin Mary, one of the clearest markers of Catholic difference in Protestant America. The man refuses them, claiming, "I'm an atheist. And besides, I'm superstitious." When Fr. Chuck asks for the ball, the man throws it away, rather limply, in a huff. Chuck then renders his only theological judgment in the film: "You even throw like an atheist."

Identifying himself as a man of sports who realizes the value of a baseball, Fr. Chuck then dutifully retrieves the ball from under a truck—only to be sprayed by a street-cleaning wagon. Despite the victory over the atheist, Fr. Chuck ends his first day in the parish all wet. His cool cannot save him from a good soaking. In the battle to navigate a new parish, round one goes to the street.

In this opening sequence, external continuities contain and sometimes even obscure the novelty of O'Malley's hip style. McCarey keeps Fr. Chuck in check through comic devices that arise organically from the urban environment in which most Catholics at the time lived—window conversations, stickball games, and street cleaners.[40] He uses this technique even more dramatically in the first scenes in which Fr. Chuck and Fr. Fitzgibbon become acquainted.

At first, the contrast between the two is sharp. With his clerical garb soaked, Fr. Chuck arrives at his first dinner with his new pastor in St. Louis Browns sweats. Shocked, Fr. Fitzgibbon mutters under his breath, "Even the bishop wouldn't do this to me!" O'Malley, unaware or at least not particularly concerned about the offense he has given, nonchalantly takes out his pipe and lights it up. Fr. Fitzgibbon stares in disbelief and asks him, "As a matter of curiosity, what made you become a priest?"

Various interruptions relieve Chuck of the responsibility of answering the question. This first encounter ends with Fr. Fitzgibbon staring in disbelief as Chuck sings his high school alma mater over the phone with a boyhood friend, now also a New York priest, Fr. Timothy O'Dowd.

The next day, when Fr. Fitzgibbon gives Fr. Chuck a tour of the church, the two finally find common ground in the conventional practices of their faith. Chuck begins where he left off the night before, flouting convention as he jumps over the hedge to get to the church stairs. Once they enter the church, however, all is silence and bliss. The church scene is fairly long, with no dialogue. On the one hand, this reflects the respect the two would have for the sanctuary, but it also suggests that the deepest bonds are beyond words.

---

[40]Contemporary audiences would have taken these devices for granted; viewers in our own day could rightly see them as almost exotic markers of a world we have lost.

In the church, both generations are equally at home and know exactly what to do. McCarey stages a particularly touching sequence in front of a side altar to St. Joseph. Fr. Chuck kneels and prays. As he rises to light a candle, he makes hand gestures to Fr. Fitzgibbon, signaling he will light two candles, one for each of them. The two shake hands. As Fr. Fitzgibbon fumbles for change to make an offering, Fr. Chuck signals that the prayer is on him and drops a coin in the offering box.[41]

This touching scene balances the satirical comments about candle burning offered by O'Malley's windowsill guide in the earlier scene even as it shows the power of devotional practice to overcome a cultural generation gap. This gap will continue to be real and provide much of the comedy in the film's presentation of the relationship between the two priests. Still, St. Anthony's provides a common ground capable of uniting the generations.

The Bishop has sent Fr. Chuck to save the parish, not to change it. Fr. Chuck may win the battle of words, but Fr. Fitzgibbon wins the battle of images: the brick, mortar, and dark wood of the neo-gothic rectory and courtyard serve as a constant visual reminder of the endurance of older ways. Though Fr. Chuck will try to raise money to pay the mortgage by selling his pop songs to a music publisher, he transforms a group of rough street kids into a very conventional Catholic boys choir that sings Latin hymns. These continuities of faith receive little explicit attention in the film. Like the real city Catholicism that inspired McCarey, the faith of *Going My Way* is instinctual, habitual, and environmental rather than theological.

The sights, sounds, and settings of St. Anthony's provide a sufficient sense of unity and continuity to cover what is in fact a multitude of discontinuities and deviations from the norms one would expect of a classic "family" film. *Going My Way* is first of all a family film with no real family in it. The would-be parents are

---

[41]Anthony Smith has offered a similar reading of the significance of this scene in his "Entertaining Catholics."

two celibate males. They "adopt" children—the street boys and a runaway teenage girl named Carol James (Jean Heather)—but cannot seem to agree at all on how to raise them. Fr. Chuck's pastoral approach to the boys—be their friend, take them to movies and ball games—may be straight out of Fr. Flanagan's playbook, but it strikes Fr. Fitzgibbon as lacking proper discipline.

His handling of Carol suggests an even greater generational divide. A young, single woman who has run away from home to pursue a career as a singer in New York, Carol is clearly in a much more dangerous situation than the delinquent boys. Still, Fr. Chuck shows no sense of urgency in handling her case. His preferred method of pastoral counseling is the piano. He coaches her on her singing style, advising this headstrong adolescent to, of all things, put *more* feeling into her singing. Fr. Fitzgibbon intrudes on this counseling session and orders Carol to return home, marry some nice young man and become a good wife and mother just like her own mother; Fr. Chuck gives her money to get an apartment and pursue her singing career.

Later, Fr. Chuck discovers that Carol has struck up a morally questionable relationship with Ted Haines, Jr., the son of the banker who holds the mortgage on St. Anthony's. In the apartment that may just be a love nest, Fr. Chuck takes to the piano once again to counsel the two. And again, Fr. Chuck's message is upbeat. He never directly questions them on their relationship, but simply assures them that he gets "a great deal of happiness out of getting people to realize that religion doesn't have to be like this [pounds dark, minor chord on the piano]." This scene ends with Fr. Chuck singing the title song, a very sentimental Johnny Burke–James Van Heusen tune about pursuing a dream—the last message any priest would want to leave with two young lovers possibly in a state of mortal sin. With its comparatively permissive approach to child guidance in matters of sex, *Going My Way* seems somewhat out of step with the family fare of its day.

The saving difference is, once again, the parish. Daniel Patrick Moynihan long ago observed that the Catholic Church was a stronger force in the lives of the American Irish than the nuclear family. The instabilities (poverty, alcoholism, abandonment) of Irish family life led many to put their hopes for stability in the Church, particularly as represented by the local parish. In *Going My Way*, the plight of the boys and Carol is secondary to the plight of St. Anthony's. The very presence of these wayward children in the story attests to the moral primacy of the parish to the family. Modern viewers who ponder the plausibility of Fr. Chuck's wonder-working powers as a counselor could easily miss the more basic issue of the parish rectory as a site for solving family problems.

Carol and the boys come to Fr. Chuck through the ministrations of an Irish policeman who brings them to the rectory. The policeman is not a particularly good Catholic. In fact, he has not been to Mass in over ten years himself. Still, by force of habit, he brings troubled youth to the rectory first, hoping to spare them a worse fate in jail or reform school. The boys are from the parish, but we never see Fr. Chuck talk with any of their parents. Instead, he "adopts" them and makes the parish the center of a more positive social environment than they seem to have experienced at home. Carol never hangs out at the parish the way that the boys do, but Fr. Chuck repeatedly brings the parish to her by keeping in touch despite her questionable living circumstances.

His somewhat glib request for Carol to "keep in touch" after her first visit to the rectory in some sense echoes Fr. Jerry's approach to Rocky Sullivan in *Angels with Dirty Faces*. Even when confronting a soul in mortal peril, personal relationships precede individual transformation. Fr. Chuck's presence in Carol's life serves to keep her within the boundaries of the film's moral universe even before her story finds its happy moral resolution in her marriage to Ted.

The heart and soul of this family film is, however, the relationship between the "parents," Fr. O'Malley and Fr. Fitzgibbon. Both Crosby and Fitzgerald received Oscars for their performances and their scenes together earned the highest praise from even the most demanding of modernist film critics.[42] In terms of the film's concern to project stability and security, the personal bond that develops between the two priests suggests an underlying continuity across the generations, despite certain obvious signs of a generation gap. In perhaps the film's most memorable scene, the two priests bond over their common ethnic heritage by sharing some Irish whiskey, while Fr. O'Malley sings Fr. Fitzgibbon to sleep with "Too-Ra-Loo-Ra-Loo-Ra (That's an Irish Lullaby)." "Swinging on a Star" won the Academy Award for best song, but "Too-Ra-Loo-Ra-Loo-Ra" got the best musical scene in the film.

That each song triumphed in its own way suggests more than anything else in the Irish films of this era the possibility that one really could be fully Irish and fully American, without ever having to choose between the two identities. That this ethnic ideal found its expression in a film about two Catholic priests suggests the persistent Irish refusal to separate religion and ethnicity and a continuing commitment to be American on their own—explicitly Catholic—terms. At a time when secular Americans were beginning to fashion a new ideal of ethnic pluralism and religious thinkers were beginning to conceive of America as a "triple melting pot" of Protestants, Catholics, and Jews, Irish Catholics insisted on ethnic and religious distinctiveness.[43]

An ethno-religious triumph in the wider realm of American popular culture, the scene must also resolve a crisis in the generational tension that lingers throughout the film. The famous scene occurs at

---

[42] Jean Renoir once stated, "McCarey understands people—perhaps better than anyone else in Hollywood." Quoted in Gehring, *Leo McCarey*, xix. The critic and author James Agee, reviewing *Going My Way* for *Time*, called McCarey's use of Barry Fitzgerald "the finest, funniest and most touching portrayal of old age that has yet reached the screen." Quoted in Gehring, *Leo McCarey*, 201.

[43] The "triple melting pot" ideal would triumph in the 1950s, but the ecumenism of *Boys Town* and *The Fighting 69th* show that the ideal was gathering steam even in the late 1930s. For the classic postwar statement, see Herberg, *Protestant, Catholic, Jew: An Essay in American Religious Sociology*.

the end of the day in which Fr. Fitzgibbon discovers that the bishop has already placed Fr. O'Malley in charge of St. Dominic's. Returning from the bishop's office, Fr. Fitzgibbon meets with Fr. O'Malley and tries to concede his defeat graciously.

Then, while waiting for the housekeeper to prepare dinner, Fr. Fitzgibbon packs his bags and sneaks out of the rectory—in effect, running away from home. On a cold and rainy night, who else but Officer McCarthy brings home the runaway, calling him a "bad boy." Fr. O'Malley then proceeds to take him upstairs and tuck him into bed, an infantilization tempered only by their sharing in the manly, adult beverage of whiskey. With no positive alternative models, the film suggests Fr. Fitzgibbon's individual dotage to be representative of a generation. This older generation may be humored. (After raising the money to pay off the mortgage through the royalties from "Swinging on a Star," Fr. Chuck tells the music publishers to put the money in the Sunday collection following Fr. Fitzgibbon's sermon.) It may also be taught. (With the mortgage paid off, Fr. O'Malley tries to teach Fr. Fitzgibbon how to play golf.) But in the end, the older generation has nothing distinct to teach the younger generation of priests.

Despite the suggestion of the obsolescence of the old, the film ends on a strong note of continuity. Fr. Fitzgibbon remains in charge of St. Dominic's, but only because the bishop has transferred Fr. Chuck to another struggling parish with an aging pastor. Conceding his own defeat, Fitzgibbon expresses his confidence that Chuck will win over his new pastor to his way of thinking. The battle of the generations will continue at St. Dominic's as well, with Chuck's old school friend Timothy O'Dowd taking over as assistant pastor.

Through an improbable series of events, which include the burning down of the old church and the building of a new one, the church even has a new mortgage—again through Mr. Hayes. As Fr. Fitzgibbon gives a speech amidst the construction of the new church, the boys choir breaks into "Too-Ra-Loo-Ra-Loo-Ra," and Fr. Fitzgibbon's mother appears, her visit from Ireland a parting gift from Fr. O'Malley. O'Malley quietly slips out of the celebration, walking through the church courtyard, the priest/cowboy headed off to clean up another parish.

The appeal and enduring reputation of *Going My Way* rests on scenes such as Fr. Fitzgibbon's reunion with his mother. As the reviewer for the *New York Post* commented, "the story is not of great importance . . . the beauty and joy of 'Going My Way' springs from the treatment of human relationships."[44] The story itself meanders and the script often suggests McCarey's laid-back, suburban California Catholicism much more than the stricter, east coast urban Catholicism he so successfully evokes through the visual ambience of the film.

In the hands of a lesser director working with lesser performers, the incongruities between text and image could have been fatal. Instead, they seemed to give the film a universal appeal. Catholics could revel in familiar imagery now receiving America's stamp of approval through a Hollywood film. Non-Catholics could be assured that the crusty old Irish priest was really as harmless as a senile grandfather; moreover, such priests were a thing of the past, while the younger priests were as American as, well, Bing Crosby.

Still, the film was much more than a referendum on Irish Catholicism. For reasons that still elude me, it seemed to represent the best that America had to offer the world. Released in the last year of World War II, the film makes only a brief mention of the war through the enlistment of Carol's husband, Ted. Nonetheless, it appeared to many soldiers to stand for all that they were fighting for. Men serving overseas actually got to see the film before its U.S. release. McCarey and Crosby received over two-hundred-thousand pieces of mail praising the film, and the following letter provides some sense of the patriotism this seemingly apolitical film inspired:

> Sometimes in the routine of training, in the worst heat of battle,
> we lose sight of the things for which we are fighting. It is a strange,

---

[44]Quoted in Gehring, *Leo McCarey*, 184.

unpatriotic feeling—you're just tired and dirty and don't give a damn. 'Going My Way' refreshed my memory as it must have refreshed the memory of thousands of little people who broke into spontaneous applause so many times during the picture.[45]

Hollywood certainly picked up on this appeal of the film, adding a special "G.I. Oscar" to *Going My Way*'s more conventional awards.[46] In the span of four years, Hollywood had baptized the Catholic priest as the guardian of wartime America: Fr. Duffy on the front lines and Fr. O'Malley on the home front.

The overwhelming critical and popular acclaim of the film seemed to call out for a sequel. McCarey resisted at first, but eventually followed up with *The Bells of St. Mary's* (1945). Though it failed to repeat *Going My Way*'s Oscar sweep, the film was even more popular at the box office than its predecessor. Like all good sequels, *Bells* offers the same thing as the original, only different. Once again, we have the easygoing Fr. Chuck pitted against a more conventional religious authority figure.

This time, however, Fr. Chuck's nemesis is a beautiful young nun, Sister Benedict (Ingrid Bergman). The situation that provides the occasion for McCarey's presentation of warm human relationships is once again financial, and once again involves real estate: Fr. Chuck is assigned to a parish in need of a new building for its parochial school. Once again, we have a family film with no (conventional) families. The troubled child in need of clerical guidance this time is Patsy Gallagher (Joan Carroll).

Abandoned by her father at an early age, she has grown up in a broken home. Her mother appears to have supported her through morally questionable relationships with various men. As Patsy approaches her teen years, her mother wants to shelter her and asks if her daughter may board at the convent. The plot weaves in and out between the two struggles: to get a new school building and to restore the girl's family life. Needless to say, both struggles have

---

[45] Ibid., 194.
[46] Ibid., 186.

a happy ending. Once again, the film's appeal lies in the portrayal and performance of personal relationships, not theology or social theory.

Still, the story departs from the conventions established by *Going My Way* in important ways. Most obviously, *Bells* is significantly less Irish than its predecessor. McCarey modeled Sister Benedict on his aunt, Sister Mary Benedict, of the Immaculate Heart Convent in Hollywood.[47] He had originally hoped to cast Irene Dunne in the role, but the final decision for Ingrid Bergman made the possibility of continuing the Irish theme out of the question. Significantly, rural life stands in for ethnicity as the common bond that will unite the battling religious authority figures.

In an early scene, Fr. O'Malley shares with Sr. Benedict some memories of his childhood. Looking out at the tiny schoolyard, Fr. Chuck laments the plight of the city children of St. Mary's. Compared to his childhood in rural Missouri, he says, with its open fields and swimming holes, their life seems dull, gray, and cramped. Sr. Benedict then reflects on her childhood in rural Minnesota, where she was something of a tomboy, enjoying all sorts of outdoor sports, especially cross-country skiing. The anti-urban note marks a significant departure from *Going My Way* and in some sense anticipates the postwar move to suburbia.

As the two share stories of rural life, Fr. Chuck laments the deteriorating condition of St. Mary's, especially when contrasted with the new, modern office building under construction right next door. The owner of the building, a Mr. Horace P. Bogardus (Henry Travers), actually wants to buy the school and tear it down to make a parking lot for his new building. Fr. Chuck has a different idea. He, too, wants to tear down the old St. Mary's, but only after he has persuaded Mr. Bogardus to donate his building to the sisters so that they can use it for their new school building.

---

[47]Ibid., 197.

This twist on the real estate dilemma of the first film is significant. Whereas Fr. Chuck came to save St. Dominic's, not change it, from the start he assumes that in order to save St. Mary's he must change it. The negative assessment of St. Mary's physical plant, if you will, is all the more striking given the visual continuities between the two films. In *Bells*, as in *Going My Way*, McCarey succeeds in creating a village ambience through his presentation of parish buildings and connecting yards. In the second film, the modern office building introduces a new architectural standard against which O'Malley finds the old, neo-gothic parish structures wanting. At the eighth-grade graduation ceremony toward the end of the film, Fr. O'Malley announces Mr. Bogardus's generous donation of his office building. Pointing to the existing and future buildings, Fr. Chuck proudly announces, "There's the old, there's the new!"

Fr. Chuck's graduation speech appears, in retrospect, darkly prophetic of the changes Irish-Catholic city culture would face in the postwar period. Still, in *Bells* as in *Going My Way*, the visual presence of Catholic priests and nuns, of physically monumental church buildings and parochial schools, seems to guarantee continuity and stability in the face of all countervailing forces. St. Mary's will go on—now new and improved, combining all the moral and spiritual authority of the past with all of the modern material conveniences of the present and future. More than any other aspect of Irish-American culture, the continued presence of Catholic churches and schools in their lives assured Irish Catholics that all other evidence to the contrary, they were still going their own way.

The title song for the first film may have been somewhat dubious as a guide to young lovers, but it spoke to the centrality of Catholicism to Irish-American cultural difference. In the middle of trying to guide Carol and Ted away from sin, Fr. Chuck reflects on his own life choices: "At one time, I had quite a decision to make—whether to write the nation's songs, or to go my way." Though couched in terms of individual choice, "going my way" meant forsaking a career in popular music for the life of a celibate Catholic priest. Fr. Chuck never completely gives up on popular music, but rather subordinates it to something higher. A generation later, many Irish Catholics would choose pop music over their faith, but in the 1940s, they could have their faith, their ethnic identity, *and* their Americanism.

Chapter 5

The Lights of Old Broadway

THE 1940S FOUND THE IRISH LOCAL HEROES in an age of nationalization—in tune, but slightly out of step, with America at large. This tension found its way into perhaps the most curious cinematic success story of the era, the Irish-American musical. Hollywood priests faced no serious rivals on the religion front, but the golden age of Irish-American music experienced a cinematic renaissance at the height of the popularity of a very different kind of music, swing.

Even as critics and pundits promoted swing as the music of democracy, *Yankee Doodle Dandy* (Michael Curtiz, 1942)—the film biography of George M. Cohan, the Irish-American song-and-dance man who ruled Broadway in the pre-jazz era of the early twentieth century—outdid all contemporary musicals in inspiring a nation in the fight against fascism.[1] For the next decade, Hollywood would continue to turn to Irish-American musicals to tell a story at odds with the swing conventions of the day. If swing music reflected American ideals of boundless freedom and individuality, Irish-American musicals told stories of individuals bounded by family, community, and place. From major productions such as *The Seven Little Foys*

---

[1] On the construction of swing as a uniquely democratic music, see Stowe, *Swing Changes: Big Band Jazz in New Deal America*. *Yankee Doodle Dandy* was the highest grossing film in Warner Brothers' history. See Sklar, *City Boys: Cagney, Bogart, Garfield*, 127.

(Melville Shavelson, 1955) to minor programmers such as *Bowery to Broadway* (Charles Lamont, 1944), Hollywood celebrated its own prehistory and helped to establish a link between the ethnic stage and the All-American screen.

Of all the genres of Irish-American film, the musical was the most consistently historical. Irish gangsters, boxers, and priests were still very much contemporary figures, but no one looking at American popular music of the thirties and forties would see it as an Irish domain. With the Jazz Age of the 1920s, African-American music finally broke free of its connection to minstrelsy to emerge as an urban, modern music in its own right. As the Irish had taken the lead in co-opting African-American music in the earlier minstrel period, so Jews continued the tradition in the Jazz Age.[2]

The ethnic transition was sharpest in musical theatre, where, through George M. Cohan, the Irish could still claim some dominance through the mid-1920s. The Columbia University-educated Richard Rogers, for example, found Cohan's music simple and sentimental, far below the standard set by the new generation of songwriters such as Irving Berlin and George Gershwin. Cohan, for his part, largely dismissed the achievements of the new Broadway, having neither the ability nor the interest to bridge this musical generation gap.[3]

Cohan and the Irish lost out in the pop marketplace of the day, but both benefited from the wave of nostalgia for all things old and

---

[2] On Irish-American popular music in the nineteenth century, see Williams, *'Twas Only an Irishman's Dream: The Image of Ireland and the Irish in American Popular Song Lyrics, 1800–1920*. The literature on minstrelsy is legion. For one recent influential reading of the Irish-black connection in music, see Lott, *Love and Theft: Blackface Minstrelsy and the American Working Class*, 49, 95. There is a growing literature on Jews and jazz. See, for example, Alexander, *Jazz Age Jews*; and Rogin, *Blackface, White Noise: Jewish Immigrants in the Hollywood Melting Pot*.

[3] On Rogers's views of Cohan, see McGilligan, "The Life Daddy Would Have Liked to Live," his introduction to McGilligan, ed., *Yankee Doodle Dandy*, 12. On Cohan's views of Rogers, see McCabe, *George M. Cohan: The Man Who Owned Broadway*, 241.

outdated that swept across America in the 1930s. Warren Susman and a host of other scholars have argued that the crisis of the Great Depression inspired Americans to pursue an unprecedented search for cultural roots, a search that produced the concept of an "American way of life."[4] The same search that led some to the folk blues of the Mississippi delta led others to the mass-produced sheet music of turn-of-the-century Tin Pan Alley.[5]

Where folk and blues stood as the music of America's rural past, Irish-American music conjured up dreams of the golden age of the American city. In what has become an all-too-familiar dynamic, yesterday's disposable commodity became today's cultural heritage. Irish-American commercial culture started to experience this transformation in the late 1930s. The old music received the endorsement of the most popular entertainer of the swing era, Bing Crosby; it also benefited from the continuing presence of the greatest star of that earlier era, George M. Cohan. In the late 1930s, as Cohan neared the end of his days, his life story became one of the most sought-after properties in Hollywood. When Warner Brothers finally secured the rights to his story, they produced in *Yankee Doodle Dandy* the first-ever musical biography, inaugurating a new genre that would survive through the swing and rock eras.[6]

Aside from its novelty as a biography, *Yankee Doodle Dandy* set itself apart from the backstage musicals of the day by its unprecedented emphasis on the family. Classic examples of the genre, such as *42nd Street* (Lloyd Bacon, 1933), generally tell an American rags-to-riches story in which individuals struggle for romantic love and career success apart from any binding ties of family or community. The family theme in *Yankee Doodle* flows naturally from Cohan's real-life work with his parents and sister in the vaudeville act The

---

[4] Susman, "The Culture of the Thirties," in his *Culture as History: The Transformation of American Society in the Twentieth Century*, 150–183.

[5] Sklar, *City Boys*, 123.

[6] McCabe, *George M. Cohan*, 245–54.

Four Cohans, but other family issues nearly prevented the film from ever being made.

Much of the struggle for creative control of the project stemmed from Cohan's concern for how Hollywood would handle the sensitive issue of his first marriage to a Jewish-American actress, Ethel Levy, and his eventual remarriage to Mary Agnes Nolan, an Irish Catholic. Divorce and remarriage were still delicate subjects for Hollywood films, and the Catholic Church—even apart from the Legion of Decency—took the strongest possible stand against them. Whatever Cohan's level of personal piety, he was a cradle Catholic and was known as such in his public life.[7] Cohan's father, Jerry Cohan, had been one of the founders of the Catholic Actor's Guild; Cohan himself had served as president of the Guild. The details of his marriage history would surely cause scandal for him personally and bring shame on his family.

Cohan did not trust the secular screenwriters of Hollywood to handle the issue properly. At first, he offered his story to the drama department at the Catholic University of America (CUA). Through the efforts of the Dominican priest, Father Gilbert V. Hartke, CUA was in fact one of the most vital centers for drama outside of New York City at the time. The Catholic University production of *Yankee Doodle Boy* would become a significant source for the story that would eventually shape the plot line of the film *Yankee Doodle Dandy*.[8]

No script survives to provide a scene-by-scene comparison between the play and the film. From the writings of those involved in the original stage production, however, it is clear that the stage play set the standard for avoiding all personal matters that might cause embarrassment. Ironically, at a time when a Catholic presence was

---

[7] Cohan died in the Church, receiving last rites and a funeral Mass at St. Patrick's Cathedral. For the first time in the history of St. Patrick's, the cathedral organ played a secular song, Cohan's "Over There." McCabe, *George M. Cohan*, 267.

[8] Ibid. On Hartke's role in this, see San Pietro, *Father Hartke: His Life and Legacy to the American Theater*, 77–79.

on the rise across a wide range of film genres, the film biography
of the most famous Irish-Catholic entertainer of his day makes no
mention at all of Catholicism.

Suspicious of Hollywood, Cohan's approval of James Cagney in
the leading role also came through local Irish-Catholic networks.
After failed efforts to secure a deal with Samuel Goldwyn and
Paramount, Cohan turned to a local New York Irish friend and
confidant, Ed MacNamara, who recommended Cagney, a close
friend and and fellow New York Irishman.[9]

Cagney began his stage career as a dancer and had proven
himself a box-office success in musicals, with his *Footlight Parade*
(Lloyd Bacon, 1933) outperforming any of his better known gangster
films.[10] Being just about the only one of the "Irish Mafia" who did
not know Cohan personally, Cagney sought out Spencer Tracy, Pat
O'Brien, and Frank McHugh for advice on how to play the role.[11]
Cagney had reasons of his own, beyond filial piety or ethnic loyalty,
for accepting the part. He had come under political suspicion for
his association with left-wing organizations and needed a role that
would shore up his credentials as a patriotic American.[12]

---

[9]One of the great lost characters of American entertainment history, MacNamara was a former policeman who had studied singing with Enrico Caruso and
hobnobbed with the New York entertainment elite. See McCabe, *Cagney*, 148.
On Cohan's failed efforts with various studios and contact with MacNamara, see
McGilligan, ed., *Yankee Doodle Dandy*, 15.

[10]Sklar, *City Boys*, 38.

[11]McCabe, *George M. Cohan*, 264. The term "Irish mafia" refers to a group of
Irish-American Hollywood performers who regularly met for marathon sessions
of Irish-style conviviality. The term reflects how, by the time of the golden age of
Hollywood, many Irish-American performers felt themselves somewhat a group
apart from the mainstream of an entertainment industry that seemed increasingly
dominated by Jewish Americans.

[12]McCabe, *Cagney*, 200–204. Though deeply honored to have earned Cohan's
approval for the role, Cagney had serious reservations about the script in its
early stages. He felt the studio made too many concessions to Cohan on content,
resulting in a script that simply was not very entertaining. Cagney insisted the
studio bring in Philip and Julius Epstein, the most famous "script doctors" in
Hollywood. Cohan never got the chance to sign off on the changes, but the final

Cohan too approached the film with some political trepidation. With the war looming in Europe, Warner Brothers clearly intended the film to be more than a nostalgic celebration of the music of a bygone era. Cohan composed the great patriotic anthems of the World War I era and the revival of those songs was to inspire a new generation to undertake the sacrifice of war once again.

Though no one would question his patriotism, Cohan was somewhat at odds with the country's current Commander-in-Chief. Like most Irish Americans, Cohan was a great supporter of Roosevelt in 1932; like some, he had soured on Roosevelt by 1936. Though Cohan identifies himself as a lifelong Democrat in the film, he had deep sympathies for Al Smith and was profoundly anti-union at a time when Roosevelt had won a landslide re-election in part for his support of industrial unionism.

In 1937, Cohan played the part of Roosevelt in an irreverent Broadway comedy, *I'd Rather Be Right*, which satirized the New Deal. The comedy of the play focuses on the travails of a young man who asks his boss for a raise so that he can marry his true love, only to have his boss respond that he will not give him a raise until President Roosevelt balances the federal budget. With a script by the great comedy team of George Kaufmann and Moss Hart and music by Lorenz Hart and Richard Rogers, no one would mistake the comedy for a right-wing attack on the New Deal.

Still, Cohan expressed his hostility to Roosevelt in more direct ways. Awarded the Congressional Gold Medal in 1935, Cohan at first refused to accept it for fear that Roosevelt would use the award as a publicity stunt to shore up support among conservative, Al Smith Democrats. At first, he decided to wait to pick it up after Roosevelt finished his second term. (When Roosevelt won re-election for an unprecedented third term, Cohan had no choice but to accept it from his political enemy.)[13]

---

shooting script owes much of its strength to the work of the Epsteins—as well as Cagney's continued input. See McGilligan, ed., *Yankee Doodle Dandy*, 39, 55.

[13]McGilligan, ed., *Yankee Doodle Dandy*, 24.

Emerging from this controversial back-story, the final film playfully evades the political and cheerfully ignores the personal. The film opens with an elderly Cohan staging his great comeback on Broadway with *I'd Rather Be Right*. The play is a critical and popular success, yet Cohan appears genuinely concerned about the president's reaction. When he receives a telegram summoning him to the White House on a "personal matter," he fears the worst.

Cohan arrives to discover that Congress has awarded him the Gold Medal of Honor for his service to the country through popular song. Cagney plays Cohan as deferential to the dignity of the office of the president and fearful of Roosevelt's response to his performance. Though nervous and unsure of the reason for his summons, Cohan quickly seeks to establish a connection to Roosevelt through the common bond of the Democratic Party. Citing the positive reviews of *I'd Rather Be Right*, Roosevelt jokingly notes that the *Herald Tribune* has declared Cohan to be a better president that Roosevelt himself; in the same spirit of fun, Cohan replies by reminding Roosevelt that the *Tribune* is a Republican newspaper.

Both Democrats, they nonetheless come from very different backgrounds—Roosevelt the country WASP patrician, Cohan the urban Irish entertainer. Against Roosevelt's real-life distaste for Irish Catholics, the film transforms ethnic difference into yet another common ground as Roosevelt declares, "That's one thing I've always admired about you Irish Americans. You carry your love of country like a flag right out in the open. It's a great quality." Cohan explains that he got his patriotism from his father, who ran away from home in Massachusetts to join the Union army. Talk of his father takes him back to his own youth, and thus he begins to tell the story of his life.

Cohan's account of his early years establishes the Yankee Doodle Dandy as both Irish and American. Just as importantly, it presents this identity as an inheritance he receives from his father. Such family ties, not romantic love, will provide the emotional core of the film; moreover, such ties are never purely emotional, but also cultural.

The flashback begins in Providence, Rhode Island, on Independence Day in 1878. George describes the age as one of boundless hope and optimism for the future, but the first scene suggests the persistence of the Irish past in a forward-looking America. His father, Jerry Cohan (Walter Huston), sings and dances to "The Dancing Master," a classic bit of stage Irish hokum performed in full Irish costume, complete with a shillelagh. The man who as a boy ran away to join the Union army has clearly not forgotten his Irish roots.

After his performance, Jerry rushes out of the theater to be with his wife, who is in labor. He finds his way back to his hotel blocked by a parade. Seeing him in his stage clothes, the marchers tell him to go to the front of the parade with the rest of the Irish. When Jerry explains his situation, he receives an express escort to the hotel on one of the parade wagons. He arrives at the hotel to find that his wife, Nellie (Rosemary De Camp), has just given birth to a baby boy. As it is the Fourth of July, Jerry suggests naming the boy George Washington Cohan; Nellie protests that the name would be too long to fit on a marquee. He then suggests dropping the middle name of Washington for some short Irish name like Dennis or Michael; they finally agree on George Michael Cohan.

Jerry then goes to the window and shouts, "It's a boy!" and the marching soldiers from the parade fire a cannon salute in his honor. The cannon fire causes the newborn George to cry and Jerry proclaims, "He's crying with a brogue!"

The cultural balance of the opening scene quickly shifts from the Irish to the American. As George recounts his youth on the stage, he follows in his father's Irish footsteps by performing "The Dancing Master"—with the significant addition of an American flag popping out of his shillelagh. Still, the Four Cohans (including George's sister Josie, played by Jeanne Cagney) are ready to perform any material people will pay to see—from wild-west shows like "Daniel Boone on the Trail" to black-face minstrelsy.

George spends his earliest years on the western circuit, literally growing up with the country as new states enter the Union. In an age in which ethnic Irish stories were still mainstream theater entertainment, George achieves his first major stage success as the lead character in the all-American *Peck's Bad Boy*. As an adult, George scores his first big hit with *Little Johnny Jones*, which features the hit song "Yankee Doodle Dandy." In terms of ethnicity, George Cohan's Yankee Doodle could not be any further from Jerry Cohan's Dancing Master.

Still, the film undercuts the trajectory of assimilation and generational discontinuity through its treatment of the relation between George's career and his family life. Unlike Jackie Rabinowitz in *The Jazz Singer*, George does not have to choose between his family and popular culture. He was born into an entertainment family that saw no contradiction between the ethnic and the American. George moves beyond the explicitly ethnic routines of his early career, but he makes this move *with* his family, not against it. Moreover, at the end of his career, he still proudly identifies himself as an *Irish* American, an identity introduced in his opening exchange with Roosevelt.

Audiences of the time would have recognized Cohan as a distinctly Irish performer. Known today for his patriotic anthems, he continued to produce explicitly Irish-themed plays well into the late 1920s.[14] At one level, the film emphasizes the American aspects of Cohan over the Irish, but the theme of intergenerational continuity prevents the film from following *The Jazz Singer*'s trajectory—that is, moving from the ethnic to the American.

George finds success not by breaking free from inherited cultural constraints, but by learning to subordinate his pride and personal ambition to the concerns of his family. Early in the film, following the success of *Peck's Bad Boy*, the Four Cohans lose a chance to

---

[14]Consider the titles of several productions from late in his career: *The O'Brien Girl* (1921), *Little Nellie Kelly* (1922), *The Rise of Rosie O'Reilly* (1923), and *The Merry Malones* (1927).

sign a long-term contract with a powerful Broadway producer when George makes unreasonable demands based on his new star status. In a later scene, as a young man and aspiring songwriter, George causes the family to lose a job at O'Rourke's Variety Theater when he convinces a young woman (who will later become his wife, Mary, played by Joan Leslie) to substitute one of his songs for her scheduled performance of "The Wedding of the Lily and the Rose."

Later, overhearing talk at the family's rooming house, George finally realizes that his actions have led to the blackballing of the Four Cohans on the vaudeville circuit. He then announces that he has found a producer for his play and is going solo. Of course, he has no money at first, but when he and his partner Sam Harris (Richard Whorf) finally get some real financial backing, he immediately telegraphs his family on the road and tells them to come back for roles in *Little Johnny Jones*. Cohan's family loyalty in fact provides the film with its signature line: "My mother thanks you, my father thanks you, my sister thanks you, and I thank you." His success is never purely individual, but always familial.

The family theme comes full circle in the moving death scene between Jerry and George. Here again, the contrast with *The Jazz Singer* is striking. Jack Robinson grants his father a dying wish that he sing *Kol Nidre* at a Yom Kippur service, but then promptly returns to the jazz singing that destroyed his relationship with his father in the first place. The reconciliation is purely sentimental and the cultural triumph of America complete. Jack wins the heart of a gentile girl and expresses his love for his Jewish mother in the American idiom of a black-face minstrel song, "Mammy."

For George and Jerry, there is no similar angst and no sense of cultural discontinuity. The only separation they have experienced has been Jerry's retirement from the stage. The bonding on Jerry's deathbed flows naturally from the lifelong bond they developed through their careers in show business. For all of George's success, there is no sense that he has somehow moved beyond his father.

Older friends, present at the deathwatch, quietly comment that Jerry was the greater performer.

The traveling nature of vaudeville life certainly limited the film's ability to link these strong family ties to a conventional notion of community rooted in place. Still, the film presents the world of the theater as a kind of moveable community—the secret brotherhood of the "trooper," rooted in the symbolic space of the American city whose Mecca was Broadway.

Little Johnny Jones, Cohan's first smash musical, featured not only the song "Yankee Doodle Boy," but also "Give My Regards to Broadway." Cohan aspired to write the songs of the nation, but for all his flag-waving, he could never imagine wanting to perform those songs anywhere other than under the bright lights of Broadway. Even as the film presents young George caught up in the romance of the frontier, it never suggests that he could call the frontier home; better to play a cowboy on Broadway than to be a cowboy in real life.

Growing up on the road and on the stage, George has no "little town blues" to lose. His path to Broadway takes him from the small time to the big time, not from innocence to experience. True, like the protagonists of much nineteenth-century fiction, George sets his sights on New York in search of a better life. At one point in the narration of his early years, George comments, "Dad seemed content with the sticks, but I was straining at the leash." Crossing generations and cultures, the film shows old Irish contentment giving way to new American ambition, but George exercises his seemingly boundless ambition within the world of the stage he has inherited from his father. Broadway is not a foreign country; it is simply the pinnacle of the only world he has ever known.

Against the overwhelmingly agrarian iconography of New Deal-era patriotism, the Yankee Doodle Dandy is a city boy through and through.[15] Aside from "Give My Regards to Broadway," the film expresses Cohan's city chauvinism in a production number of the title song from his 1906 musical, *Forty-Five Minutes from Broadway*. The lyrics of the title song present the world outside of New York as something like a foreign country:

> Only forty-five minutes from Broadway,
> Think of the changes it brings;
> For the short time it takes,
> What a diff'rence it makes
> In the ways of the people and things.
> Oh! What a fine bunch of rubens,
> Oh! What a jay atmosphere;
> They have whiskers like hay,
> And imagine Broadway
> Only forty-five minutes from here.

Though delivered in a spirit of good fun, these lyrics do point to a country/city theme that recurs throughout the film. Significantly, country life actually serves as the setting for the final breakup of the Four Cohans. After they rise to the top of Broadway, the Cohans, like many successful New York performers of the time, purchase a house in the country, complete with small farm animals. With the family all together to celebrate Jerry's birthday, George's sister Josie announces that she is leaving the act to get married, while Jerry and Nellie announce they are retiring to live a quiet country life. George protests, "You can't put an actor out to grass. The fresh air kills him!" A throwaway line at one level, it also points to the urban basis of their family solidarity.

The film steers George's city chauvinism clear of elitism through its emphasis on his urban populism. George may have had some fun at the expense of country bumpkins, but the film presents him as something of a city bumpkin, always struggling to convince critics and high-brow performers that he is something more than a flag-

---

[15] For the classic study of this phenomenon, see Stott, *Documentary Expression in Thirties America*.

waving writer of cheap musical comedies. The film works the Cohan hit "Mary" into this dimension of the story.

He writes the song for his sweetheart Mary (who takes the place of the two real-life wives), but ultimately gives it to Faye Templeton (Irene Manning), a high-class Broadway performer he has been trying to woo in his efforts to raise his standing in the eyes of critics. The dutiful Mary forgives him, and the film gives the last word to populism through its handling of Cohan's effort at producing a serious drama, *Popularity*. The play fails miserably with critics and audiences alike. Initially angered by the bad reviews, Cohan quickly concedes defeat and places an ad in all the New York papers apologizing to his public for producing such a terrible play and advising them to avoid it at all costs.

George's recognition of his populist roots is timely. No sooner does he finish drafting his apology than the streets come alive with news of the sinking of the Lusitania and the entry of the United States into the Great War in Europe. George tries unsuccessfully to enlist in the army. Turned down because of his age, he quickly learns that he can serve his country through his unique talents of songwriting. As he leaves the recruiting office dejected, he hears a bugler playing a march, which inspires a melody that becomes the great anthem of the First World War, "Over There."

In this sequence of events, the film compresses the chronology of both Cohan's career and the country's entry into World War I, but all with the narrative effect of establishing Cohan as a man of the people and the nation—rather than of the critics. This emphasis on populist patriotism over technical quality reflects only a partial truth about Cohan's career. The film accurately presents Cohan's ongoing battle with the critics, but completely ignores his role as a stage innovator, the man who in fact invented the modern Broadway musical.

Where earlier musicals had simply been a series of production numbers only loosely tied together by any kind of plot, Cohan made great strides toward integrating music and story. He followed

Harrigan and Hart in trying to present the stage as a mirror of city life, yet pushed their realism beyond the accepted norms of his day. At the same time, Cohan also polished up and refined the rough working-class theater of Harrigan and Hart for a more genteel middle-class audience.[16]

Despite the debacle of *Popularity*, the real-life Cohan did have later success in developing more complex characters, such as the Shaughraun-like vagabond of *The Tavern* (1920) or the title role in *The Song and Dance Man* (1923). No less a dramatist than Eugene O'Neill saw Cohan as the spiritual father of all Irish-Americans of the theater and cast Cohan successfully in his *Ah, Wilderness* (1933); the youthful J. D. Salinger was completely bowled over by Cohan's performance.[17]

The choice of the filmmakers to ignore the more innovative aspects of Cohan's art reaffirms the place of Irish-American entertainers in Hollywood lore as urban traditionalists. Again, the contrast with jazz stories is revealing. George Gershwin, one of the generation of composers who sneered at Cohan, received his own film biography treatment with *Rhapsody in Blue* (Irving Rapper, 1945). The film very clearly presents jazz as the music of innovation. *Rhapsody in Blue* overcomes the generational split of *The Jazz Singer* by presenting Gershwin's father, Papa Morris Gershwin (Morris Carnovsky) as enthusiastically accepting a technical standard for assessing his son's music: in a recurring comic scene early in the film, Papa Gershwin proudly charts his son's success by noting the increasing length of his compositions.

If the immigrant father cannot quite see beyond quantity, the film makes clear that Gershwin is progressing in quality as well. The title composition, "Rhapsody in Blue," debuts at New York City's Aeolian Hall as part of a larger "educational" program organized by

---

[16]Cohan once summed up this aesthetic in the following words: "Speed! Speed! And lots of it. That's the idea of the thing. Perpetual motion." See McCabe, *George M. Cohan*, 56, 68.

[17]Ibid., 228.

Paul Whiteman, the leading jazz bandleader of the 1920s. Titled "An Experiment in Modern Music," the program traces the development of music from the "primitive" rhythms of the African jungle to the modern symphony, with Gershwin's composition coming in second to the top of this evolutionary hierarchy.[18]

This emphasis on technical virtuosity even shapes the one Irish contribution to the genre of jazz biopic, *The Fabulous Dorseys* (Alfred E. Green, 1947). True to life and Hollywood conventions, the brothers Tommy and Jimmy Dorsey (who play themselves) fight constantly, but as jazz musicians they fight over the very technical issue of musical arrangements. Both aspire to the technical heights of a "real musician" such as Art Tatum, the African-American jazz giant who makes a cameo appearance in the film.

Yankee Doodle Dandy never directly confronts the technical divide between Irish-American and jazz aesthetics, but it does point to an equally important generational divide. In a scene late in the film, after Cohan has retired, the film shows George trying to talk to some swing kids whose car has overheated as they drove past his retirement home. The younger generation has never heard of him. They ask him what movies he has starred in, and he clarifies that he was a star of the stage, the "legitimate theater."

The generations do not even seem to speak the same language: the jitter buggers talk jive while Cohan deciphers the older show-biz slang of a *Variety* headline, "STIX NIX HIX PIX" (rural audiences reject movies with rural themes). As the kids leave, Cohan overhears them referring to him as a "nice old guy." The shock of his irrelevance propels him out of retirement and into *I'd Rather Be Right*. Cohan triumphs in the new age of swing. As he carried on the traditions of his father, so, too, he reconciles the musical generations of a nation.

---

[18]The same emphasis on technical development shapes more current and racially sensitive re-workings of Whiteman's project, such as Ken Burns's documentary, *Jazz*.

The film ends with an explicit appeal to national unity across the generational divide. Returning to the framing device of the meeting with Roosevelt, Cohan receives the Congressional Gold Medal of Honor, which specifically cites his patriotic songs, "You're a Grand Old Flag" and "Over There." As he leaves the president's office, he tap dances down the White House stairs and walks out into the street, where a new generation of soldiers for a new world war march to Cohan's theme song for the First World War, "Over There."

In 1942, Americans did not need the songs of George M. Cohan to inspire them to fight against Japan and Germany; they had Irving Berlin and a whole generation of jazz/swing songwriters to provide World War II with its official soundtrack. They did, however, need Cohan's songs to transform the war into a battle for an American way of life that stretched beyond the present moment into the past.[19] Cohan's Irishness may be relatively thin compared to that of characters in other Irish-American films of the period, but the linking of even a nominal ethnic identity to the battle for America marks a sea change from the 100-per-cent Americanism of World War I and the nativist revival that helped to defeat Al Smith in the 1920s.

The fight against the racial ideologies of Nazi Germany put an end to public nativism and led to an unprecedented celebration of ethnic diversity in America.[20] The success of *Yankee Doodle Dandy* inspired a minor but enduring genre of Irish-American musicals that proved the golden age of Irish-American popular music had appeal even apart from the explicit flag-waving of Cohan's patriotism.

The end of Cohan's career marked the end of the Irish-American dominance of Broadway at a time when New York set the musical

---

[19]This is, of course, the theme of Warren Susman's classic essay on the thirties. For a more extended treatment of the development of the idea of an American way of life, see Pells, *Radical Visions and American Dreams: Culture and Social Thought in the Depression Years.*

[20]On this development, see Gleason, "Americans All," in Gleason, *Speaking of Diversity*, 153–87.

standard for the nation. In the decade or so following *Yankee Doodle Dandy*, the Irish-themed musicals moved back in time and place, to a more local and ethnically Irish milieu. The Tin Pan Alley tunes revived by Bing Crosby received biopic treatment in two Technicolor films celebrating the great songwriters of the turn of the century, Ernest R. Ball and Chauncey Olcott.

Irish Eyes Are Smiling (Gregory Ratoff, 1944), the Ball story, is a slight effort distinguished only by the involvement of Damon Runyon and its suggestion that by the mid-1940s one could still present the urban Irish as a kind of exotic other. At the beginning of the film, Ball (Dick Haymes) forsakes the classical music world of the Cleveland Conservatory of Music to pursue a career in the rough-and-tumble world of Irish-American popular music. Throughout his struggle for commercial success, he chases the love of his life, Mary "Irish" O'Neill (June Haver), a tough but morally pure Irish-American showgirl.

My Wild Irish Rose (David Butler, 1947), the Olcott story, is a much more successful effort deeply rooted in the traditions of popular Irish-American narrative. This second attempt to strike *Yankee Doodle* gold benefits from solid source material in Rita Olcott's biography of her husband, as well as the proven ability of Warner Brothers to handle Irish class and cultural issues. Part *Yankee Doodle Dandy* and part *Gentleman Jim*, the film presents Olcott as a working-class Irishman seeking to rise in the social world while remaining loyal to his family and his ethnic roots.

The film opens with a page out of *Gentleman Jim*. Chauncey Olcott (Dennis Morgan) is a Buffalo, New York tugboat operator who aspires to a career as a singer. He sets his sights high, seeking to ingratiate himself with Lillian Russell (Andrea King), the most popular singer of her day. He attends a Russell concert with his half brother, Joe Brennan (Clifton Young).

Somewhat like the Walter Lowrie character in *Gentleman Jim*, Joe is the voice of Irish-American low expectations. When Chauncey suggests he is a better singer than one of the men in the show, Joe replies, "Aw, forget it, Chauncey, and stick to tugboats. You could be a good deck hand someday." Chauncey next boasts that he will dance with Lillian Russell before the night is over, to which Joe responds, "Come on, let's go home, we don't belong here. . . . Chauncey, we're tugboat people and you gotta get onto yourself."

Ignoring Joe's advice, Chauncey decides to try to meet Russell after the show. He finds her stage door crowded with wealthy businessmen/admirers and passes himself off as a steamboat tycoon. Each man vies for Russell's attention, but they all end up going out to dinner with her together. Chauncey confides his stage aspirations to Russell. She pegs him as an Irishman from the start and has her guard up against his blarney. But when he sings for her, she concedes he has a fine voice. Russell's approval inspires him to pursue a career as a singer.

True to the tradition of Irish-American popular narrative, Chauncey's ambition first puts him at odds with his family. Also true to this tradition, Chauncey redeems himself through the choice of a career recognized as legitimate within Irish-American culture itself. Following his evening with Lillian Russell, Chauncey finds himself back at home with Joe, his mother (Sara Allgood), and his stepfather, Captain Brennan (George Cleveland). Joe and the Captain kid Chauncey about his dreams of becoming a star, while his mother counsels him to focus on a more practical career: "When are you going to have your fill of this, Chauncey? When are you going to settle down to hard work like the Captain and Joe here, like your father before you? You know, if you work hard enough, one day you'll own your own tugboat, and that should be good enough for any man."

Chauncey, in turn, justifies his dreams in terms of his mother and the great tradition of Irish singers: "It might be good enough for me, mother, but it's not good enough for you. The boys at the barber shop say I have a singing voice suited for the theatre, and could become another William Scanlan."

The film here reworks the Sullivan-Corbett battle of generations into a musical setting. Mrs. Brennan at first dismisses his dreams— "Stop comparin' yourself in the same breath with a fine Irish singer like William Scanlan." Next, she suggests that any occupation as lucrative as the theater must be sinful. Finally, she relents, but gives him only a guarded blessing: "If a man's voice is heaven sent, I guess it becomes his duty to share it with the whole world," but she doubts that Chauncey has "much talent for this actin' business." Mrs. Brennan gives Chauncey his father's watch for good luck, but makes him vow to use a stage name until he has become a success.

Like *Yankee Doodle Dandy*, *My Wild Irish Rose* legitimizes the pursuit of success by placing it in the context of family duties and obligations. No lone, isolated American individual, Olcott understands himself as heir to traditions—both familial (his father's name) and ethnic (William Scanlan)—that he must respect in order for his success to have meaning.

The film introduces a strong love interest in the character of Rose Donovan (Arlene Dahl), but the convoluted plot twists that serve to keep the lovers apart also lead the story on a tour through a thickly Irish world of urban politics and entertainment. Olcott begins his professional career when he enters a bar attracted by the singing of a bartender whose voice has "the quality of Scanlan." The barman identifies himself as a displaced New Yorker, once "known as the best 'Singing Barman' of the Bowery." He offers to sell the bar to Chauncey in exchange for the cost of the fare back to New York. Chauncey instead offers him his own Studebaker carriage.

As the two negotiate the final deal, a woman in a runaway carriage cries out for help. Chauncey rescues the woman (Rose), introduces himself as Jack Chancellor (the stage name he adopts to keep his promise to his mother) and shares his aspirations to become a professional singer. To deflect his romantic overtures, Rose confesses she is just visiting Buffalo and will soon be traveling back to New York, where her father is a high-ranking alderman.

Rose returns home and Chauncey begins a series of misadventures—including involvement with a traveling minstrel show and a professional wrestler named "Iron Duke" Muldoon (George O'Brien)—that eventually land him in New York. Rose, accompanied by her father, John Donovan (Alan Hale), and her fiancé, Terry O'Rourke (William Gould), attend a performance of Chauncey's minstrel troupe. She insists on meeting Chauncey after the show, and the clear attraction that exists between the two disturbs both her father and her fiancé. Her father has no respect for minstrel performers, but he is a close friend of the great Irish tenor William Scanlan (William Frawley). Consequently, Chauncey's pursuit of love and fame will be intertwined throughout the rest of the film.

Most of this plot is a series of coincidences that have little to do with Olcott's actual rise to the top of the New York stage. Like *Irish Eyes*, *My Wild Irish Rose* is completely silent on the professional relationship between Olcott and Ball. In the film, Chauncey gets his first big break by running into Lillian Russell at a booking agency, and he gets his next big break when he crosses paths with William Scanlan at "Iron Duke" Muldoon's gym. Chauncey earns a spot in Scanlan's show, and as Scanlan's health declines, Chauncey eventually takes over singing duties, hiding behind scenery while Scanlan lip-syncs to fool the audience.

Scanlan's doctor finally orders him to retire. Performing at a theater in Boston on St. Patrick's Day, Scanlan officially passes the mantel of king of the Irish tenors on to Olcott. The crowd at first rejects the new king, but Olcott quickly wins them over by singing "A Little Bit of Heaven." A medley of hits follows, culminating in his singing "Mother Machree" to his own mother—a scene whose ethnic continuities contrast sharply with the ethnic disconnect of "Mammy" in *The Jazz Singer*.

Having won the respect of his mother, Chauncey now focuses on winning the love of Rose. When Mr. Donovan asks Chauncey to sing at a rally for his re-election as alderman, Rose and Chauncey rekindle their romance and elope. Donovan is outraged that an Irishman would marry his daughter in front of a mere justice of the peace, but he reconciles with Chauncey when they all agree to make the marriage right with a proper (Roman Catholic) church wedding. The film then ends with yet another medley of hits, finishing with the title song, "My Wild Irish Rose."

Wild Irish Rose falls short of the technical standards of *Yankee Doodle Dandy*, but the songs of Olcott and Ball live on in St. Patrick's Day celebrations as surely as Cohan's still provide the soundtrack for the Fourth of July. Ironically, the Irish-American biopic would find cinematic redemption in the story of an entertainer whose music would not survive in either holiday: Eddie Foy.

Foy was a contemporary and rival of Cohan's. He appears (played by his son, Eddie Foy, Jr.) as a character in a brief but significant scene in *Yankee Doodle Dandy*. As the two debate their relative merits, Cohan, in praise of himself, says, "Cohan's done alright. He gave the world 'Yankee Doodle Dandy.' What's Foy done for his country?" Foy responds, "He gave 'em seven kids." Foy's boast would become the basis for the one truly worthy sequel to *Yankee Doodle Dandy*—that is, *The Seven Little Foys*. The Cohan-Foy rivalry that earned a brief comic scene in the former film inspired one of the most memorable scenes in Hollywood musical history: James Cagney as George M. Cohan and Bob Hope as Eddie Foy trading taps on top of the dinner table at a Friar's Club banquet.[21]

Despite this memorable scene, the film's success lies in its Academy Award-nominated story rather than in its songs: the story of Foy's professional rise, personal fall, and ultimate redemption through his relationship with his children. The film carries on the

---

[21] Foy did not produce a body of music that could carry a film on its own. He did, however, live a life that inspired tremendous loyalty and enduring admiration among the ex-vaudevillian New Yorkers who went on to become Hollywood movie stars. Cagney once commented that Foy was always there to give him a free meal when he was a struggling, starving actor. And Cagney refused to take any payment for his show-stopping cameo in the film. See McCabe, *Cagney*, 291.

family theme of earlier Irish-American musicals, but invests it with genuine pathos. The story speaks to the domestic concerns of the 1950s as much as Cohan's patriotism spoke to the international concerns of the 1940s, but with a note of dissonance.

Released at the height of the Baby Boom, the film celebrates a vision of family life rooted in an older, Irish-American entertainment world at odds with postwar suburban ideals. An absent father, Eddie Foy becomes present not by forsaking work for home, but by incorporating home into work. Rather than make himself into a conventionally dutiful father, Foy transforms his children into Irish-American troopers.

The Seven Little Foys goes far beyond *Yankee Doodle Dandy* in presenting the dark side of family life on the vaudeville circuit. Where *Yankee Doodle Dandy* strikes a note of continuity, *The Seven Little Foys* tells a story of conversion. The film opens with the triumphant debut of Eddie Foy and the Seven Little Foys at the Palace Theatre in New York in 1913, but uses this performance as a framework for a flashback narrative in which Eddie Foy, Jr. tells the story of the transformation of his father from bachelor song-and-dance man to a dedicated family man.

At the start of the flashback, Foy appears as a bachelor version of Jerry Cohan, performing an Irish song-and-dance routine, in full Irish costume, complete with shillelagh. Performing in Chicago, he dreams of making it in New York. At this point, the similarities with Jerry end. Backstage after his number, Foy gulps beer and refuses to give up his dressing room to an Italian ballet duo, Madeleine (Milly Vitale) and Clara Morando (Angela Clarke). Foy dismisses all chivalry with a quip: "I'm not interested in dogs, women, or children—in order of their importance." The young, beautiful Madeleine appeals to him directly, only to be rebuffed as a foreigner; when she protests that he himself is Irish, he simply responds, "Isn't everybody?"

Madeleine, strangely attracted to Eddie, continues her verbal sparring as the two prepare for their next performances. At the same time, Barney Green (George Tobias), a talent scout for the Schubert Brothers, has arrived to scout Foy for a New York show. Later, when the Morando's act runs overtime, Eddie fears he will lose his chance to impress Green. Dressed in his baggy-pants clown outfit, he tries to disrupt their performance; the audience, including Barney, bursts out laughing.

Thinking Foy part of the act, Barney offers to sign Eddie and the Morando sisters together. Eddie refuses at first and the Morandos return to Italy. Eddie eventually relents, and Madeleine agrees to sign—on the condition that Eddie marries her. When a quick pregnancy prevents Madeleine from performing, the Schuberts drop the whole act and Eddie has to start all over as a solo act.

Foy, like Cohan, will eventually rise to the top of the New York stage. Still, against the narrative convention of *Yankee Doodle Dandy*, *Seven Little Foys* severs the connection between moral transformation and professional success. The film shows how Foy gets his big break by calming a crowd during the famous Iroquois Theater fire in Chicago, but this isolated act of heroism has no bearing on his personal moral life. Instead, Foy's professional success drives him away from his family. As the film alternates between visuals of theater marquees and Catholic Church baptisms, the narrator, Eddie Foy, Jr., comments: "Eight shows a week at the theater and a matinee at St. Patrick's Cathedral."

That the film shows baptisms rather than hospital births is of no small significance. Eddie's relationship to the Church as much as to his family serves as an indicator of the state of his soul. A good provider, Eddie is an absent father. He shows up for the baptisms, but does little more. After one baptism, he quips "Thank you, Father. I can just make the second act."

Eddie buys Madeleine her dream house in New Rochelle, but generally sleeps in on Sunday mornings. The parish priest, Father O'Casey (Lester Mathews), vows that on the day Eddie Foy shows up for Sunday Mass, he will have all the church bells in New Rochelle ring. Still, to the entertainment world that is his real community,

Eddie is both a personal and professional success. The Friars Club in New York presents him with an award as the Outstanding Father of the Year.

The Friars Club dinner is the turning point of the film. It provides the occasion for the film's musical high point, the Hope/Cagney tabletop duet. Still, pride goeth before the fall. Any illusions Eddie may have had that he really was an outstanding father are shattered when he returns home to discover that Madeleine is dead. She had in fact been sick for quite some time, but kept it a secret from Eddie for fear of interfering with his work; Eddie's long absences from home made her secret all too easy to keep. Eddie learns of her death as he crosses paths with a priest leaving the Foy home in New Rochelle, presumably having just administered last rites. The priest does not even recognize Eddie as Madeleine's husband.

This personal tragedy plunges Eddie into depression and professional failure. Madeleine's death leads him to reconnect with his family in the worst possible way: drinking and reading the racing form while spoiling his children with presents and letting them run wild. His friend and agent, Barney Green, tries to rouse him out of his guilty stupor. He realizes Eddie is unfit for domesticity, so he suggests that Eddie connect to his children by bringing them into show business.

Eddie rejects the suggestion. The two argue, but Barney gets the last word: "What made me think that because the Cohans turned out alright the Foys would too? The Cohans had a father!" Professional rivalry provides the incentive that guilt alone could not. Eddie immediately knocks a bottle of beer out of one of his son's hand, spanks him, and begins transforming his family into Eddie Foy and the Seven Little Foys.

The reconciliation that Eddie achieves with his family is neither easy nor conventional. His children resent his new presence as much as they did his former absence. At first, they resist his efforts to make them into performers. He eventually whips them into shape. The new act debuts successfully in Pittsburgh, but they all must pay their dues on the regional vaudeville circuit.

Despite their steady success, the children resent the grind of life on the road. They look forward to returning home for Christmas, yet learn that their father has booked them for a holiday show in New York instead. The Christmas show is a success, but immediately after it the police come and take the children away from Eddie, charging him with violating child labor laws. At the climactic scene in juvenile court, Eddie makes his case for custody not as a father, but as a song-and-dance man.

He concedes that the children did not want to enter show business, but pleads that he had no other choice: "If I was a carpenter, I would have brought them up as carpenters and not be in court." Show business is the only thing he knows, the only way he can raise his children. The children then come to Eddie's defense, claiming they were only pretending to be unhappy, because "he'd have slugged us if we said we liked him."

To discern whether Eddie is in fact guilty of violating child labor laws, the judge then asks the children to give a demonstration of their act. They proceed intentionally to perform so badly that the judge lets Eddie off the hook by claiming that he cannot construe anything the children have shown him as properly coming under laws governing "entertainment." Eddie gets to keep his children not as a suburban father, but as an urban entertainer.

In the great Catholic tradition of *Going My Way*, the Church, not the home, has the last word in family life. The film ends on Sunday morning, with Eddie once again asleep as Aunt Clara takes the children to church. This time, however, Eddie wakes up, realizes everybody has left, and races off to join them at Mass. First he shows up by mistake at the Episcopal Church; the Reverend directs him to the Catholic Church and then spreads the word to all of the other Protestant Churches to ring their bells in honor of Eddie Foy attending church on Sunday.

Eddie catches up with his children just as they are entering the Catholic church. One of the youngest tries to sneak out, but Eddie finds him hiding behind the door and drags him in, saying, "If I go, everybody goes!" Eddie's attendance at Mass puts the finishing touches on his moral rehabilitation, but reinforces the distinctly Irish-Catholic terms of that moral transformation.

Eddie does not become someone new so much as he becomes what he should have been from the start. The comic confusion with the Episcopal church affirms a kind of 1950s ecumenism even as it makes clear that for Eddie there is no substitute for the Catholic Church. The film measures Eddie's Catholic spiritual transformation not by abstract religious principles, but by the accepted public standards of urban Irish Catholicism: showing up for Mass on Sunday.

The film biographies of Cohan, Ball, Olcott and Foy sustained the golden age of Irish-American music in the popular imagination well into the 1950s. The real-life success of these figures kept their film renderings at some distance from Irish-American narrative traditions that were more skeptical of success and celebrity. Some of the richest storytelling in the musical genre actually came in the formula pictures that sought to evoke turn-of-the-century New York at several rungs below Broadway royalty.

The Betty Grable vehicle, *Sweet Rosie O'Grady* (Irving Cummings, 1943), for example, takes a song from that era as the starting point for a Bowery Cinderella story in which a New York burlesque queen ultimately forsakes marriage to an English duke to marry the Irish-American reporter who challenged her to stay true to her Irish roots.

Strawberry Blonde (Raoul Walsh, 1941), a Raoul Walsh/James Cagney collaboration, takes a line from the song "The Band Played On" as the musical hook for a reworking of Irish American James Hagan's play about a working-class man who, nearly destroyed by his attraction to a wealthy, glamorous redhead, finds contentment in the love of a decent, honest working-class nurse. Still, among all the Irish-American-themed musicals of this period, no single film expresses the idea of redemption through failure better than the 1944 Universal production, *Bowery to Broadway*.

Bowery to Broadway is just the sort of film destined to fall through the cracks of film history. It is a programmer pure and simple, a mid-level production clearly designed to put people in the seats through the lure of another song-filled, nostalgic trip down memory lane to a simpler time of 1890s New York. It is, nonetheless, a memorable film.

The story follows the rivalry between two showmen from the Gilded Age, Michael O'Rourke (Jack Okie) and Dennis Dugan (Donald Cook). As the title suggests, the two begin their rivalry on the Bowery, at the low end of the entertainment spectrum. With the encouragement of a slumming Lillian Russell, they take their rivalry uptown. The two eventually join forces and come to rule Broadway, but success destroys the relationships that sustained them during the tough Bowery years.

In the end, Dugan and O'Rourke see the error of their ways and reunite with all their old Bowery friends. The success of *Yankee Doodle Dandy* may show how Americans of the 1940s loved a winner, but the persistence of films such as *Bowery to Broadway* proves that American audiences of that decade could still find cautionary tales on the perils of ambition compelling.

The presentation of the O'Rourke–Dugan rivalry at the beginning of the film places the viewer firmly in the world of earlier films like *The Bowery*. O'Rourke, proprietor of the Crystal Palace, and Dugan, owner of the Shamrock Gardens, are the theatrical equivalent of tavern owners Steve Brody and Chuck Connors. As in the earlier film, a Bowery rivalry once again appears as a contest of brains (Dugan) versus brawn (O'Rourke).

At first, brawn seems to have the upper hand, as O'Rourke gets one up on Dugan by stealing his headline act, Bonnie La Tour (Evelyn Ankers), "That Bowery Sweetheart." Dugan responds by barging into La Tour's dressing room at the Crystal Palace to demand the return of his costumes—including the one she is wearing. As

Dugan struggles with La Tour over her costume, O'Rourke calls the police and has him arrested, declaring, "You see, Officer? Even on the Bowery a woman ain't safe with men like Dugan."

In the spirit of good sportsmanship, O'Rourke then pays for Dugan's bail. A priest, Fr. Kelley (Andy Devine), delivers the bail. He apparently has acted as emissary for Dugan in the past: "You know, if you and Michael ever get arrested at the same time, I'll have to be using my own money to get [you] out." The presence of a priest as intermediary between two Bowery showmen is an authentic period detail, but also attests to the generic standing priests had attained within the Irish-American films of the 1940s.

Father Kelley will soon come to the rescue again as Dugan enacts his revenge. Rather than simply trying to steal back Bonnie La Tour, Dugan sets up O'Rourke to bring himself down. Pretending to wallow in his defeat, Dugan plants the word on the street that he lost La Tour just at the point when he had planned to cast her in his most daring production to date—a show featuring her and ten "Parisienne Models" in flesh-colored tights!

O'Rourke quickly steals the idea, only to have his show halted by the Murray Hill Society for Social Reform, who call in the police to arrest O'Rourke on charges of obscenity: "It's a disgusting display of the human anatomy. Ten girls in flesh-colored tights!" Fr. Kelley dutifully arrives at the police station with the bail money. O'Rourke asks him for help in getting back at Dugan, but Fr. Kelley replies, "Oh, that I couldn't do. He's one of my boys, too. And besides, it was Dennis that called me to get you out."

Mike meets up with Denny only to learn that the supposed Murray Hill reformers were actually some of Denny's own men. Angry at first, Mike quickly concedes an honorable, underhanded victory to Denny: "A bunch of phonies. I oughta . . . Denny, you're wonderful! What a pal. What a brain!" The two share a good laugh, but O'Rourke soon proves himself not completely lacking in the brains department. Turning the raid to his own purposes, he re-opens the La Tour show as "The Show That Shocked Murray Hill."

Denny grumbles—"Ah, that lucky Mick. Doing a land-office business on an idea that should have put him in the poor house"—but actually does fairly well himself on O'Rourke's overflow.

Losing the battle for Bonnie La Tour exposes a deeper discontent in Denny. Talking to his friend Joe Kirby (Frank McHugh), he declares that he is through with the Bowery: "Look at it. A beer-and-pretzel business! Nine parts saloon and one part intelligence! Maybe it's all right for Mike, but a man with my ideas. . . . " Before he can finish his rant, he looks out through the window and spies Tom Harvey (Thomas Gomez), "the biggest politician in Tammany Hall," with Lillian Russell (Louise Allbritten) riding down the street in a carriage. Harvey and Russell are clearly slumming, but Dugan sees this chance encounter as a possible ticket out of the Bowery.

The two first enter O'Rourke's Crystal Palace. From the start, Mike's rough, clumsy hospitality grates on Russell. Denny senses Mike will not know how to handle a classy performer like Russell properly and quickly devises a plan to lure her over to his Shamrock Gardens. Congratulating Mike on his high-class clientele, Denny suggests he honor Russell by inviting her to sing one of her big hits, "The Bamboo Tree." Mike snaps at the bait only to have Russell leave in a huff after being pressed into service on her night off.

Denny then whisks her over to his Shamrock Gardens, where he hosts her in style, quietly toasting her while his own musicians pay tribute to her by themselves performing "The Bamboo Tree." Honored, Russell then joins in to sing with Dugan's chorus. Dugan succeeds in winning the respect of Russell. She suggests he take his business uptown and offers to put him in touch with the right people. To O'Rourke, who has stood by watching Dugan's triumph, she remarks, "I'm sure you'll enjoy a long and successful career on the Bowery." Defiant to the end, O'Rourke vows to follow Dugan uptown to continue their rivalry.

The rivalry continues on 14th Street, but a near-fatal accident in the middle of a performance leads the two to join forces to take on Broadway itself. Peggy Fleming (Susanna Foster), a young protégé of Denny's, is crippled in a fall during a lavish production number. Guilt stricken, Denny vows to quit show business altogether. Fr. Kelley, a constant presence throughout the story, tries to console Denny by insisting he is not to blame for the accident. Furthermore, Peggy's injury frees her to marry her true love, Denny's songwriter, Ted Barry (Turhan Bey), proving that some good has come from her life in the theater.

Mike then arrives to inform everyone that the fire marshal has closed down his 14th Street theater, so he is moving uptown to 42nd Street—that is, to Broadway! Clearly trying to goad Denny back into the business, Mike boasts, "I ain't the kind of guy who quits climbing a mountain when I'm twenty feet from the top." The two spar on their relative merits as showmen until Father Kelley finally suggests that they take this moment of transition as an opportunity to join forces, "to fight side by side instead of toe to toe." The two agree to go into business together and the scene ends with them comically arguing over who gets first billing in the partnership.

Dugan and O'Rourke succeed in securing financial backing for their first Broadway show, *Remember April*. Right from the start, success threatens to compromise old friendships. The show's big-time Broadway director, Walter Rogers (Richard Lane), demands that they replace an old dance duo, The Dancing Kirbys, with Irene and Vernon Castle, "the greatest dance team in the country." Mike and Denny protest and defend the Kirby's talent and showmanship. Rogers responds: "Look, gentlemen, show business is no place for sentiment. This isn't the Bowery; it's Broadway. The Kirbys are old hat; they don't belong here."

Joe and Bessie Kirby (Rosemary DeCamp), meanwhile, have overheard the argument from the hallway. Although they had worked all their lives to make it on Broadway, they agree to sacrifice their dreams for the success of the show. Just as Rogers is ready to leave the show because of Dugan and O'Rourke's refusal to drop the Kirbys, Joe and Bessie walk into the room and announce that they are retiring from show business to open a dance school. The Kirbys' retirement frees Dugan and O'Rourke to sign the Castles without betraying their friends. The scene ends with the Kirbys lamenting their loss. As they enter an elevator, the attendant asks, "Going up?" Joe replies, "Going down."

The rest of the film will suggest the opposite. Joe and Bessie work out a simple, happy life as dance teachers, while success nearly destroys Dugan and O'Rourke. *Remember April* is a big hit and runs for two years. A string of hit shows follows, with titles including *Gay Widows*, *Sweetheart Parade*, and *The Golden Goddess*. As in the old Bowery days, however, Denny aspires to more than simply financial success.

In pursuit of class and sophistication, he signs Marina (Maria Montez), "the greatest international personality of the century," to their next show, *Song of Romance*. As with his earlier encounter with Lillian Russell, O'Rourke shows himself out of his league by trying to promote her as he would any American celebrity. Dugan knows how to handle her correctly, and the show turns out to be the biggest success ever to hit Broadway.

Still, with the turn toward classier entertainment, Denny takes complete creative control of the business and marginalizes O'Rourke. Further, his budding romance with Marina leaves little time for the male camaraderie of earlier times. Mike finally breaks down and confides his problems to the Kirbys.

> *Mike:* Two years of producing nothing, doing nothing. Just sitting around.
>
> *Bessie:* I know what you mean. It's just business. Not show business. Not the part that gets under your skin—the all night rehearsal . . . the put-it-together, pull-it-apart . . . going crazy over sets and costumes . . . will a number click or won't it.
>
> *Joe:* Yeah, Mike. Bessie and I know what you mean.
>
> *Mike:* You know . . . she hit the nail right on the head. It's just business. It ain't show business.

The thematic gauntlet thrown down, much of the rest of the film will focus on the efforts of Mike, the Kirbys, and the rest of the old Bowery gang to rescue show business from just business.

Predictably, Mike's renewed resolve drives him apart from Denny. Mike tries to interest Denny in a new musical that their old friend Ted has been writing for Marina, but Denny responds that he wants to take a break from musical productions. Despite the success of *Song of Romance*, Denny is convinced that Marina is worthy of more sophisticated fare. The story here takes a page from the *Popularity* interlude in *Yankee Doodle Dandy*. Denny's respect for Marina's past as a dramatic actress in Europe—as well as his concern for her romantic present with him—lead him to insist that her next play on Broadway be a serious drama.

Denny proposes an American production of *Dark Autumn*, a Hungarian drama for which Marina won high praise in Europe. Mike and Denny argue but cannot come to any agreement. Denny decides to produce *Dark Autumn* without Mike. The play fails miserably at the box office, as do subsequent serious dramas with titles such as *Death Walks Softly* and *Flame in the Wind*.

Mike continues to produce musicals on his own, but they fail as well. Marina eventually realizes that Denny's love for her is driving him away from all his friends and making him miserable. She also realizes that her love alone cannot bring Denny happiness. She decides to break up with Denny in order to free him to rebuild his life with his old friends.

With Marina out of the picture, the old gang works on getting O'Rourke and Dugan back together. Peggy and Ted work on Mike while Bessie and Joe work on Denny. Mike and Denny eventually run into each other in front of their now closed 42nd Street Theatre. As the two begin to reminisce about old times, a street vendor joins in a conversation with them, unaware of their identity. The vendor recalls seeing Dugan and O'Rourke shows as far back as their days on the Bowery; in the spirit of the Bowery, he offers them "a real old-style coney hot dog," which they each take with the works.

Though the film does not make clear how long the theater has been closed, the image of the boarded-up theater and the tone of the conversation with the vendor make Dugan and O'Rourke appear as names from a bygone era. The vendor, a wizened street historian, then offers his assessment of their achievement.

> *Vendor:* What a pair, that Dugan and O'Rourke. Scrappin' all the time. Ha! Ha! But did they know how to put on shows! Talk about real dancing, real singing. Ain't got anything like it these days.
>
> *Mike:* Good shows, were they?
>
> *Denny:* Oh, good for their time.
>
> *Vendor:* Good for anytime. They was real entertainment, they was.
>
> *Denny:* Times have changed.
>
> *Vendor:* Times has, but people hasn't. Them shows would be just as good today. . . .

Inspired by their conversation with the vendor, the two reconcile and return to doing what they do best, making musicals.

Reunited, they can finally produce the musical Ted had written right before Denny took his detour into high drama with Marina. The show will star none other than Bessie Jo Kirby (Ann Blyth), daughter of the Dancing Kirbys, who will finally realize her parents' dream of having a Kirby on Broadway. The show is titled *Bowery to Broadway*, and the film closes with two romantic production numbers: "As They Did It On the Bowery," the film's "song specialty" featuring the great Hollywood dancers Donald O'Connor and Peggy Ryan in a routine to the song "He Took Me for a Sleigh Ride in the Good Old Summer Time"; and "As They Do It On Broadway," a lavish, "classy" production number featuring Bessie Jo and the entire ensemble singing "Sing What's in Your Heart."

Even as they mend their personal and professional relationship, Dugan and O'Rourke reconcile past and present, Bowery and Broadway, through music. With the show a clear hit, Mike proclaims, "Gee,

Denny, this is just like old times." Finally, the film even reconciles friendship and romantic love. At the end, Mike reveals that none other than Marina herself has been the silent-angel backer for the show. Denny and Marina embrace as Mike looks on approvingly.

Both improbable and believable, *Bowery to Broadway* is Hollywood formula storytelling at its best. That is, improbable circumstances and coincidences work to tell a story worthy of belief. Lacking any real show-stopping numbers, the film never made it into the pantheon of classic musicals. Still, with solid character performances and a story that suggests an ideal beyond fame and fortune, it holds up much better than many of the better-remembered musicals of the era. The film's ideal synthesis of Bowery and Broadway spoke to a persistent narrative hope that it is possible to achieve something like middle-class prosperity without having to forsake one's working-class roots.

In the larger context of the 1940s, Bowery and Broadway serve as metaphors for a wide range of binary oppositions, not the least being that of stage and screen. Hollywood musicals celebrated the life of the stage even as they worked to destroy it. The stage entertainment that did survive in a few urban centers like New York would accrue tremendous cultural capital during the postwar years, but Hollywood—and television—completely replaced vaudeville as the mainstream venue of national American popular culture.

All the Hollywood moguls were New Yorkers by birth and upbringing. They grew up with the stage and paid homage to it through a generation of film musicals. The backstage movie musical expressed a classic American desire to have it all, stage and screen. With its ethnic and historical dimensions, the Irish-American musical was central to Hollywood's efforts to present film as a continuation of an earlier stage tradition.

In the context of Irish-American musicals, the conceit that the national media could actually work to save local life in the present found its most revealing expression in *Duffy's Tavern* (Hal Walker, 1945). An idiosyncratic case of a film in which art tries to show life imitating art, *Duffy's Tavern* takes Fr. O'Malley's parish-saving antics as a model for the "real-life" Bing Crosby's miraculous powers to induce postwar economic recovery. Using characters from a popular Irish-themed radio show, the film tells the story of how an all-star cast of Hollywood celebrities descend upon a New York City neighborhood to help a group of returning servicemen get back to work and return to the life they lived before the war. The show's grand finale features a comic performance of the life of Bing Crosby that culminates with his success in *Going My Way*, complete with all the stars taking their turn at verses from "Swinging on a Star." By the end of the film, order is restored and all is right with this still very local—and Irish—world.

Duffy's Tavern will make no one's top-ten list. It is very much a film of its time and for the moment. At one level, it is simply a glorified variety show featuring the stars of Paramount Studios. Crosby was Paramount's biggest star at the time, and the film gave the studios' other stars a chance to bask in his reflected glory. Still, Crosby and Paramount share a significant degree of advertising space with another pop culture phenomenon of the time, the *Duffy's Tavern* radio show.

A popular—and at times top-ranked—radio show during the 1940s, *Duffy's Tavern* featured Ed Gardner as Archie, the amiable, though not-too-bright, manager of an Irish-American bar on the Lower East Side of New York. Tin Pan Alley tunes such as "When Irish Eyes Are Smiling" and "The Sidewalks of New York" provided the theme music. Each episode would begin with Archie answering a ring of the phone with, "Duffy's Tavern, where the elite meet to eat—Archie the manager speakin', Duffy ain't here. . . . Oh, hello, Duffy." It would then go on with a series of comic skits and dialogues featuring a colorful cast of local, working-class characters who frequented the tavern. Celebrities would also appear as themselves, dropping in to perform a song or participate in a comedy skit. Crosby himself appeared once in 1943 as part of a promotional campaign for *Going My Way*. Paramount's decision to continue a promotional partnership with the low ethnic humor of *Duffy's Tavern* suggests a lesson learned from the success of *Going My Way*: at a time of unprecedented nationalization through war, Americans wanted an America that still affirmed the life of local community.

For all of its lightness, the film *Duffy's Tavern* never reduces community to warm fuzzy feelings. The central dilemma of the film is economic: returning servicemen need jobs. The record factory that had employed many of the local men before the war is now closed due to a shortage of shellac. Archie comes to the rescue, providing temporary "employment" to fourteen factory workers. According to Archie, "The policy of Duffy's Tavern is that Duffy's takes care of its pals."

Duffy himself, on vacation in Canada, knows nothing of this. Meanwhile, the fourteen "waiters" have cost the tavern twelve hundred dollars in food, drink, and wages. Archie fears not. He believes himself to be the intended of Peggy O'Malley, daughter of Michael O'Malley, owner of the National Phonograph Record Company. The impending nuptials will put him in an ideal position to encourage O'Malley to reopen the factory as soon as possible, thus solving his own money problems.

He is wrong on both counts. Peggy has no romantic interest in Archie whatsoever and her father has gambled away the money he needs for the shellac. Archie's effort to raise the money needed to avoid embezzlement charges provides most of the comedy in the film.

Crosby (as a presence) appears early in the film. In an effort to impress Peggy, Archie tries to spruce up Duffy's by placing "auto-graphed" (by himself) pictures of celebrities on the wall, including one of Crosby. He asks Finnegan (Charles Cantor), a regular, for advice:

> *Archie:* And when she sees who me own private friends are and how they send me their own private autographs...I wonder how I ought to sign this one? Uh...
>
> *Finnegan:* Duh—how about "The Groaner?"

> *Archie:* Yeah, yeah...not too much familiarity and just
> enough contempt.

Archie and Finnegan clearly speak at a far cultural and class remove from an Irish American such as Crosby's Fr. O'Malley. Finnegan has a speech impediment that makes most of his words barely decipherable. Archie speaks with an exaggeratedly clear enunciation that only heightens the comedy of his inability to use words and idioms correctly.

As a national celebrity, Crosby became a local hero of sorts not by adopting the working-class accents of the Duffy's Tavern crowd, but through a self-deprecating humor that made him a regular guy despite his sophistication and success. Crosby employed this comic convention in his earlier appearance on the *Duffy's Tavern* radio show, in which Archie introduces Bing alternately as Bob Hope's sidekick and Bob Crosby's older brother. Finnegan's suggestion of "The Groaner" merely follows Crosby's own repeated public mockery of his reputation as "The Crooner."

Later in the film, Archie's attempt to recruit Bing for the block party show becomes yet another occasion for Bing to play the butt of an ego-deflating joke. As a crowd of celebrities mill about in the hotel lobby, Crosby stands next to Dorothy Lamour, his female sidekick from the *Road* pictures. A woman spies the pair and cries out, "Oh, Mr. Crosby, please. You've got to do it. You must! Its—it's the biggest moment of my life!" She then asks him to hold her baby while she gets Dorothy Lamour's autograph.

Archie's efforts at fame by association make no impression on Peggy O'Malley (Marjorie Reynolds), but Crosby will help to bring together the true lovers of the film, Peggy and Danny Murphy (Barry Sullivan), the leader of the out-of-work servicemen. Both neighborhood kids, the two meet when Danny confronts Mr. O'Malley (Victor Moore) on his failure to get the shellac needed to re-open the record factory. In the exchange, the film introduces the Crosby connection. O'Malley tries to dodge Danny's questions by saying he would be a fool not to look for shellac "with a Bing Crosby master just lying there crying." Danny refuses to accept O'Malley's evasions and storms off in anger. Peggy follows him.

> *Peggy:* Mind if I walk along?
>
> *Danny:* Sidewalk's public.
>
> *Peggy:* You're quite a fighter, aren't you? Hot-headed, too.
>
> *Danny:* The name's Murphy.
>
> *Peggy:* Mine's O'Malley.
>
> *Danny:* What does that make us—besides Irish?

Despite Peggy's efforts at peace-making, Danny never softens up until they pass by his true love, the old record factory: "This is like coming back to your girl and finding out she's not your girl." The two enter the building and Danny gives Peggy a tour that is nothing less than a celebration of the romance of production: "You should have seen this place when it was really humming. Mac and Chuck over there at the stampers. Lou and Joe over there making the biscuits. . . . That's what they press the records from. . . . Over there's where the whole thing starts in this studio. They make the master recording on wax. . . . These are the pressers. When we're going full blast, these babies can turn out five or six hundred records an hour."

This scene reflects more than a little of the industrial populism of the New Deal/Popular Front aesthetics of the 1930s. In a non-Marxist way, Danny presents a vision of a community united in production. The romance derives not simply from the technical process of producing records, but the camaraderie and solidarity of cooperative labor. Only after imaginatively reconnecting to the world of productive work does Danny feel man enough to respond to Peggy's affection.

At this point, Bing enters. Danny's tour of the production process concludes in the playback room, "the room where the finished product comes to life." Danny comes across "that Bing Crosby master your old man was talking about" and plays it for Peggy. The voice of Bing sings,

> Learn to croon, if you want to win your heart's desire.

> Sweet melodies of love inspire romance.
> . Just whisper da-da-dee-da-da-da,
> And when you do,
> She'll whisper da-da-dee-da-da,
> And nestle closer to you.
> Please lend a little ear to my pleas.

Of Bing, Danny declares, "He's still the Boss." The two dance and reminisce about where they were when they first heard the song. Danny recalls his college days at State U. He sardonically notes how he was voted most likely to succeed, but his budding romance with Peggy gets the better of his bitterness. As the two leave the factory for a ferry ride, Danny shuts off the record machine, blows a kiss to the Crosby master and says, "Thanks, Boss."

Romance comes more easily than economic recovery. Danny finds a supplier for the shellac but learns that O'Malley has no money to buy it. At the same time, Archie learns that Duffy is sending a certified public accountant to check the books. Danny needs three thousand dollars for the shellac and Archie needs twelve hundred dollars to avoid prison. After several people make fund-raising suggestions, Archie suggests a block party, "like the steamfitters and welders had last year up on 18th Street."

O'Malley objects that that party succeeded because they got a big star—Rudy Vallee—to perform. Recalling Archie's earlier boasts, Finnegan tells everyone that Archie is a close personal friend of Bing Crosby, who just happens to be in town with other celebrities on a war bond drive. Archie's efforts to meet the stars at the hotel provide the slapstick comedy that dominates the next section of the film, as Archie and O'Malley don various disguises to sneak their way into celebrity hotel rooms to make their pitch for the block party. The police finally catch up with the two as they try to pass themselves off as masseurs to Betty Hutton. Peggy, who works as an operator at the hotel, intervenes and explains their plight to the stars.

The next scene opens with a sign announcing the celebrity block party:

Tonite
MONSTROUS BLOCK PARTY!
REAL LIVE MOVIE STARS
(In Their Own Flesh and Blood!)
MASTER OF CEREMONIES
ARCHIE
Of
DUFFY'S TAVERN

Archie introduces a number of comic sketches and musical numbers featuring Paramount stars such as Betty Hutton, Paulette Goddard, Brian Donlevy, Eddie Bracken, and Cass Dailey. One local dance team from Duffy's Tavern, Johnny Coy and Miriam Franklin, pitch in with a tap-ballet titled "Johnny Comes Marching Home."

As the stars entertain the audience, Danny tries to get the factory up and running to raise the money to pay back Duffy and keep Archie out of jail. Danny contacts O'Malley's old distributor, who agrees to pay Danny the cash he needs if he can deliver fifteen hundred Crosby platters by the morning. The finances get a bit cloudy at this point, but we can assume that the celebrities will raise the money to buy the shellac, while Danny and his men will produce the records to pay back Duffy.

Improbable, yes, but a revealing improbability nonetheless. Were the celebrities simply to bail out Archie, Danny and his men would lose their dignity, even their manhood, as objects of charity. The returning servicemen of *Duffy's Tavern* are not asking for a handout, just a hand.

The earlier nostalgia for production past becomes a nearly social- ist utopia of workers' control and solidarity. O'Malley offers Danny and his men not simply jobs, but part ownership of the company. Even Peggy gets into the act, with Danny conceding inter-gender cooperation, if not equality: "Come on, Peggy. You can be of some help, too."

The film cuts back and forth from stage performances to factory work. Despite their heroic efforts, Danny and his crew fall one hundred records short of the fifteen hundred that they promised the distributor. Still, when the distributor arrives, he is satisfied. When he asks who he makes the check out to, Peggy says, "Danny!" Danny signs the check over to Duffy's daughter just in time to save Archie from arrest. Danny then announces his engagement to Peggy and asks Archie to be the best man at his wedding.

As Crosby put the neighborhood back to work, so he entertains them at play. The block party extravaganza concludes with a production number celebrating the life of Crosby himself, from birth to *Going My Way*. Archie introduces the grand finale: "And now we come to the big piece of resistance. A sketch with Dorothy Lamour, Robert Benchley, and Bing Crosby—a man who ain't the father of his country, but you certainly got to give him credit for trying. See you later." The jokes reveal something of Crosby's standing as both a patriotic icon and a family man. Crosby's family of four sons, modest by the Catholic standards of the day, set him apart from most other Hollywood stars. Crosby could hardly make a public appearance without someone making some joke about the size of his family, and those jokes only expanded in range after he won an Academy Award for portraying a celibate Catholic priest.

His sons often appeared on his radio show and his oldest, Gary, recorded a few songs. The boys appear in *Duffy's Tavern* as well, as the skit begins with the *New Yorker* writer Robert Benchley (also a Paramount contract player) arriving at the Crosby home to baby-sit while Bing is away. As he strolls through a set with several house fronts, Benchley identifies Crosby's by the sight of a stork picketing the house with a placard reading, "Unfair"—yet another poke at Crosby's very un-Hollywood-like family size.

Benchley arrives to find the boys arguing about a call strike while playing baseball. To make peace, he offers to tell them a story. First, he suggests "a real Horatio Alger success story—about the rise of Frank Sinatra." Gary reminds "Uncle Robert" that "that's one name we don't mention around here!" By this time, the rivalry between Sinatra and Crosby for the title of King of the Crooners was in full gear, and Crosby handled it publicly with much the same kind of humor he treated other celebrity relationships.[22] Benchley then goes on to tell the boys the very un-Horatio-Alger-like story of their father.

At the first sight of Bing as a baby, his mother screams in horror. As a youth, Bing does poorly in school so he can stay after to flirt with the teacher (played by Dorothy Lamour). Barry Fitzgerald makes an appearance as a "gone-fishing" father who cannot answer the simplest questions a young boy might ask. Bing is cheap on dates in high school; as an adult, his idea of romancing a girl is sitting with her on a porch swing while he reads the racing form. He attends Gonzaga College but never gets past his sophomore year. He finally leaves college to take the entertainment world by storm—as the camera cuts to images of Bing standing in the rain in New York, Chicago, and even Hollywood (where it never rains).

The story then jumps to the success of *Going My Way*. Bing leads all the Paramount stars in "Swinging on a Star," with each performer making up new verses that satirize their own screen personas. This production number ends with Crosby and Lamour trading barbs that play off their *Road* movie connections and the usual Bing jokes. Crosby sings,

> If you don't care what the public must endure
> You might grow up to be Lamour.

She fires back,

> Or would you dress in any old thing,
> Have a funny name such as B-b-b-Bing
> Have Sinatra sneer when you sing,
> Or would you rather be a snob?

Crosby's response deflects the charge of snobbery to his other *Road* companion, Bob Hope:

> A snob is an actor who will tell you he's tops.

---

[22] See Samuel L. Chill, "Rivalries: The Mutual Mentoring of Bing Crosby and Frank Sinatra," in Prigozy and Raubicheck, eds., *Going My Way: Bing Crosby and American Culture*, 116–22.

> He even brags about his flops.
> Now when this boy plays golf, he never counts his strokes,
> And that's not all—he tells those beat-up jokes.
> But if you're like a friend of mine called Bob,
> You might grow up to be a snob.

The *Road* tie-in is fairly predictable, but the snob joke does not quite follow the conventions of Hope-Crosby banter, on or off the screen. In the *Road* films, Hope always played the buffoon, while their off-screen jokes focused on golf and professional success rather than cultural sophistication. In the context of *Duffy's Tavern*, however, the deflection of snobbery to Hope serves to identify Crosby as a regular guy.

Indeed, the film clearly wishes to present Hollywood itself as a kind of regular guy. Hollywood stars support the nation through a war bond drive, yet they also help to save a neighborhood through a block party. By the end of the film, the local actually seems to take precedence over the national—the bond drive providing an occasion for the block party, rather than the other way around. The film even eschews the conventional pitch to buy bonds that the studio heads tagged on to so many films of the era.

The end of the film simply brings us back to the beginning, with Archie on the phone with Duffy. In one sense, nothing has changed. At the beginning of the film, Archie thought he would solve all his financial problems by marrying Peggy O'Malley. At the end of the film, he informs Duffy that he may no longer need his job at the tavern: "From the way a certain party has been reacting to me, don't be surprised if one of these days you're referring to me as Mr. Betty Hutton."

Archie's misread of Betty Hutton's affections calls comic attention to the gap between a local Irish bartender and a Hollywood celebrity, but it also echoes his earlier misread of a local girl, Peggy O'Malley. In both instances, Archie confidently predicts his romantic success due to his "maggotism" (magnetism). His brush with Hollywood stardom appears to have left him unchanged. He is still a working-class bartender and still clueless when it comes to women. In this sense, the Bowery as local, ethnic, and working-class triumphs over Broadway as national, American, and middle-class. Still, the object of Archie's romantic delusion has changed; local girl Peggy O'Malley gives way to national celebrity Betty Hutton. In a subtle, comic way, the film ends where so many other Irish-American films begin—on the Bowery looking up at Broadway.

Conclusion

The Suburbs of America

NOTHING LASTS FOREVER, least of all in Hollywood. The presence of Irish-American stories in Hollywood cinema peaked in 1945. Beyond the lust for novelty that drives American popular culture in general, the decline of Irish-American storytelling in Hollywood cinema reflects a broad range of political and social changes. If the Holocaust and suburbanization each, in very different ways, silenced discussion of European ethnicity, postwar prosperity seemed to render the urban folk wisdom of Irish America obsolete. Ironically, the very success of these films of the 1930s and 1940s may have paved the way for the assimilation of the postwar period.

The election of John F. Kennedy as the first Irish-Catholic president of the United States might not have been possible without Father Chuck. The Kennedy victory in 1960 redeemed the political humiliation of the Irish in 1928, yet in many ways betrayed the cultural victory the Irish had achieved in the wake of Smith's defeat. Kennedy seemed to confirm the fears that Al Smith refused to accept were true: the Irish could only be accepted as American if they completely rejected every distinguishing mark of their Irishness and assimilated to the standards of WASP America. The Irish-American films of the decade and a half from *Going My Way* to Kennedy's election continued to work within an urban ethic even as they pointed to its passing.

In all these developments, it is impossible to overestimate the profound influence of the Holocaust on the place of ethnicity

197

in American culture. America had initially responded to Hitler's anti-Semitism and his doctrines of Aryan racial superiority by re-imagining American democracy in terms of cultural and ethnic pluralism. Irish-American films, particularly the priest films, were an important part of this new vision of America. With widespread awareness of the death camps, the ideal of tolerance quickly mor-phed from pluralism to a new model of assimilation whose moral legitimacy proceeded from the sincere commitment to accept and affirm the dignity of every individual regardless of race or religion.

The lesson the west took from Hitler was less the need for greater tolerance than the equation of ethnic identity and violence. Thus, Hollywood's showcase treatment of anti-Semitism, *Gentle-man's Agreement* (Elia Kazan, 1947), attacks the bigotry that would deny Jewish Americans full access to the freedoms and opportu-nities available to non-ethnic Americans. Nowhere does the film suggest that the pursuit of ethnic distinctiveness should serve as a standard by which to measure American-style toleration. Represen-tative of the mood of the times is the complete failure of another postwar film with a Jewish-American theme, Bing Crosby's remake of *Abie's Irish Rose* (A. Edward Sutherland, 1946).

A staple of American popular culture for over twenty years, the story now struck viewers and critics alike as offensive. At one level, the film perpetuated old stereotypes now deemed the breeding ground of hate; at another level, its story of assimilation through intermarriage implicitly challenged American pretensions to toler-ance. Serious treatments of race and ethnicity in films of this period were long on righteous denunciations of intolerance but very short on acknowledging the cultural costs of tolerance.

In the world of Irish-American cinema, the new mood was per-haps best captured by the transformation of that foundational genre, the gangster film. At one level, all seemed right with the world. James Cagney was back on top with one of his most memorable gangster roles, that of Cody Jarrett in *White Heat* (Raoul Walsh, 1949). Nearly fifty years old at the time of the shooting of the film, Cagney showed no signs of slowing down. His Cody Jarrett is Tommy Powers and Rocky Sullivan to the nth degree.

The film's dramatic conclusion—Cody's suicidal ignition of an oil refinery amidst psychotic shouts of "top of the world"—seemed a gangster death appropriate for a nuclear age. Still, for all the accolades Cagney earned, his Cody Jarrett stands in stark contrast to his previous gangsters by his conspicuous lack of ethnicity. Cody is a rural American gangster much more in the John Dillinger tradition. In his self-destructive rise to the top of the crime world, he is much more a Rico Bandello than a Tommy Powers. In keeping with the turn to psychological themes in *noir* crime films, the rich social world of Cagney's earlier films gives way to a Freudian mother-love complex.

The turn from ethnicity to psychology afflicted the boxing film as well. *Body and Soul* (Richard Rossen, 1947) retains only traces of ethnicity in its story of Charlie Davis, a Jewish boxer struggling to get to the top. Charlie's struggles are in the end personal rather than communal. By the early 1960s, films like *Requiem for a Heavyweight* (Ralph Nelson, 1962) would confirm the boxer-as-existential-hero as the new standard for the genre.

The grit and pathos of urban life in general drew some of the leading artists of the postwar generation to Irish-themed stories, though to a much different effect than in the prewar generation. Elia Kazan stands as a case in point. The most respected director of the era, the man largely responsible for introducing the new, psychologically oriented "method" style of acting to a broad film-going public, Kazan made his feature film directorial debut with *A Tree Grows in Brooklyn* (1945), a film adaptation of Betty Smith's popular novel of the travails of a poor Irish girl growing up in turn-of-the-century Brooklyn. The characters—most especially the loving, but alcoholic, father—could have come from any Warner Brothers film of the 1930s. The choice of story, however, works directly against the narrative conventions of those earlier films.

In a gentle and sentimental manner, the story tells of the efforts of Francie Nolan (Peggy Ann Gardner) to find some escape from the dreariness of her tenement life with her long-suffering mother and ne'er-do-well father. She finds hope for her future in the world of books she encounters through her public school education. For all its Irish characters and setting, this story goes against the grain of the dominant traditions of Irish-American popular narrative. For Irish Catholics, the public school was more often than not perceived as a hostile outside force dedicated to seducing Irish children away from their primary ethnic and religious loyalties. Critics and audiences alike loved the film, but its vision of the school stands in sharp contrast to, say, the parochial school of *The Bells of St. Mary's*. That latter film also presents a young Irish girl in a troubled family situation, but it never suggests that she could transcend the limitations of her ethnic world through education.

Kazan drew on stories from a much rougher urban Irish terrain for his greatest film, *On the Waterfront* (1954). The film has it all: gangsters, boxers, priests, and even a trace of Bowery Cinderella. Once again, however, the story departs from the earlier narrative conventions. Earlier films presented moral conflicts within the confines of the ethnic community, while *On the Waterfront* tells of the need to betray tribal loyalties for a higher good.

A crusading priest, Fr. Barry (Karl Malden) struggles to persuade a failed boxer, Terry Malloy (Marlon Brando), to testify before a federal crime commission to expose the corruption of the leaders of the labor unions that control the docks of New York. Unlike Jerry Connolly, Fr. Barry is an outsider with no childhood connection to Terry; he appeals to some local loyalties, but his strongest appeal is to abstract principles of justice that transcend those loyalties. For much of the film, Terry refuses to testify on the basis of his duty to the leaders of his union, including his own brother, Charlie (Rod Steiger).

Charlie's murder at the hands of the union bosses severs all remaining ties to the union and Terry testifies against the big union leader, Johnny Friendly (Lee J. Cobb). Rejected by his fellow long-shoremen as a snitch, Terry eventually fights his way back into their brotherhood and ends the film as a local hero of sorts. His return to the community is bloody and sacrificial, suggesting reconciliation on local terms. Still, the damage had been done. The film presents tribal loyalties as a mask for corruption and violence. Salvation comes through having the courage to stand outside of one's community.[1]

At the same time as stories such as these cast doubt on the moral authority of the urban Irish-American community, Old-World Ireland arose as an alternative basis of Irish identity. As William Williams has shown in his masterful work, 'Twas Only an Irishman's Dream, the Irish image in America has vacillated between old- and new-world emphases.[2] After a generation of Tin Pan Alley songs that directed affections toward the Ould Sod, the city films of the 1930s and 1940s reestablished America as the geographic center of popular Irishness.

The 1950s saw the balance tip back to Ireland, largely through the towering influence of one film: *The Quiet Man* (John Ford, 1952). Irish-American John Ford won an Academy Award for his direction of this sentimental, whimsical tale of Sean Thornton (John Wayne), an Irish-American boxer who returns to his ancestral home in Innisfree to live a quiet rural life far from the dirt, noise, and violence of the American city where he grew up.

Pushing every button and pulling every heartstring available in transatlantic Irish popular culture, the film has been the bane of all

---

[1] The film has most often been read as an apology for Kazan's own testimony before the House Un-American Activities Committee, in which he identified members of the Communist Party he had come to know in Hollywood. See Navasky, *Naming Names*. For a definitive study of the local Irish world that inspired the film, see Fisher, *On the Irish Waterfront: The Crusader, the Movie, and the Soul of the Port of New York*.

[2] Williams, *'Twas Only an Irishman's Dream*. See in particular Chapters 8 and 9 on the shift from the theater of Harrigan and Hart in the 1880s to that of Chauncey Olcott in the 1890s.

subsequent Irish and Irish-American directors seeking to create a "serious" Irish cinema. Still, beneath all the b'gosh-and-be-gorrah antics, the film actually tells a sophisticated story of the meaning of community, one that resonates with the Irish city films of an earlier era. Sean quickly realizes that past family claims alone cannot earn him membership in the small, rural Irish community. If he is going to start his life over again in Ireland, he must do so on Irish, not American terms.

He falls in love with a tough, rural Irish version of the Bowery Cinderella in Mary Kate Danaher (Maureen O'Hara). Like her American cousins, Mary Kate's love for an outsider threatens her loyalty to communal traditions. Mary Kate's brother, Red Will (Victor McLaughlin), refuses to grant his permission for her to marry Sean; without this permission, Mary Kate must marry without her dowry, to her great shame in the eyes of the community. Sean dismisses these local traditions as nonsense, but ultimately fights Red Will for her honor and finally gains full acceptance into the community.[3] The continuity of themes ultimately could not compensate for the fundamental shift in place. For the vast majority of Americans, *The Quiet Man* forever marked the end of Irish culture in America.

The Irish in America may not have followed Sean Thornton back to Ireland, but many did flee the city for the comparatively rural world of the suburbs. John Ford himself would directly address the passing of an Irish-American urban world in his film adaptation of Edwin O'Connor's popular novel of Boston politics, *The Last Hurrah* (1958). The subject matter was quite a departure for Ford who, for all his public Irishness, never really directed a significant film dealing with urban Irish-American culture.

Ford is clearly out of his element in the film. Despite strong performances by many of the aging greats of Irish-American cinema, the film adds little to O'Connor's novel. Based in part on the declin-

---

[3]For this reading, I am indebted to Luke Gibbons's excellent reading of *The Quiet Man* in Rockett, Gibbons, and Hill, *Cinema and Ireland*.

ing years of real-life Boston mayor James Michael Curley, the story bemoans the passing of a more personal, if often corrupt, politics in favor of an impersonal media-based politics of image, captured in particular by the increasing role of television in political campaigns.

If *The Quiet Man* offers the hope of paradise regained in the Old World, *The Last Hurrah* suggests the impossibility of passing on even the morally ambiguous traditions of the past. Frank Skeffington (Spencer Tracy), a big-city mayor nearing the end of his political career and hoping to pass some of his hard-earned wisdom on to the next generation, offers his nephew, Adam Caulfield (Jeffrey Hunter), an inside look at his last campaign for mayor.

Adam is a college-educated, middle-class journalist whose parents have sheltered him from the rough-and-tumble world of urban Irish politics. In the course of following his uncle through the campaign, Adam discovers the world he has lost and finds it in many ways superior to the safe, morally self-righteous, middle-class world of his own upbringing. For all of Skeffington's flaws, he clearly appears superior to his rival, Kevin McCluskey (Charles Fitzsimmons), a squeaky-clean, college-educated front man for an old WASP reform coalition that has fought Skeffington for decades. Skeffington loses the election, but wins the cultural war. Still, he has no successor. He has won Adam's heart, but Adam is not a politician. He is a writer, a journalist/anthropologist who merely charts modernity's destruction of yet another venerable, traditional way of life.

The election of John F. Kennedy to the presidency of the United States put to rest any doubts that may have remained after O'Connor's great novel. Kennedy was a Kevin McCluskey who had to be taken seriously. A model of Irish-American assimilation, Kennedy spoke the language of WASP idealism, nowhere more than in his famous inaugural speech on "The New Frontier." Ethnically, Kennedy was at most a *Quiet Man* Irishman—that is, he distanced himself from the urban world of Irish American culture but freely invoked all of the sentimental conventions of Old-World Ireland. His religion, rather than his ethnicity, proved the major obstacle to his election.

Campaigning in the long shadow of Al Smith, Kennedy took a much stronger stand on the total separation of his faith from his public life.[4] The three years of his presidency proved him a man of his word on the religion front, while his assassination in November of 1963 made him into a secular saint, a martyr for a whole range of liberal social-justice movements for which he showed somewhat lukewarm support as president. Still, Kennedy's ethno-religious background was enough for the Irish to consider him one of their own. His election and assassination put to rest all questions as to whether the Irish could be accepted as full Americans.

The Kennedy moment did, however, raise the question of whether one could be American and still be Irish. Again, for many Irish Americans, a sentimental connection to the Ould Sod was a sufficient sign of ethnic distinction. As many Irish Americans participated in the great migration from the city to the suburbs in the decades following the end of World War II, they cut themselves off from the places so central to their cultural traditions.

Television took over the central storytelling role once controlled by Hollywood cinema, and newly suburban Irish Americans could, for a brief time, watch Jackie Gleason replay their hard-scrabble urban past on episodes of *The Honeymooners*.[5] Increasingly, those in search of connection to ethnic roots would turn to the old-world model of the Clancy Brothers, whose performances on *The Ed Sullivan Show* introduced a new generation of Irish Americans to the drinking and fighting songs of old Ireland. The Clancy Brothers' repertoire quickly augmented the Tin Pan Alley tunes re-popularized by Bing Crosby and the Irish-American musicals of the 1940s, but all this remained distinctly ethnic, never generally American in the

---

[4]For a recent study of the role of Catholicism in Kennedy's election, see Carty, *A Catholic in the White House?: Religion, Politics and John F. Kennedy's Presidential Campaign*.

[5]See Lipsitz, *Rainbow at Midnight: Labor and Culture in the 1940s*.

way that Irish-American culture had once been. Hollywood, facing increasing competition from television, could no longer risk money on films that might have only limited ethnic appeal. As a consequence, the decade of the 1960s was perhaps the low point in the history of Irish-American film narrative.

Suburban, middle-class, college-educated Irish Americans in search of cultural identity showed little interest in keeping the old urban traditions alive. Daniel Patrick Moynihan spoke for a generation of intellectuals whose flight from that urban world sent them to Ireland for inspiration. College and university literature departments sang the praises of Yeats and Joyce, not Cagney and Crosby. The embrace of Irish literary modernism became part of a generational revolt against lower-middle-class Irish-American Catholicism.

The younger generation lambasted Irish Americans for failing to embrace the Irish modernists as their own, and they criticized the older generation for failing to recognize homegrown Irish-American modernists such as Eugene O'Neill and F. Scott Fitzgerald. For the educated, Irish literary modernism became a way of asserting ethnic identity against the general American Irish trend toward assimilation. It retains much of this power and purpose today.

Recent decades suggest new developments. Modernism has certainly lost much of its edge. After fifty years or so of canonical status, it has a much harder time presenting itself as anything other than the cultural establishment. Traditional Ireland has lost some of its distinct but related authority through a similar process of failure through success. The seemingly overnight modernization brought about by the rise of the Celtic Tiger has made it more difficult to think of Ireland as a rural retreat from urban modernity. At the same time, the end of the IRA's armed campaign to bring the Northern counties into a united republic has deprived contemporary Ireland of the violent edge that stood as a stinging rebuke to the comfort and security of middle-class, suburban Irish America. Rootless, cosmopolitan Americans in search of cultural roots now travel to

Ireland only to find rootless, cosmopolitan Irish. In this setting, the dying Irish ghettos of New York, Boston, and Chicago have taken on something like the status of tribal homelands.[6]

After decades of domination by Italian-American stories, the gangster genre has slowly returned to its Irish roots with films such as *State of Grace* (Phil Joanou, 1990), *Miller's Crossing* (Ethan and Joel Cohen, 1990), *Road to Perdition* (Sam Mendes, 2002), *Gangs of New York* (Martin Scorsese, 2002), and *The Departed* (Martin Scorsese, 2006). As much as the earlier turn to modernism, the appeal of these films suggests a dissatisfaction—with the norms of middle-class American life—that one can only see as hopeful.

Still, there is a danger. For all the high quality of many of these films, they render a life that can only appear as exotic to contemporary middle-class audiences. The urban films of the 1930s and 1940s told stories much closer to the actual lives of the urban people who saw them. Compared to this earlier time, today's films are thus both more violent and graphic, yet less realistic. The modern viewer reconnects to a violent, local past only to return, refreshed and regenerated, to the virtual reality of a life lived increasingly in cyberspace.

Irish Americans of an earlier age wanted middle-class prosperity and working-class roots; today, they want middle-class prosperity, working-class roots—and middle-class freedom. In a letter to F. Scott Fitzgerald, the Irish-American writer John O'Hara once commented, "I suspect that Al Smith is the only Irishman who isn't a climber at heart."[7] The Irish-American films of the 1930s and 1940s told the story of Al Smith most powerfully in their rejection of social climbing. Americans who wish to make claims for ethnic identity today have much to learn from the stories these films tell.

---

[6]Of all these ghettos, South Boston has emerged as the gold standard of tribalism. See Lukas, *Common Ground: A Turbulent Decade in the Lives of Three American Families*; O'Connor, *South Boston, My Hometown: The History of an Ethnic Neighborhood*; and MacDonald, *All Souls: A Family Story from Southie*.

[7]Fanning, *The Irish Voice in American Fiction*, 252.

References

Addams, Jane. *Twenty Years at Hull House*. Mineola, NY: Dover, 2008.

Akam, Everett Helmut. *Transnational America: Cultural Pluralist Thought in the Twentieth Century*. Lanham. MD: Rowman & Littlefield, 2002.

Alexander, Michael. *Jazz Age Jews*. Princeton, NJ: Princeton University Press, 2003.

Appleby, R. Scott. *Church and Age Unite!: The Modernist Impulse in American Catholicism*. Notre Dame, IN: University of Notre Dame Press, 1992.

Barton, Ruth, ed. *Screening Irish America*. Dublin: Irish Academic Press, 2009.

Basinger, Jeanine. *Silent Stars*. New York: Alfred A. Knopf, 1999.

———. *A Woman's View: How Hollywood Spoke to Women, 1930–1960*. New York: Alfred A. Knopf, 1993.

———. *The World War II Combat Film: Anatomy of a Genre*. Middletown, CT: Wesleyan University Press, 1986.

Beauchamp, Cari. *Without Lying Down: Frances Marion and the Powerful Women of Early Hollywood*. New York: Scribners, 1997.

Black, Gregory D. *Hollywood Censored: Morality Codes, Catholics, and the Movies*. New York: Cambridge University Press, 1994.

Brinkley, Alan. *Voices of Protest: Huey Long, Father Coughlin, and the Great Depression*. New York: Knopf, 1982.

Broderick, Francis L. *Right Reverend New Dealer, John A. Ryan*. New York: MacMillan, 1963.

Brownlow, Kevin. "The Irish in Early Hollywood," delivered at the conference "Screening Irish America," University College at Dublin, April 13, 2007.

Burns, Walter Noble. *The One-Way Ride: The Red Trail of Chicago Gangland from Prohibition to Jake Lingle.* Garden City, NY: Doubleday, Doran, 1931.

Cagney, James. *Cagney by Cagney.* Garden City, NY: Doubleday, 1976.

Carty, Thomas J. *A Catholic in the White House?: Religion, Politics and John F. Kennedy's Presidential Campaign.* New York: Palgrave MacMillan, 2008.

Casey, Marion R. "Ireland, New York and the Irish Image in American Popular Culture, 1890–1960," Ph.D. New York University, 1998.

Cawelti, John G. *Adventure, Mystery, Romance: Formula Stories as Art and Culture.* Chicago: University of Chicago Press, 1976.

Cohen, Henry. *The Public Enemy.* Madison: University of Wisconsin Press, 1981.

Couvares, Francis G. "Hollywood, Main Street, and the Church: Trying to Censor the Movies Before the Production Code," in Couvares, Francis G., ed. *Movie Censorship and American Culture.* Washington: Smithsonian Institution Press, 1996.

Curran, Joseph M. *Hibernian Green on the Silver Screen: The Irish and American Movies.* Westport, CT: Greenwood Press, 1989.

Di Battista, Maria. *Fast-Talking Dames.* New Haven, CT: Yale University Press, 2003.

Diner, Hasia R. *Erin's Daughters in America: Irish Immigrant Women in the Nineteenth Century.* Baltimore, MD: The Johns Hopkins University Press, 1983.

Douglas, Ann. *The Feminization of American Culture.* New York: Farrar, Straus and Giroux, 1998.

Dunne, Finley Peter. *Mr. Dooley in Peace and in War.* Urbana: University of Illinois Press, 2001.

English, T. J. *Paddy Whacked: The Untold Story of the Irish American Gangster.* New York: Regan, 2005.

Erenhalt, Alan. *The Lost City: The Forgotten Virtues of Community in America*. New York: Basic Books, 1995.

Evans, Sara. *Born for Liberty*. New York: The Free Press, 1989.

Fanning, Charles. *The Irish Voice in American Fiction*. Lexington: University of Kentucky Press, 1990.

Fiedler, Mari Kathleen. "Fatal Attraction: Irish-Jewish Romance in Early Film and Drama," *Eire-Ireland* 20, no. 3 (Fall 1985): 6–18.

Finan, Christopher M. *Alfred E. Smith: The Happy Warrior*. New York: Hill and Wang, 2002.

Fisher, James T. *On the Irish Waterfront: The Crusader, the Movie and the Soul of the Port of New York*. Ithaca, NY: Cornell University Press, 2009.

Fitzgerald, Maureen. *Habits of Compassion: Irish Catholic Nuns and the Origins of New York's Welfare System, 1830–1920*. Urbana: University of Illinois Press, 2006.

Gabler, Neal. *An Empire of Their Own: How the Jews Invented Hollywood*. New York: Anchor, 1989.

Gans, Herbert J. *The Urban Villagers: Group and Class in the Life of Italian Americans*. New York: The Free Press of Glencoe, 1962.

Gehring, Wes D. *Leo McCarey: From Marx to McCarthy*. Lanham: The Scarecrow Press, 2004.

Giddins, Gary. *Bing Crosby, A Pocket Full of Dreams: The Early Years, 1903–1940*. Boston: Little, Brown, 2001.

Giovacchini, Saverio. *Hollywood Modernism: Film and Politics in the Age of the New Deal*. Philadelphia: Temple University Press, 2001.

Glazer, Nathan, and Daniel Patrick Moynihan. *Beyond the Melting Pot: The Negroes, Puerto Ricans, Jews, Italians and Irish of New York City*. Cambridge, MA: MIT Press, 1963.

Gleason, Philip. *Speaking of Diversity: Language and Ethnicity in Twentieth-Century America*. Baltimore, MD: The Johns Hopkins University Press, 1992.

Gordon, Mary. "Father Chuck: A Reading of *Going My Way* and *The Bells of St. Mary's*, or Why Priests Made Us Crazy," in Thomas

J. Ferraro, ed., *Catholic Lives, Contemporary America*. Durham, NC: Duke University Press, 1997: 76–103.

Gorn, Elliot J. *The Manly Art: Bare-Knuckled Prize Fighting in America*. Ithaca, NY: Cornell University Press, 1986.

Handlin, Oscar. *Al Smith and His America*. Boston: Little, Brown, 1958.

Harris, Stephen L. *Duffy's War: Fr. Francis Duffy, Wild Bill Donovan, and the Irish Fighting 69th in World War I*. Herndon, VA: Potomac, 2007.

Herberg, Will. *Protestant, Catholic, Jew: An Essay in American Religious Sociology*. New York: Doubleday, 1955.

Higham, John. *Strangers in the Land: Patterns of American Nativism, 1865–1925*. New York: Atheneum, 1963.

Isenberg, Michael T. *John L. Sullivan and His America*. Urbana: University of Illinois Press, 1994.

Jacobs, Diane. *Christmas in July: The Life and Art of Preston Sturges*. Berkeley: The University of California Press, 1994.

Jones, John Paul. *The Irish Brigade*. New York: R. B. Luce, 1969.

Kirstein, Lincoln. "James Cagney and the American Hero," *Hound & Horn* 5 (1932): 465–67.

"Kitty Foyle: LIFE's Pictures of the U.S. White Collar Girl Reappear in RKO Movie," LIFE (December 9, 1940): 87–90.

Leff, Leonard J., and Jerold L. Simmons, *The Dame in the Kimono: Hollywood Censorship and the Production Code from the 1920s to the 1960s*. New York: Grove Weidenfeld, 1990.

Lipsitz, George. *Rainbow at Midnight: Labor and Culture in the 1940s*. Urbana: University of Illinois Press, 1994.

Lott, Eric. *Love and Theft: Blackface Minstrelsy and the American Working Class*. New York: Oxford University Press, 1995.

Lukas, J. Anthony. *Common Ground: A Turbulent Decade in the Lives of Three American Families*. New York: Knopf, 1985.

Macdonald, Michael Patrick. *All Souls: A Family Story from Southie*. Boston: Beacon, 1999.

McCabe, John. *Cagney*. New York: Knopf, 1997.

————. *George M. Cohan: The Man Who Owned Broadway*. New York: De Capo, 1980.

McGilligan, Patrick, ed. *Yankee Doodle Dandy*. Madison: University of Wisconsin Press, 1981.

Meagher, Timothy J., *Inventing Irish America: Generation, Class and Ethnic Identity in a New England City, 1880–1928*. Notre Dame, IN: University of Notre Dame Press, 2001.

Merwin, Ted. "The Performance of Jewish Ethnicity in Anne Nichols' *Abie's Irish Rose*," *Journal of American Ethnic History* 20, no. 2 (Winter 2001): 3–37.

Moore, Colleen. *Silent Star*. Garden City, NY: Doubleday, 1968.

Moore, R. Laurence. "Tocqueville, American Catholics, and American Democratic Culture," a talk delivered at the Cushwa Center for the Study of American Catholicism on April 12, 2001. For an overview of that talk, see "Cushwa Center Lecture," *American Catholic Studies Newsletter* 28, no. 2 (Fall 2001): 7–8.

Morley, Christopher. *Kitty Foyle*. New York: Grosset & Dunlap, 1939.

Morris, Charles. *American Catholic: The Saints and Sinners Who Built America's Most Powerful Church*. New York: Vintage, 1998.

Mumford, Lewis. "The Corruption of Liberalism," *New Republic* 102 (May 6, 1940): 603–08.

Munby, Jonathan. *Public Enemies, Public Heroes: Screening the Gangster from* Little Caesar *to* Touch of Evil. Chicago: University of Chicago Press, 1999.

Muscio, Giulana. *Hollywood's New Deal*. Philadelphia: Temple University Press, 1997.

Navasky, Victor S. *Naming Names*. New York: Hill and Wang, 2003.

Negra, Diane. *Off-White Hollywood: American Culture and Ethnic Female Stardom*. New York: Routledge, 2001.

O'Connor, Stephen. *Orphan Trains: The Story of Charles Loring Brace and the Children He Saved and Failed*. Chicago: University of Chicago Press, 2004.

O'Connor, Thomas H. *South Boston, My Hometown: The History of an Ethnic Neighborhood*. Boston: Quinlan, 1988.

Ó Maitiú, Séamas. *The Humours of Donnybrook: Dublin's Famous Fair and Its Suppression*. Dublin: Irish Academic Press, 1995.

Ousler, Fulton, and Will Ousler. *Father Flanagan of Boys Town*. Garden City, NY: Doubleday, 1949.

Pells, Richard. *Radical Visions and American Dreams: Culture and Social Thought in the Depression Years*. Middletown, CT: Wesleyan University Press, 1973.

Pope, S. W., ed. *The New American Sport History: Recent Approaches and Perspectives*. Urbana: University of Illinois Press, 1996.

Prigozy, Ruth, and Walter Raubicheck, eds. *Going My Way: Bing Crosby and American Culture*. Rochester, NY: University of Rochester Press, 2007: 116–22.

Quinn, Peter. *Looking for Jimmy: A Search for Irish America*. New York: The Overlook Press, 2007.

Rockett, Kevin, Luke Gibbons, and John Hill. *Cinema and Ireland*. Syracuse, NY: Syracuse University Press, 1989.

Roddick, Nick. *New Deal in Entertainment: Warner Brothers in the 1930s*. London: British Film Institute, 1983.

Rogers, Ginger. *Ginger: My Story*. New York: Harper Collins, 1991.

Rogin, Michael. *Blackface, White Noise: Jewish Immigrants in the Hollywood Melting Pot*. Berkeley: University of California Press, 1998.

Rotella, Carol. *Good with Their Hands: Boxers, Bluesmen, and Other Characters from the Rustbelt*. Berkeley: University of California Press, 2002.

Ruth, David E. *Inventing the Public Enemy: The Gangster in American Culture, 1918–1934*. Chicago: University of Chicago Press, 1996.

San Pietro, Mary Jo. *Father Hartke: His Life and Legacy to the American Theater*. Washington: Catholic University Press, 2002.

Schapp, Jeremy. *Cinderella Man: James J. Braddock, Max Baer, and the Greatest Upset in Boxing History*. New York: Mariner, 2006.

Shannon, Christopher. *Conspicuous Criticism: Tradition, the Individual, and Culture in Modern American Social Thought*. Scranton, PA: University of Scranton Press, 2006.

Shelley, T. J. "'What the Hell is an Encyclical?': Governor Alfred E. Smith, Charles C. Marshall, Esq., and Father Francis P. Duffy," *U.S. Catholic Historian* 15, no. 2 (Spring 1997): 87–107.

Sklar, Robert. *City Boys: Cagney, Bogart, Garfield*. Princeton, NJ: Princeton University Press, 1992.

Slayton, Robert. *Empire Statesman: The Rise and Redemption of Al Smith*. New York: The Free Press, 2001.

Smith, Alfred E. *Up to Now: An Autobiography*. New York: Viking, 1929.

Smith, Anthony B. "Entertaining Catholics: Bing Crosby, Religion and Cultural Pluralism in 1940s America," *American Catholic Studies* 114, no. 4 (Winter 2003): 1–19.

Sollars, Werner. *Beyond Ethnicity: Consent and Descent in American Culture*. Oxford: Oxford University Press, 1988.

Sterne, Evelyn Savidge. *Ballots and Bibles: Ethnic Politics and the Catholic Church in Providence*. Ithaca, NY: Cornell University Press, 2003.

Stott, William. *Documentary Expression in Thirties America*. New York: Oxford University Press, 1973.

Stowe, David W. *Swing Changes: Big Band Jazz in New Deal America*. Cambridge, MA: Harvard University Press, 1998.

Susman, Warren I. *Culture as History: The Transformation of American Society in the Twentieth Century*. New York: Pantheon Books, 1984.

Swindell, Larry. *Spencer Tracy: A Biography*. New York: World, 1969.

Treat, Roger L. *Bishop Sheil and the CYO*. New York: Julian Messner, 1951.

Walsh, Frank. *Sin and Censorship: The Catholic Church and the Motion Picture Industry*. New Haven: Yale University Press, 1996.

Warshow, Robert. *The Immediate Experience: Movies, Comics, Theatre, and Other Aspects of Popular Culture*. Garden City, NY: Doubleday, 1960.

"White Collar Girl: Research Notes for Ginger Rogers' Film Version
    of Christopher Morley's Best-Selling Novel, *Kitty Foyle*," LIFE
    (March 25, 1940): 81–87.

White, William Allen. "Al Smith, City Feller." *Colliers* 78 (August 21,
    1926): 8–9.

Whitfield, Eileen. *Pickford: The Woman Who Made Hollywood.* Lex-
    ington: University of Kentucky Press, 1997.

Williams, William H. A. "Green Again: Irish-American Lace-Curtain
    Satire," *New Hibernia Review* 6, no. 2 (Summer 2002): 9–24.

———. *'Twas Only an Irishman's Dream: The Image of Ireland and
    the Irish in American Popular Song Lyrics, 1800–1920.* Urbana:
    University of Illinois Press, 1996.

Wright, Richard. *Native Son.* New York: Harper, 1940.

Index